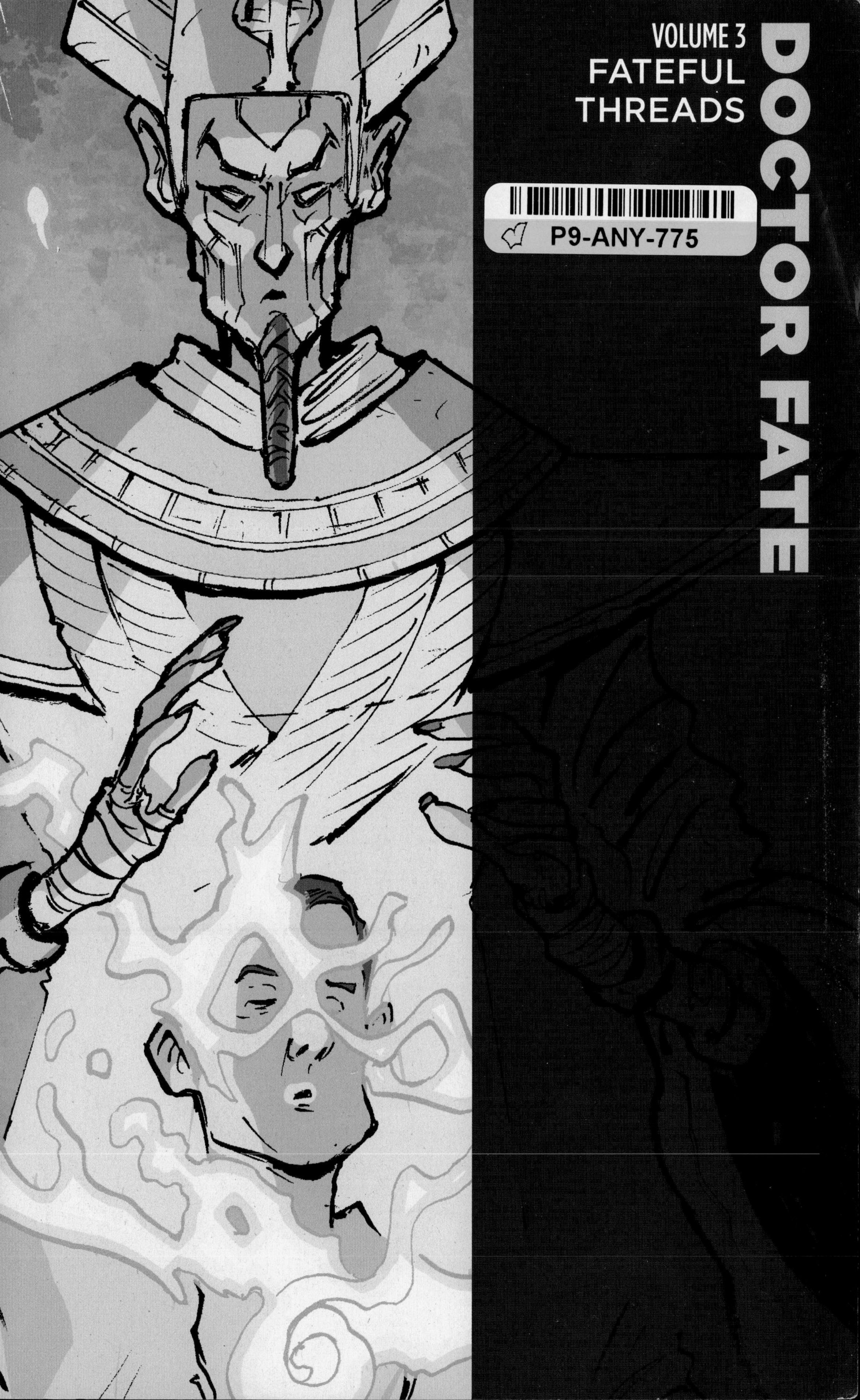
VOLUME 3
FATEFUL
THREADS
DOCTOR FATE
P9-ANY-775

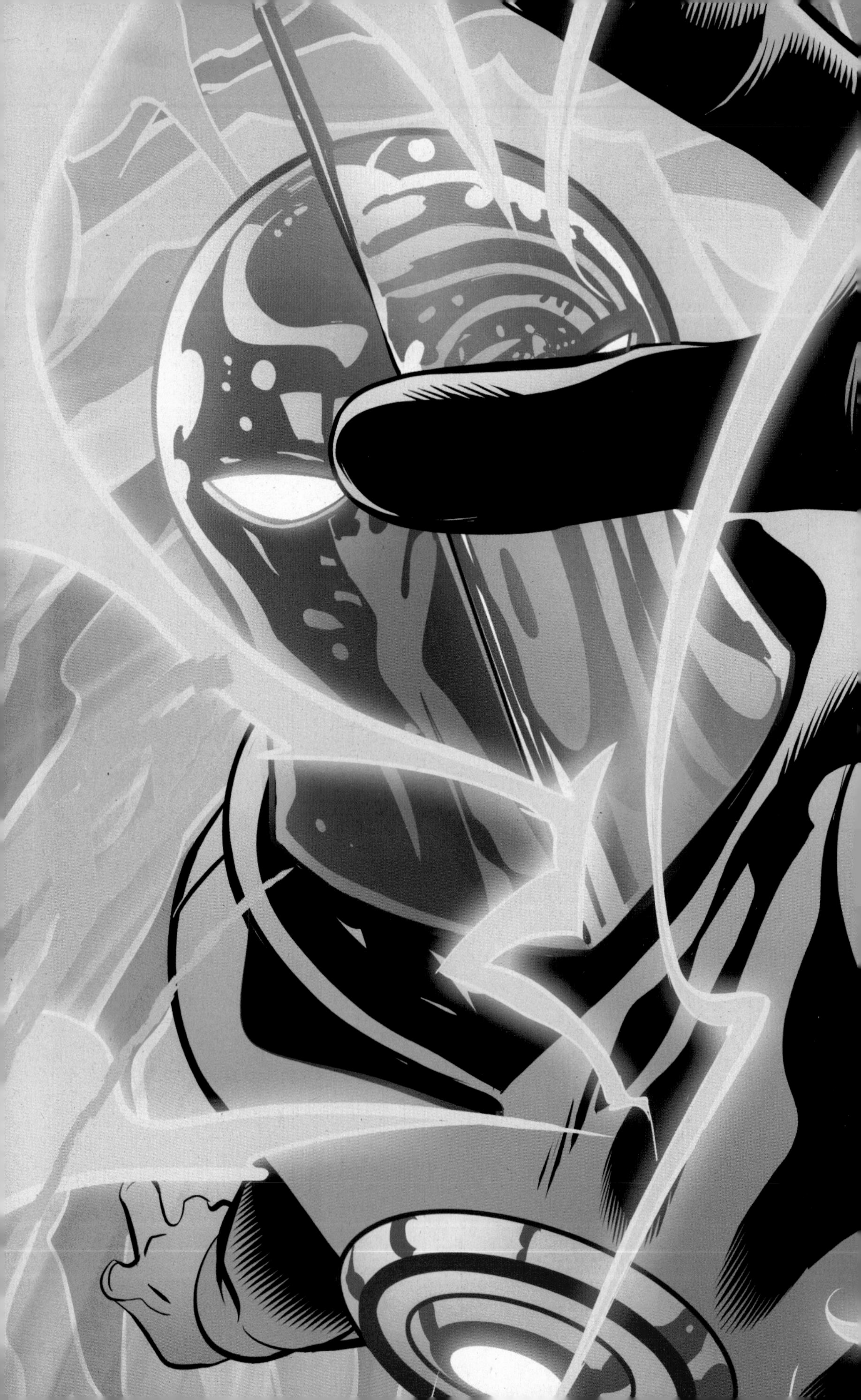

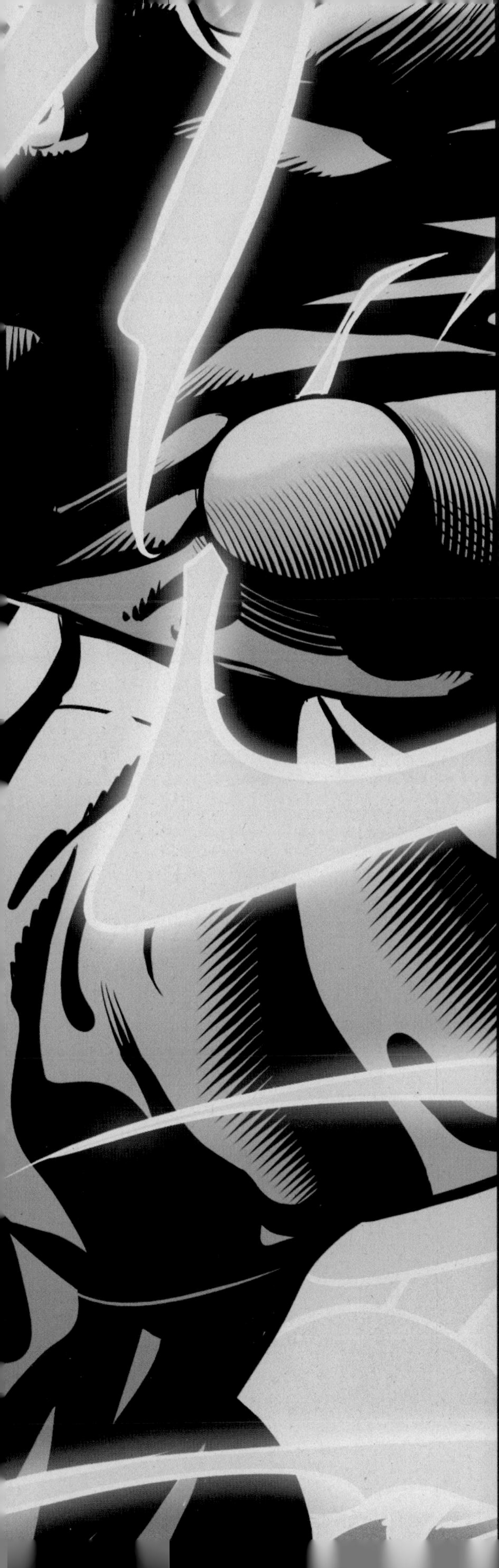

DOCTOR FATE

VOLUME 3
FATEFUL THREADS

WRITTEN BY
PAUL LEVITZ

ART BY
SONNY LIEW
BRENDAN McCARTHY
IBRAHIM MOUSTAFA
INAKI MIRANDA
BRENO TAMURA

COLOR BY
LEE LOUGHRIDGE
MARK HARRISON
EVA DE LA CRUZ
BRENDAN McCARTHY

LETTERS BY
SAIDA TEMOFONTE

COLLECTION COVER ART BY
BRENDAN McCARTHY

DAVID WOHL Editor – Original Series
JEB WOODARD Group Editor – Collected Editions
ROBIN WILDMAN Editor – Collected Edition
STEVE COOK Design Director – Books
DAMIAN RYLAND Publication Design

BOB HARRAS Senior VP – Editor-in-Chief, DC Comics

DIANE NELSON President
DAN DiDIO Publisher
JIM LEE Publisher
GEOFF JOHNS President & Chief Creative Officer
AMIT DESAI Executive VP – Business & Marketing Strategy,
Direct to Consumer & Global Franchise Management
SAM ADES Senior VP – Direct to Consumer
BOBBIE CHASE VP – Talent Development
MARK CHIARELLO Senior VP – Art, Design & Collected Editions
JOHN CUNNINGHAM Senior VP – Sales & Trade Marketing
ANNE DePIES Senior VP – Business Strategy, Finance & Administration
DON FALLETTI VP – Manufacturing Operations
LAWRENCE GANEM VP – Editorial Administration & Talent Relations
ALISON GILL Senior VP – Manufacturing & Operations
HANK KANALZ Senior VP – Editorial Strategy & Administration
JAY KOGAN VP – Legal Affairs
THOMAS LOFTUS VP – Business Affairs
JACK MAHAN VP – Business Affairs
NICK J. NAPOLITANO VP – Manufacturing Administration
EDDIE SCANNELL VP – Consumer Marketing
COURTNEY SIMMONS Senior VP – Publicity & Communications
JIM (SKI) SOKOLOWSKI VP – Comic Book Specialty Sales & Trade Marketing
NANCY SPEARS VP – Mass, Book, Digital Sales & Trade Marketing

DOCTOR FATE VOLUME 3: FATEFUL THREADS

DC Comics, 2900 West Alameda Ave., Burbank, CA 91505
Printed by Solisco Printers, Scott, QC, Canada. 3/31/17. First Printing.
ISBN: 978-1-4012-7241-8

Library of Congress Cataloging-in-Publication Data is available.

PEFC Certified

This product is from
sustainably managed
forests, recycled and
controlled sources

PEFC/26-31-02   www.pefc.org

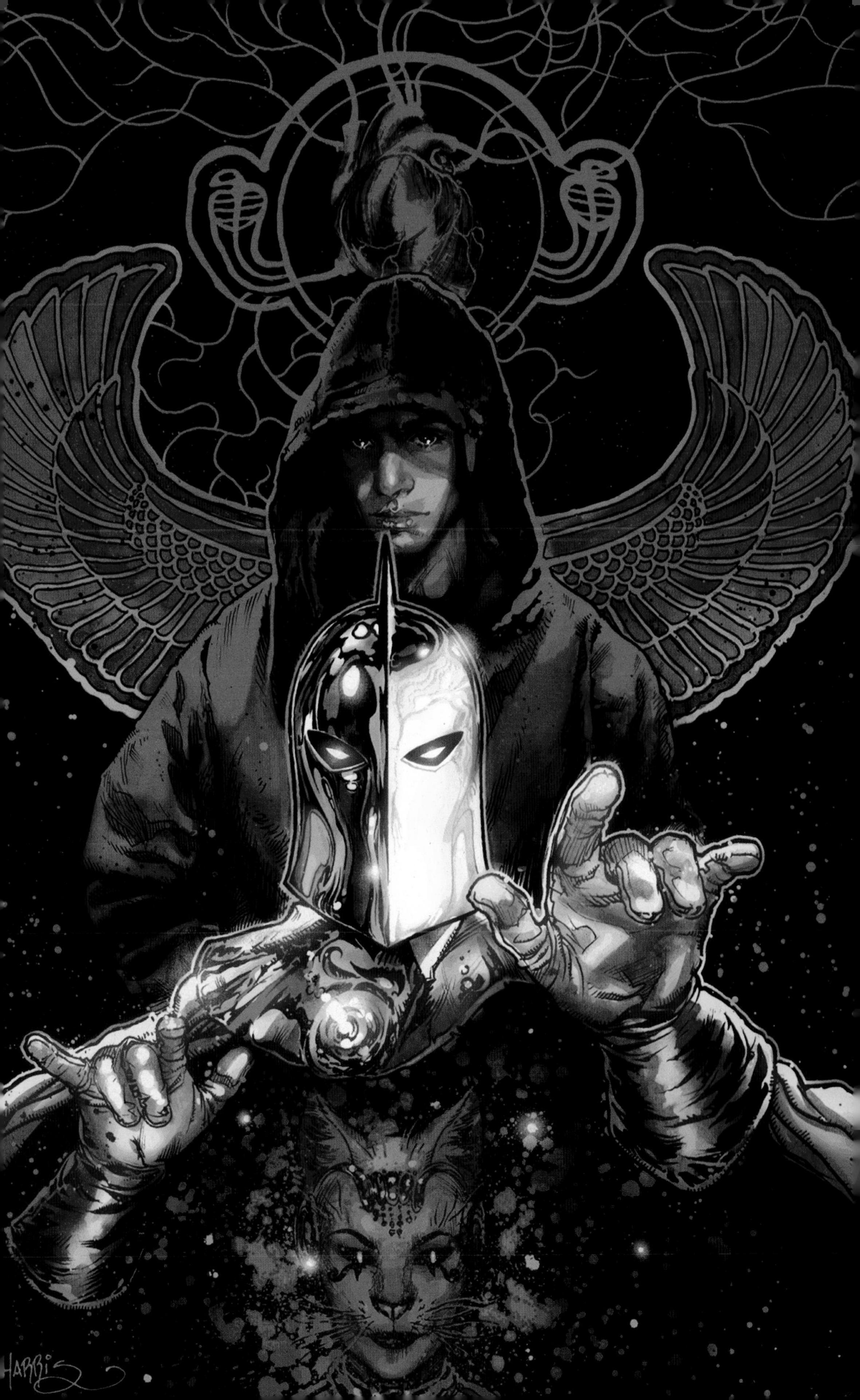
HARRIS

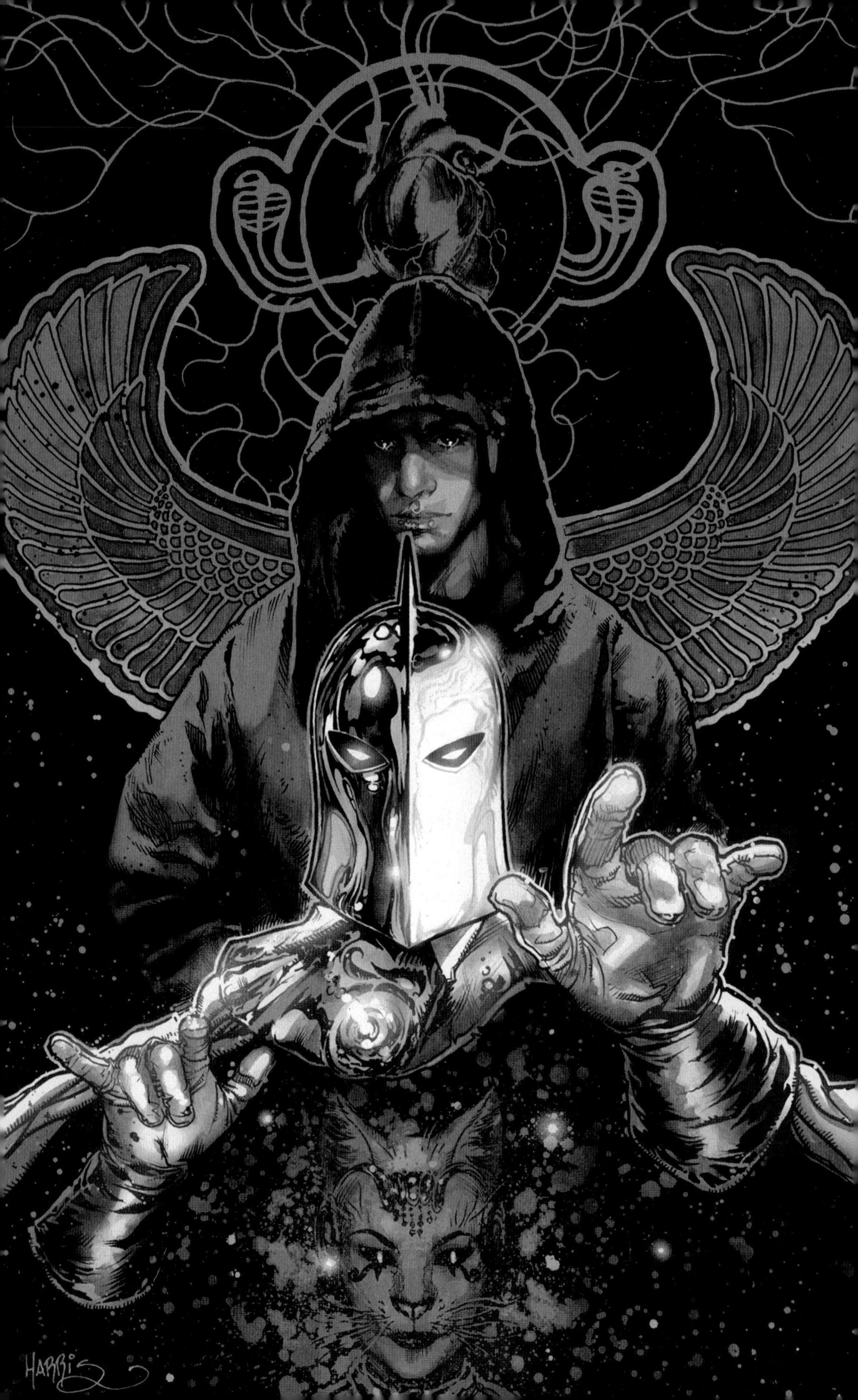
HARRIS

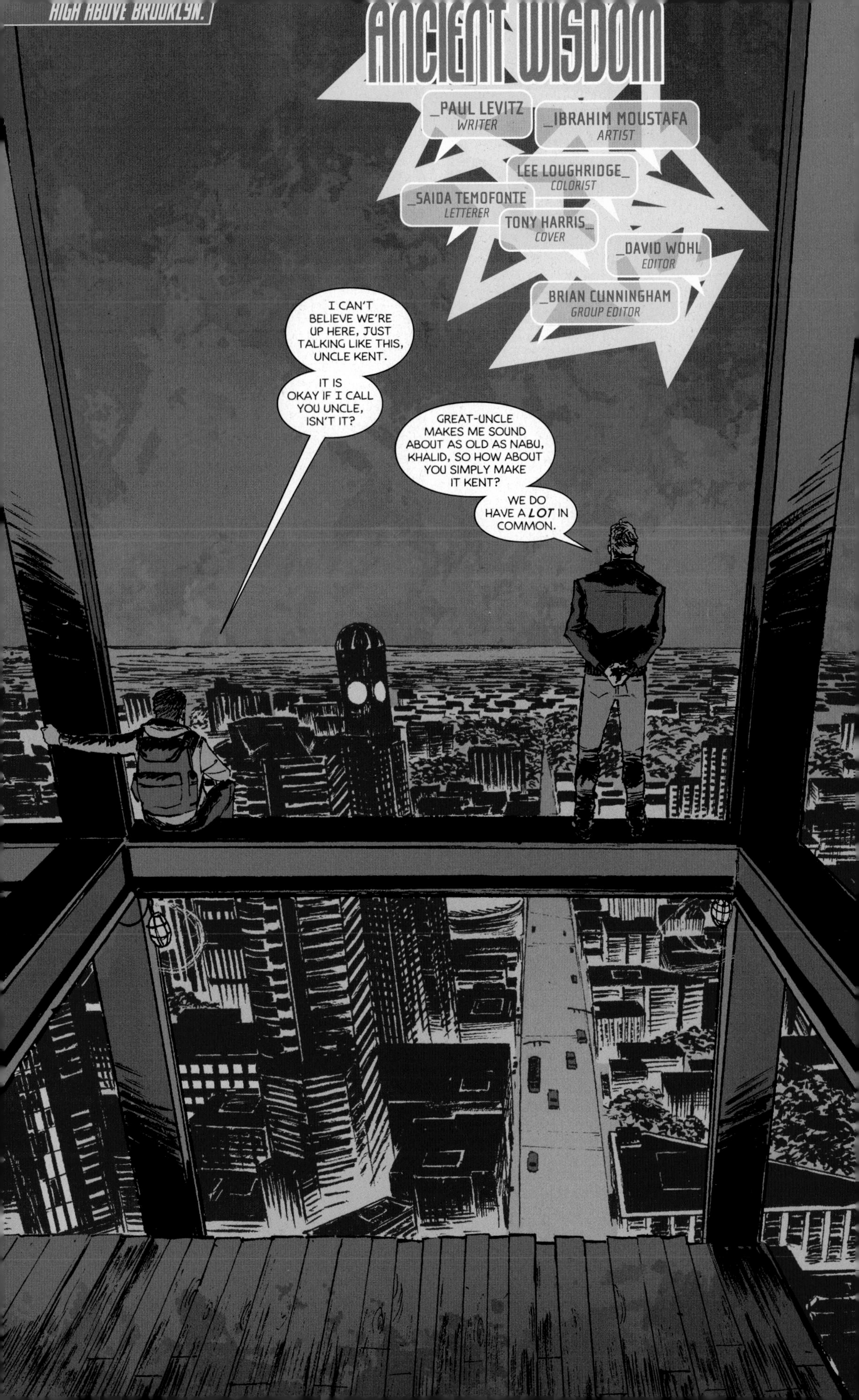
HIGH ABOVE BROOKLYN.
ANCIENT WISDOM
_PAUL LEVITZ WRITER
_IBRAHIM MOUSTAFA ARTIST
LEE LOUGHRIDGE_ COLORIST
_SAIDA TEMOFONTE LETTERER
TONY HARRIS_ COVER
_DAVID WOHL EDITOR
_BRIAN CUNNINGHAM GROUP EDITOR
I CAN'T BELIEVE WE'RE UP HERE, JUST TALKING LIKE THIS, UNCLE KENT.
IT IS OKAY IF I CALL YOU UNCLE, ISN'T IT?
GREAT-UNCLE MAKES ME SOUND ABOUT AS OLD AS NABU, KHALID, SO HOW ABOUT YOU SIMPLY MAKE IT KENT?
WE DO HAVE A LOT IN COMMON.

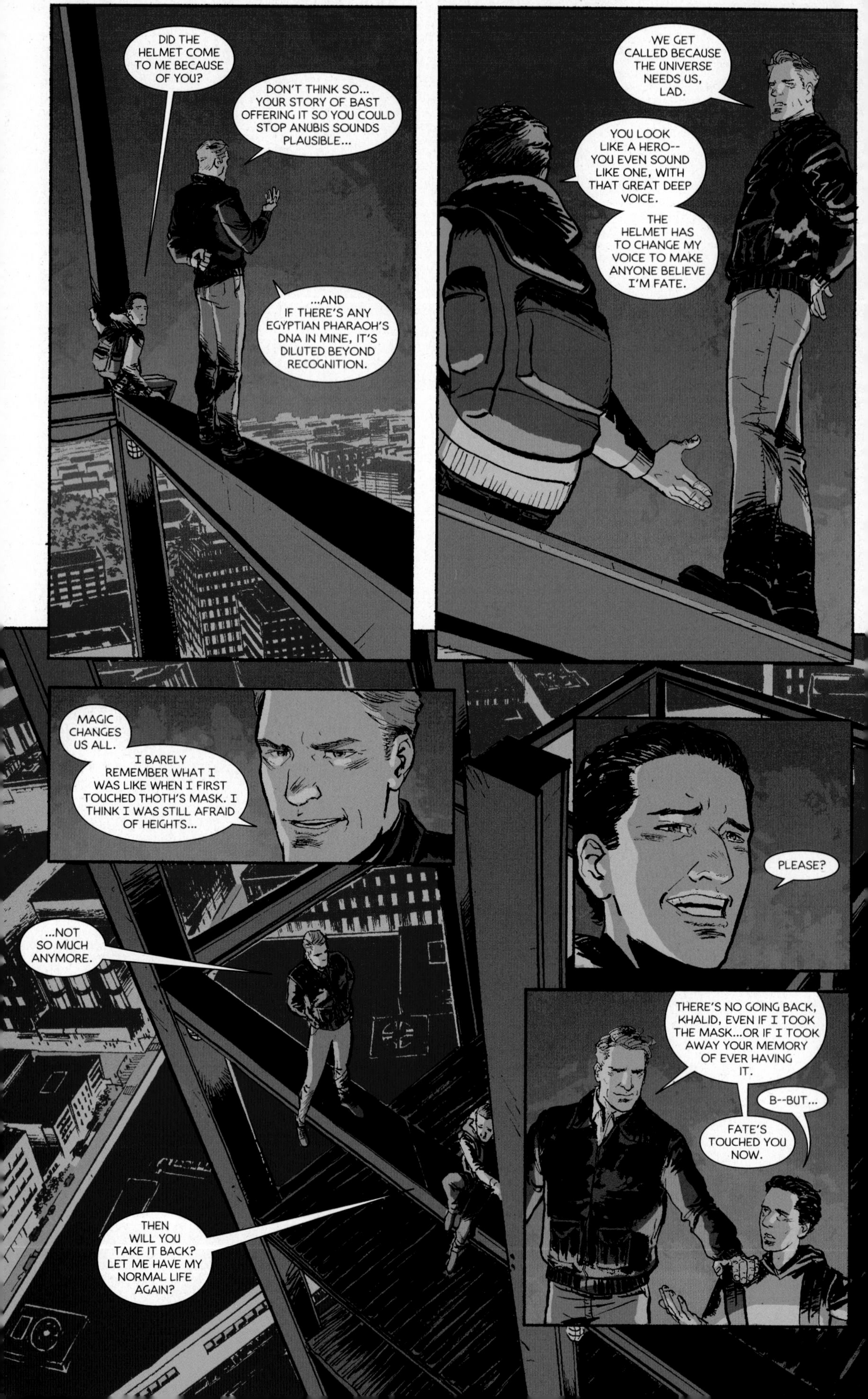

DID THE HELMET COME TO ME BECAUSE OF YOU?
DON'T THINK SO... YOUR STORY OF BAST OFFERING IT SO YOU COULD STOP ANUBIS SOUNDS PLAUSIBLE...
...AND IF THERE'S ANY EGYPTIAN PHARAOH'S DNA IN MINE, IT'S DILUTED BEYOND RECOGNITION.
WE GET CALLED BECAUSE THE UNIVERSE NEEDS US, LAD.
YOU LOOK LIKE A HERO-- YOU EVEN SOUND LIKE ONE, WITH THAT GREAT DEEP VOICE.
THE HELMET HAS TO CHANGE MY VOICE TO MAKE ANYONE BELIEVE I'M FATE.
MAGIC CHANGES US ALL.
I BARELY REMEMBER WHAT I WAS LIKE WHEN I FIRST TOUCHED THOTH'S MASK. I THINK I WAS STILL AFRAID OF HEIGHTS...
...NOT SO MUCH ANYMORE.
THEN WILL YOU TAKE IT BACK? LET ME HAVE MY NORMAL LIFE AGAIN?
PLEASE?
THERE'S NO GOING BACK, KHALID, EVEN IF I TOOK THE MASK...OR IF I TOOK AWAY YOUR MEMORY OF EVER HAVING IT.
B--BUT...
FATE'S TOUCHED YOU NOW.

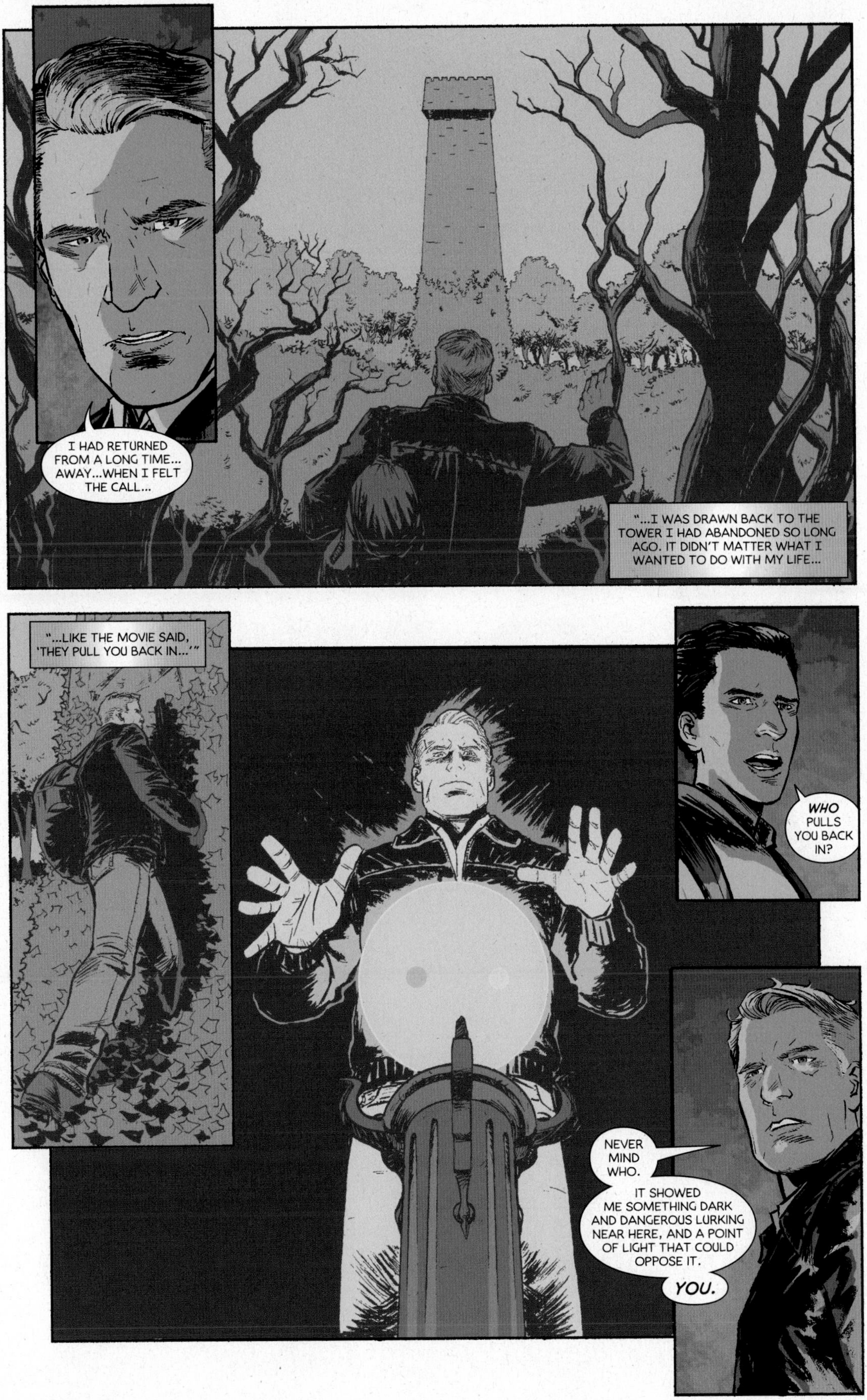
I HAD RETURNED FROM A LONG TIME... AWAY...WHEN I FELT THE CALL...
"...I WAS DRAWN BACK TO THE TOWER I HAD ABANDONED SO LONG AGO. IT DIDN'T MATTER WHAT I WANTED TO DO WITH MY LIFE...
"...LIKE THE MOVIE SAID, 'THEY PULL YOU BACK IN...'"
WHO PULLS YOU BACK IN?
NEVER MIND WHO.
IT SHOWED ME SOMETHING DARK AND DANGEROUS LURKING NEAR HERE, AND A POINT OF LIGHT THAT COULD OPPOSE IT.
YOU.

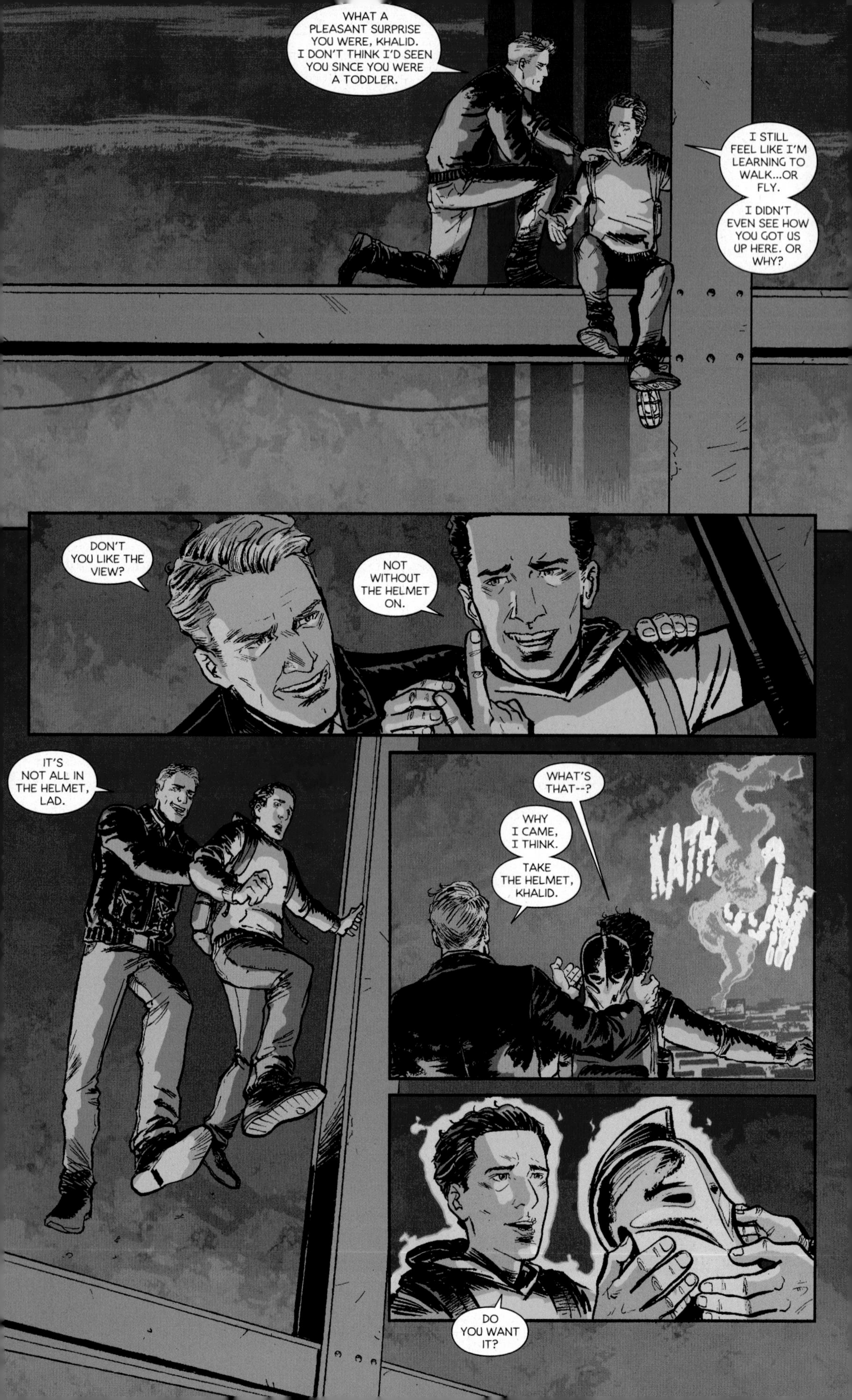

WHAT A PLEASANT SURPRISE YOU WERE, KHALID. I DON'T THINK I'D SEEN YOU SINCE YOU WERE A TODDLER.
I STILL FEEL LIKE I'M LEARNING TO WALK...OR FLY.
I DIDN'T EVEN SEE HOW YOU GOT US UP HERE. OR WHY?
DON'T YOU LIKE THE VIEW?
NOT WITHOUT THE HELMET ON.
IT'S NOT ALL IN THE HELMET, LAD.
WHAT'S THAT--?
WHY I CAME, I THINK.
TAKE THE HELMET, KHALID.
DO YOU WANT IT?

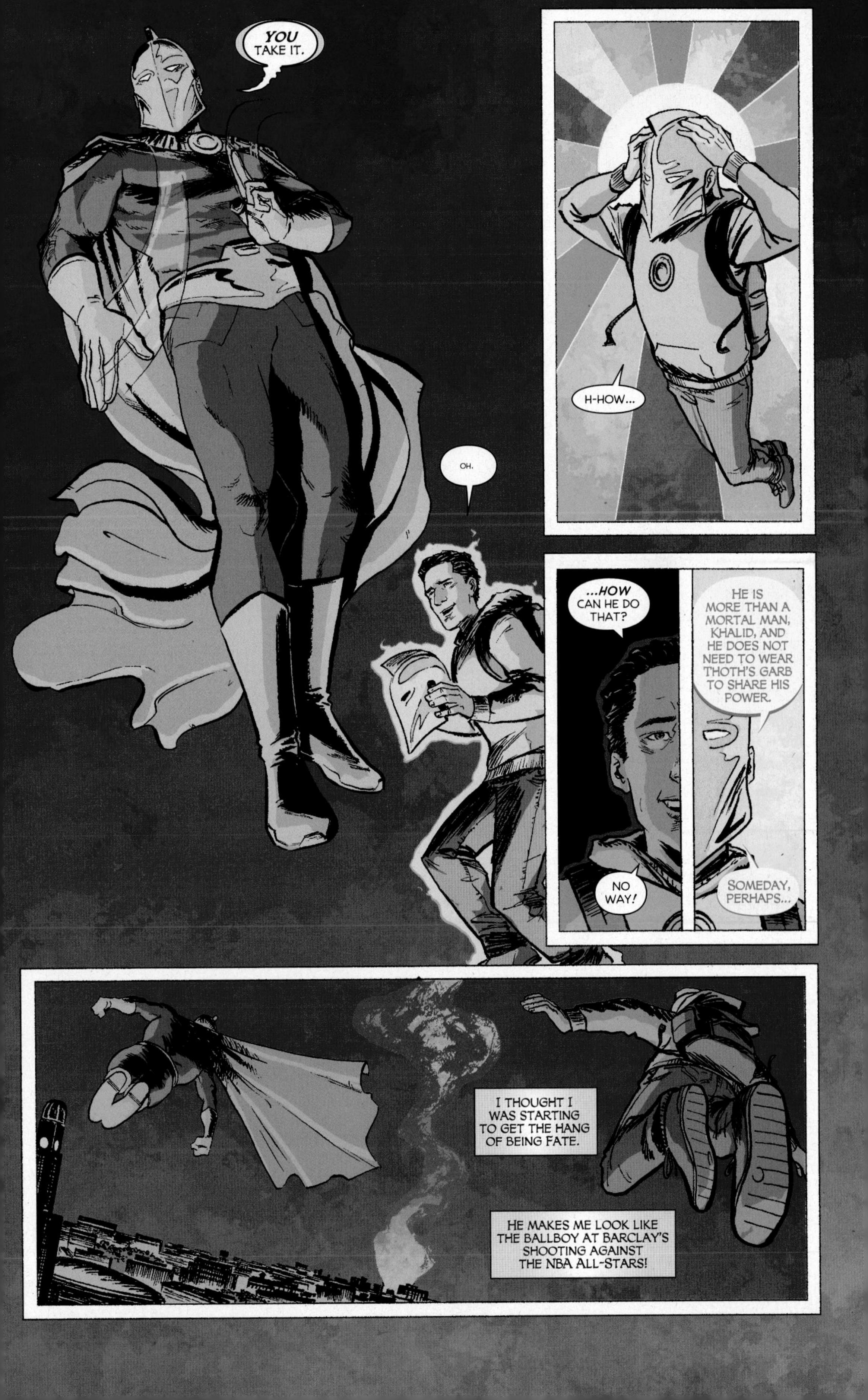

YOU TAKE IT.
H-HOW...
OH.
...HOW CAN HE DO THAT?
HE IS MORE THAN A MORTAL MAN, KHALID, AND HE DOES NOT NEED TO WEAR THOTH'S GARB TO SHARE HIS POWER.
NO WAY!
SOMEDAY, PERHAPS...
I THOUGHT I WAS STARTING TO GET THE HANG OF BEING FATE.
HE MAKES ME LOOK LIKE THE BALLBOY AT BARCLAY'S SHOOTING AGAINST THE NBA ALL-STARS!

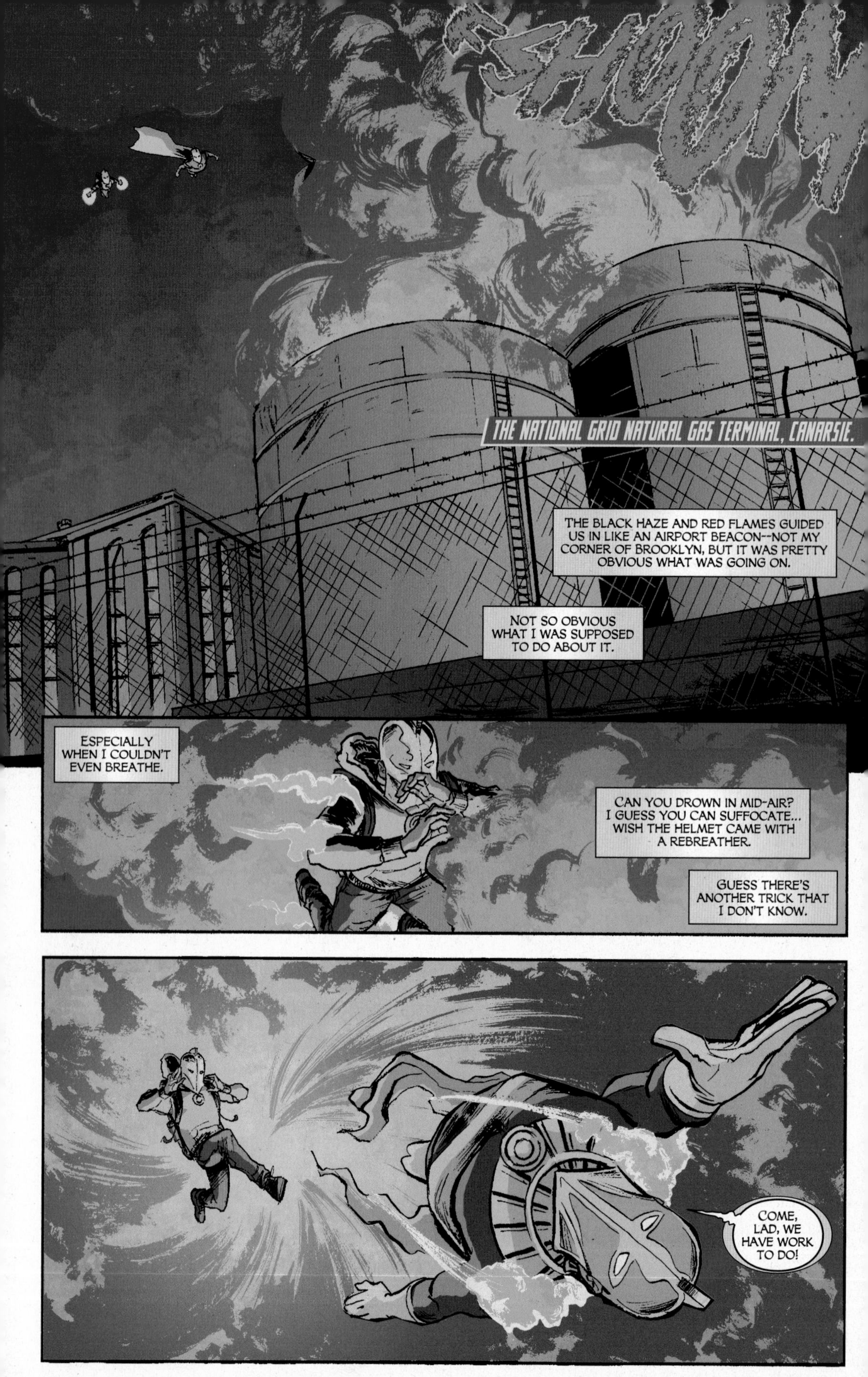
THE NATIONAL GRID NATURAL GAS TERMINAL, CANARSIE.
THE BLACK HAZE AND RED FLAMES GUIDED US IN LIKE AN AIRPORT BEACON--NOT MY CORNER OF BROOKLYN, BUT IT WAS PRETTY OBVIOUS WHAT WAS GOING ON.
NOT SO OBVIOUS WHAT I WAS SUPPOSED TO DO ABOUT IT.
ESPECIALLY WHEN I COULDN'T EVEN BREATHE.
CAN YOU DROWN IN MID-AIR? I GUESS YOU CAN SUFFOCATE... WISH THE HELMET CAME WITH A REBREATHER.
GUESS THERE'S ANOTHER TRICK THAT I DON'T KNOW.
COME, LAD, WE HAVE WORK TO DO!

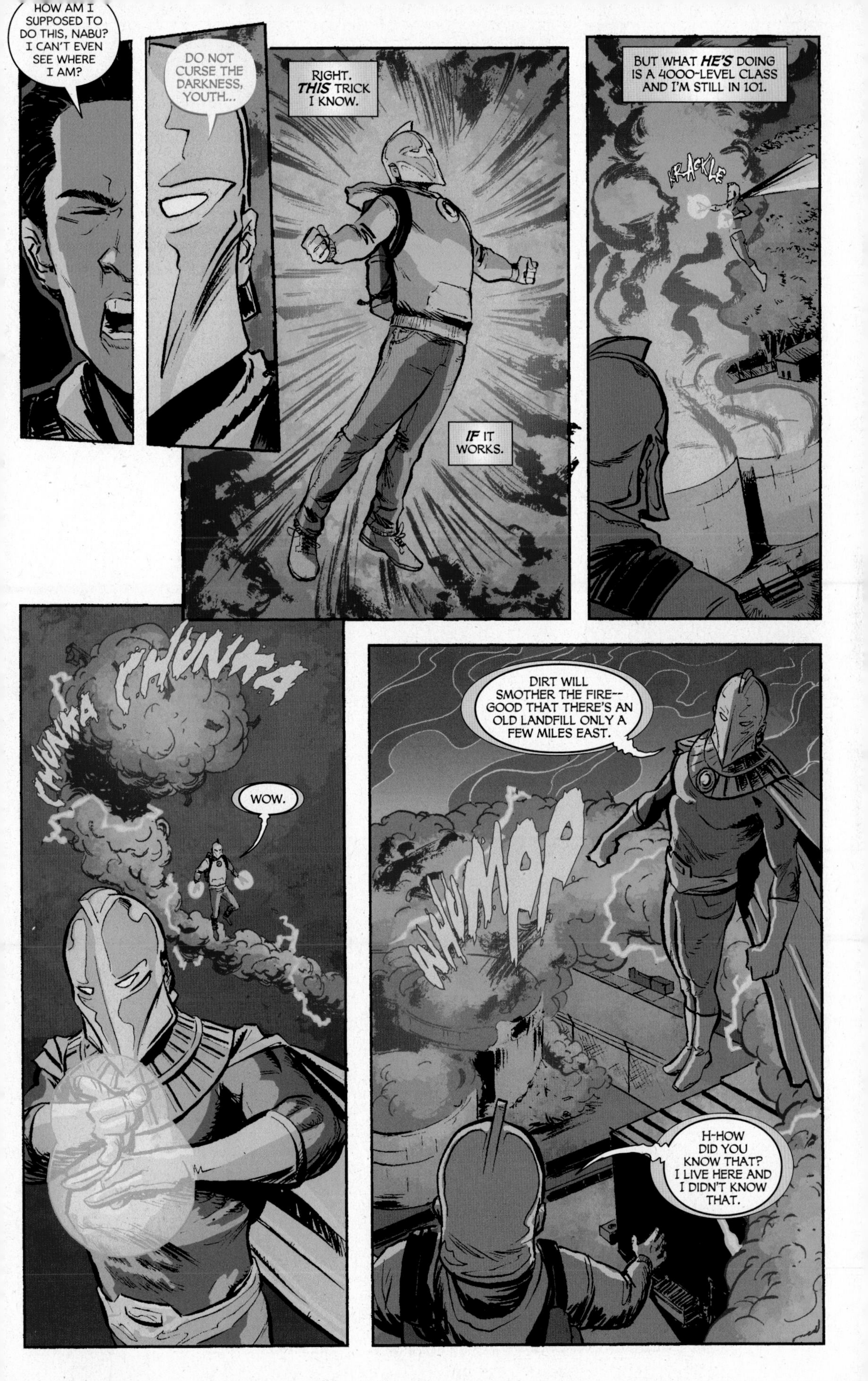
HOW AM I SUPPOSED TO DO THIS, NABU? I CAN'T EVEN SEE WHERE I AM?
DO NOT CURSE THE DARKNESS, YOUTH...
RIGHT. THIS TRICK I KNOW.
IF IT WORKS.
BUT WHAT HE'S DOING IS A 4000-LEVEL CLASS AND I'M STILL IN 101.
KRACKLE
CHUNKA CHUNKA
WOW.
DIRT WILL SMOTHER THE FIRE--GOOD THAT THERE'S AN OLD LANDFILL ONLY A FEW MILES EAST.
WHUMPP
H-HOW DID YOU KNOW THAT? I LIVE HERE AND I DIDN'T KNOW THAT.

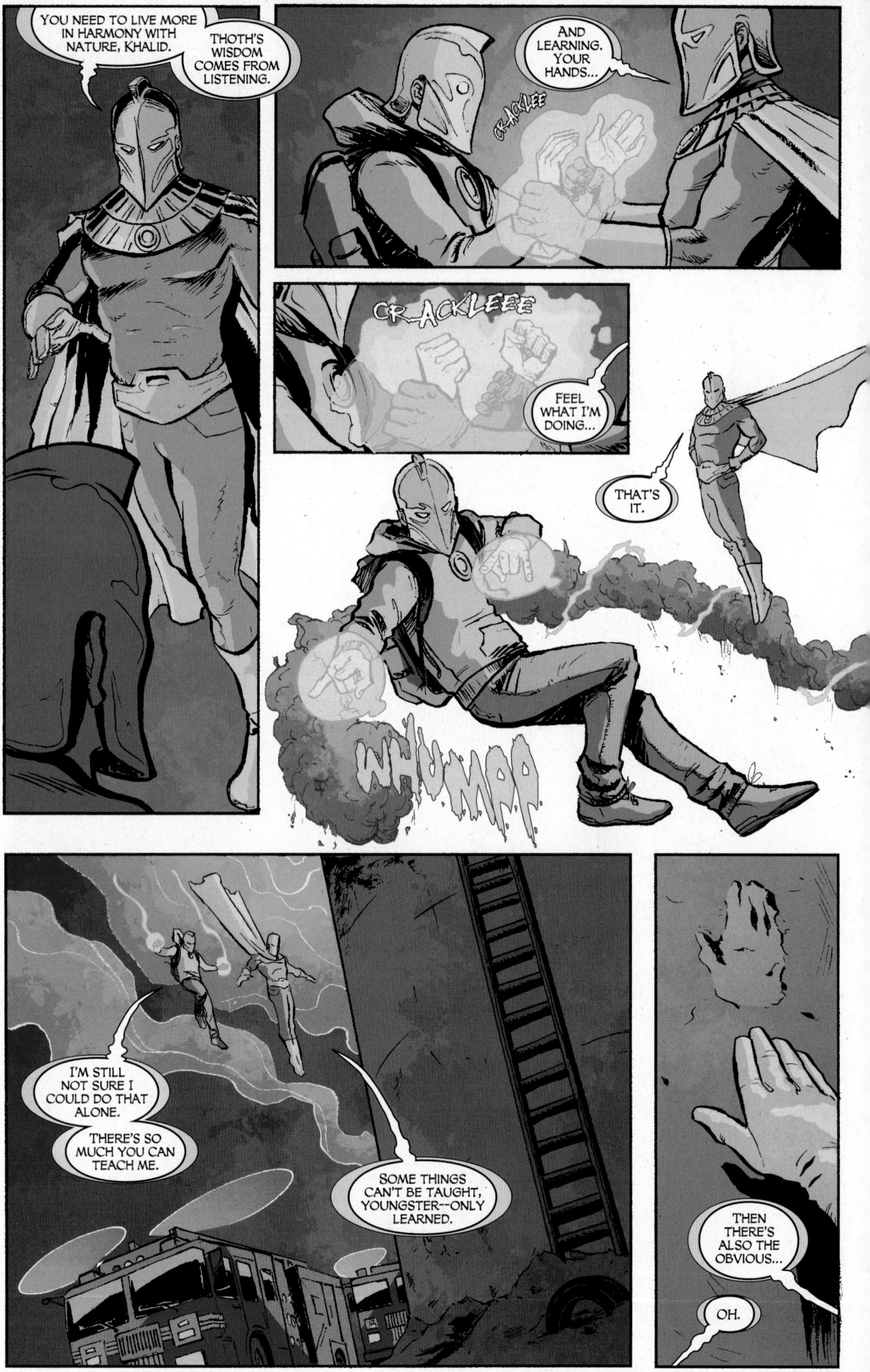
YOU NEED TO LIVE MORE IN HARMONY WITH NATURE, KHALID.
THOTH'S WISDOM COMES FROM LISTENING.
AND LEARNING. YOUR HANDS...
CRACKLEE
CRACKLEEE
FEEL WHAT I'M DOING...
THAT'S IT.
WHUMPP
I'M STILL NOT SURE I COULD DO THAT ALONE.
THERE'S SO MUCH YOU CAN TEACH ME.
SOME THINGS CAN'T BE TAUGHT, YOUNGSTER--ONLY LEARNED.
THEN THERE'S ALSO THE OBVIOUS...
OH.

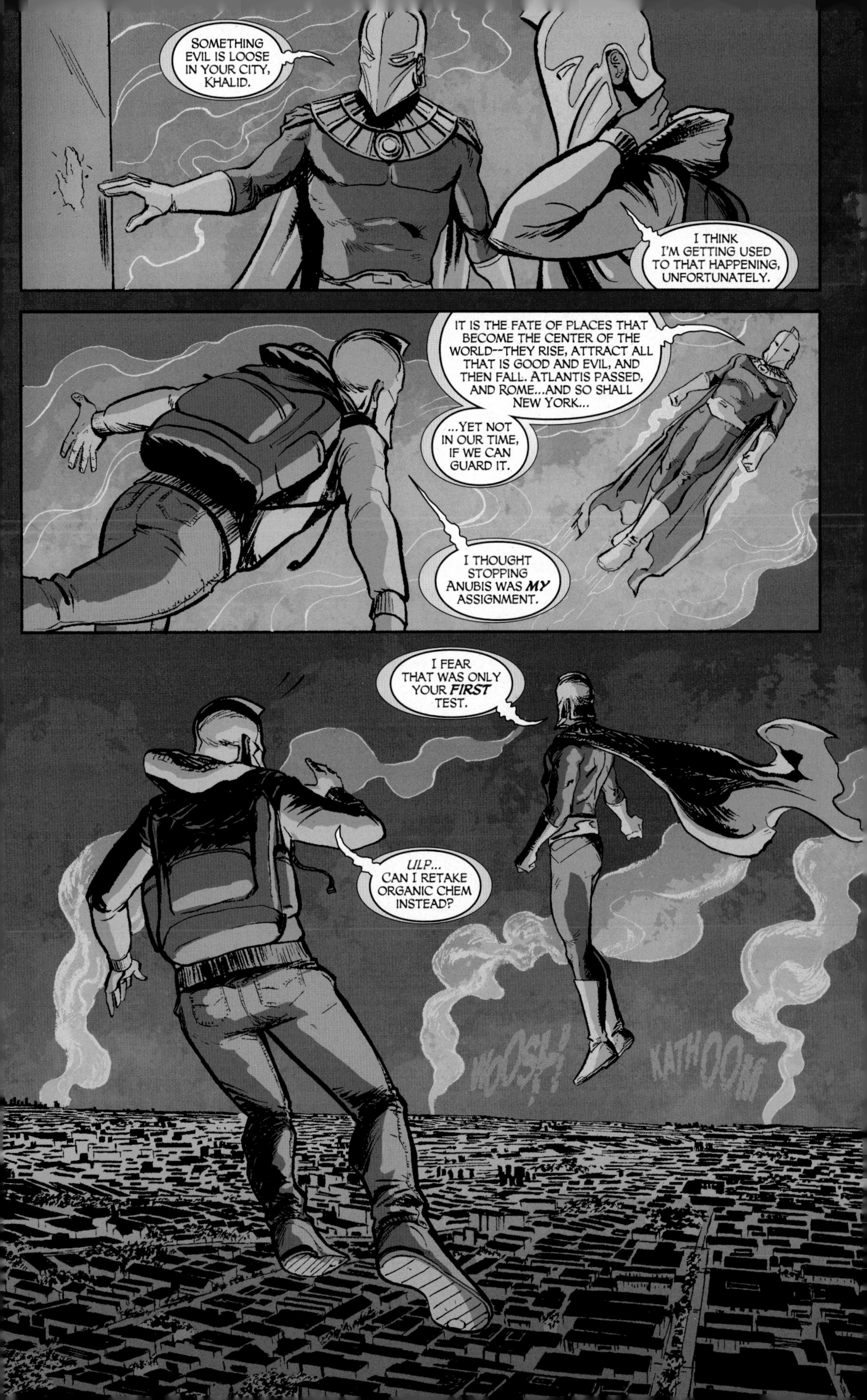
SOMETHING EVIL IS LOOSE IN YOUR CITY, KHALID.
I THINK I'M GETTING USED TO THAT HAPPENING, UNFORTUNATELY.
IT IS THE FATE OF PLACES THAT BECOME THE CENTER OF THE WORLD--THEY RISE, ATTRACT ALL THAT IS GOOD AND EVIL, AND THEN FALL. ATLANTIS PASSED, AND ROME...AND SO SHALL NEW YORK...
...YET NOT IN OUR TIME, IF WE CAN GUARD IT.
I THOUGHT STOPPING ANUBIS WAS *MY* ASSIGNMENT.
I FEAR THAT WAS ONLY YOUR *FIRST* TEST.
ULP... CAN I RETAKE ORGANIC CHEM INSTEAD?
WOOSH!
KATHOOM

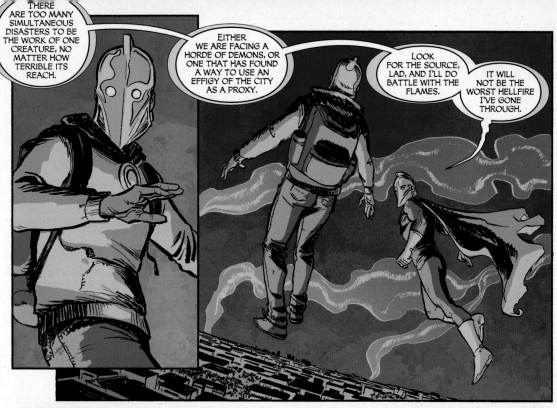

THERE ARE TOO MANY SIMULTANEOUS DISASTERS TO BE THE WORK OF ONE CREATURE, NO MATTER HOW TERRIBLE ITS REACH.

EITHER WE ARE FACING A HORDE OF DEMONS, OR ONE THAT HAS FOUND A WAY TO USE AN EFFIGY OF THE CITY AS A PROXY.

LOOK FOR THE SOURCE, LAD, AND I'LL DO BATTLE WITH THE FLAMES.

IT WILL NOT BE THE WORST HELLFIRE I'VE GONE THROUGH.

GREAT...I THOUGHT I WAS FINALLY GETTING A MENTOR, AND HIS IDEA OF GUIDANCE IS AN OMINOUS VERSION OF THE NIKE SLOGAN.

HOW EXACTLY AM I SUPPOSED TO FIND THE "SOURCE"?

HE SAID SOMETHING COULD BE BURNING THE CITY IN EFFIGY... OH...

LISTEN TO HIS WORDS OF WISDOM, KHALID.

WOOOOSH

GOT IT.

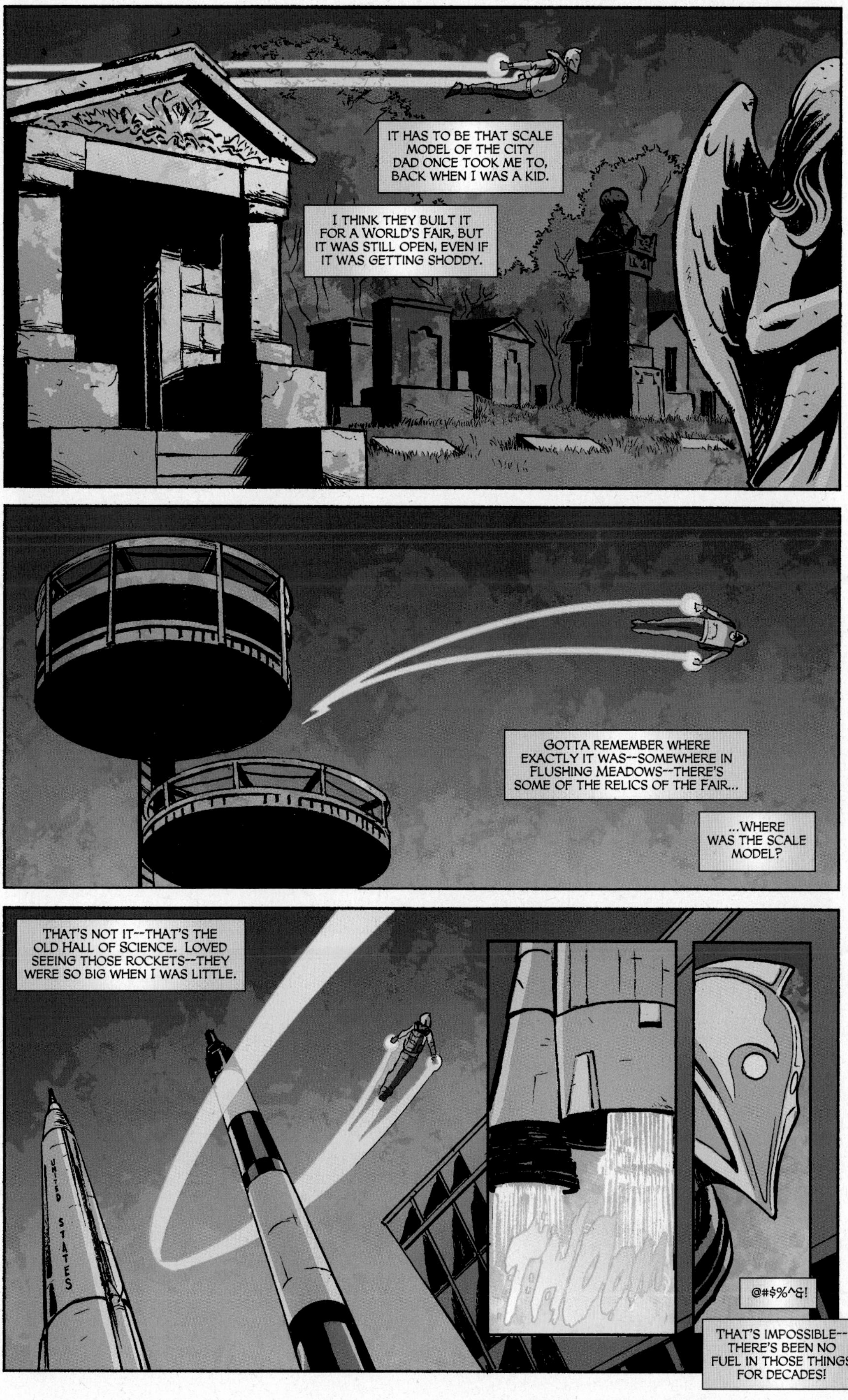
IT HAS TO BE THAT SCALE MODEL OF THE CITY DAD ONCE TOOK ME TO, BACK WHEN I WAS A KID.
I THINK THEY BUILT IT FOR A WORLD'S FAIR, BUT IT WAS STILL OPEN, EVEN IF IT WAS GETTING SHODDY.
GOTTA REMEMBER WHERE EXACTLY IT WAS--SOMEWHERE IN FLUSHING MEADOWS--THERE'S SOME OF THE RELICS OF THE FAIR...
...WHERE WAS THE SCALE MODEL?
THAT'S NOT IT--THAT'S THE OLD HALL OF SCIENCE. LOVED SEEING THOSE ROCKETS--THEY WERE SO BIG WHEN I WAS LITTLE.
UNITED STATES
@#$%^&!
THAT'S IMPOSSIBLE--THERE'S BEEN NO FUEL IN THOSE THINGS FOR DECADES!

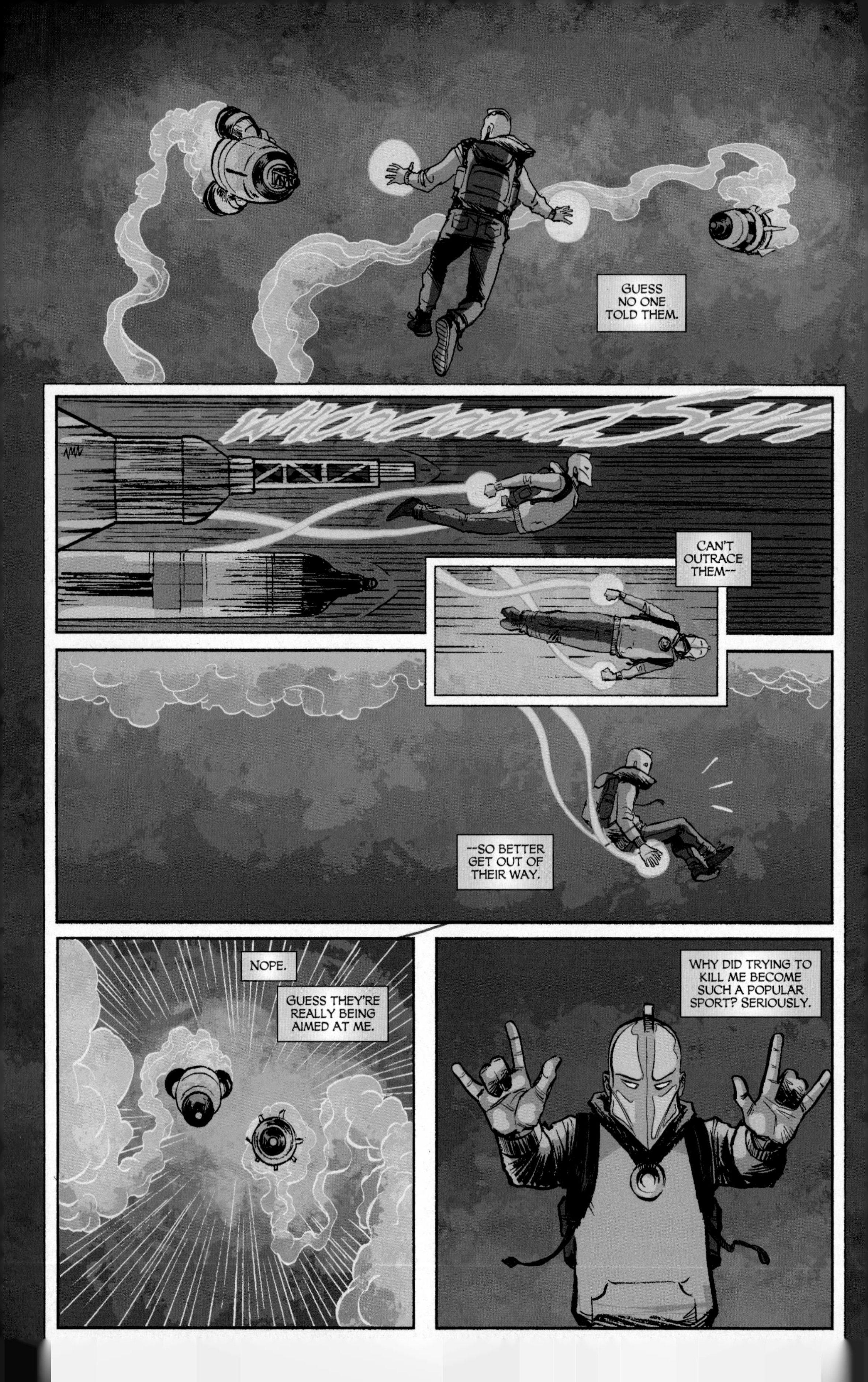
GUESS NO ONE TOLD THEM.
WHOOOOOOOOSHH
CAN'T OUTRACE THEM--
--SO BETTER GET OUT OF THEIR WAY.
NOPE.
GUESS THEY'RE REALLY BEING AIMED AT ME.
WHY DID TRYING TO KILL ME BECOME SUCH A POPULAR SPORT? SERIOUSLY.

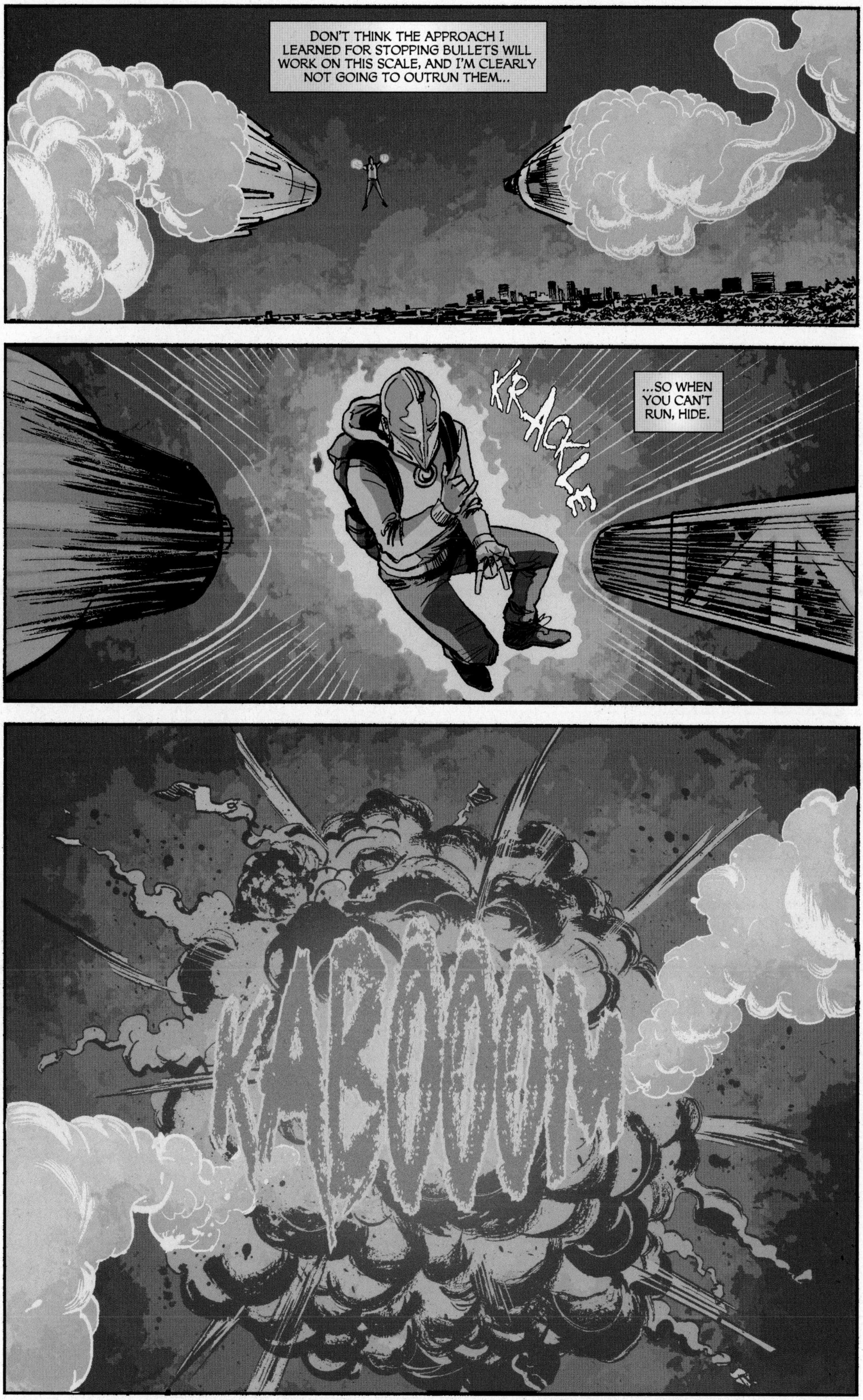
DON'T THINK THE APPROACH I LEARNED FOR STOPPING BULLETS WILL WORK ON THIS SCALE, AND I'M CLEARLY NOT GOING TO OUTRUN THEM...
KRACKLE
...SO WHEN YOU CAN'T RUN, HIDE.
KABOOOOM

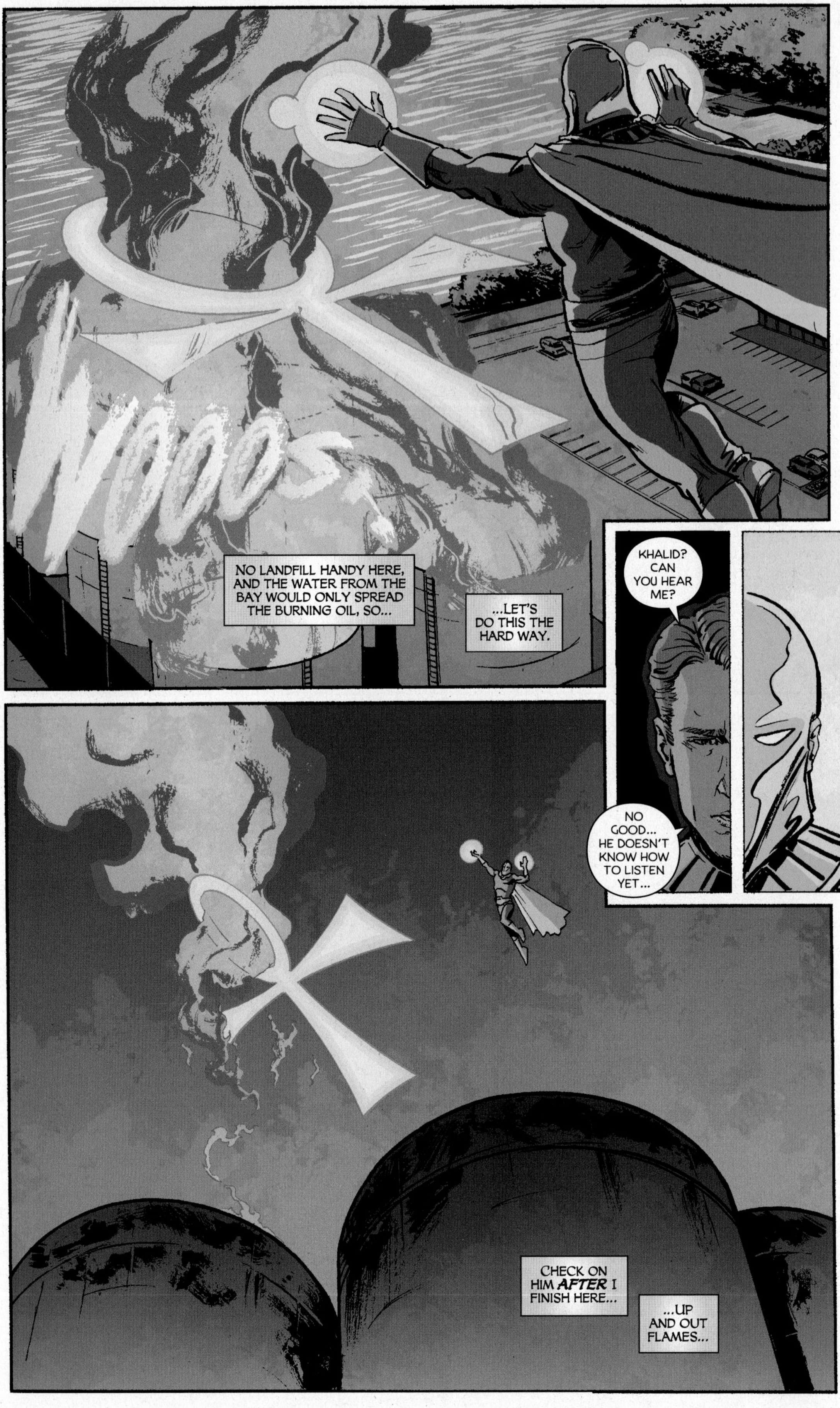
WOOOSH
NO LANDFILL HANDY HERE, AND THE WATER FROM THE BAY WOULD ONLY SPREAD THE BURNING OIL, SO...
...LET'S DO THIS THE HARD WAY.
KHALID? CAN YOU HEAR ME?
NO GOOD... HE DOESN'T KNOW HOW TO LISTEN YET...
CHECK ON HIM AFTER I FINISH HERE...
...UP AND OUT FLAMES...

THAT WORKED! FIGURED IF I COULD GO THROUGH THINGS LIKE WALLS, THE SAME TRICK MIGHT LET THINGS GO THROUGH ME.

FEELS LIKE I'VE BEEN SITTING IN AN OVEN, THOUGH.

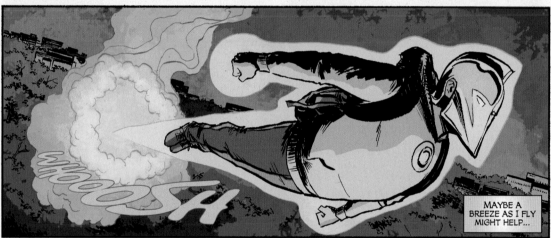

MAYBE A BREEZE AS I FLY MIGHT HELP...

THEY'LL HAVE A LOT TO CLEAN UP BEFORE THEY CAN REOPEN IN THE MORNING, BUT AT LEAST NO ONE GOT HURT.

ESPECIALLY ME.

WHATEVER'S WRECKING NEW YORK BY EFFIGY NOTICED I WAS GETTING CLOSE--AND I AM.

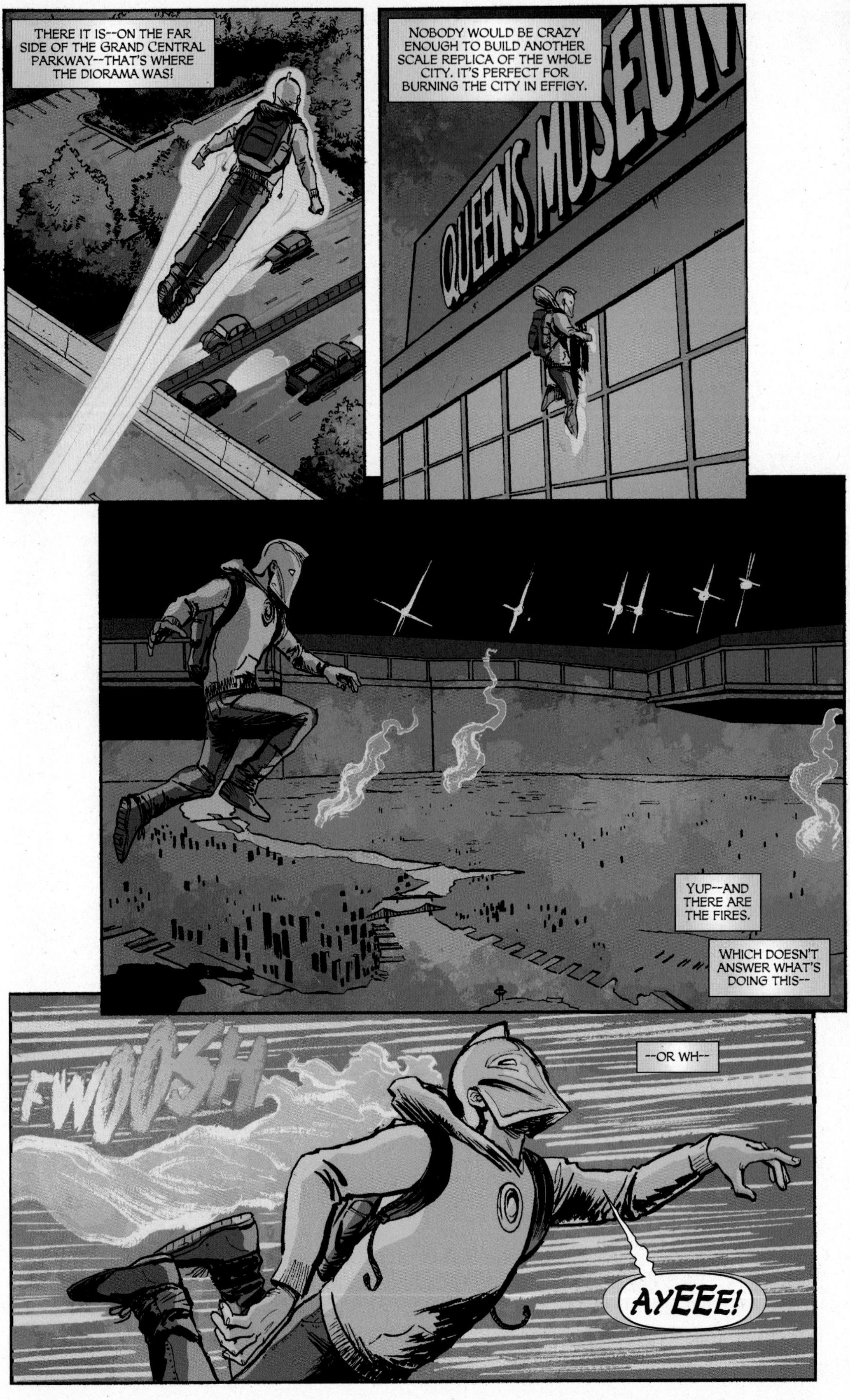
THERE IT IS--ON THE FAR SIDE OF THE GRAND CENTRAL PARKWAY--THAT'S WHERE THE DIORAMA WAS!
NOBODY WOULD BE CRAZY ENOUGH TO BUILD ANOTHER SCALE REPLICA OF THE WHOLE CITY. IT'S PERFECT FOR BURNING THE CITY IN EFFIGY.
QUEENS MUSEUM
YUP--AND THERE ARE THE FIRES.
WHICH DOESN'T ANSWER WHAT'S DOING THIS--
FWOOSH
--OR WH--
AYEEE!

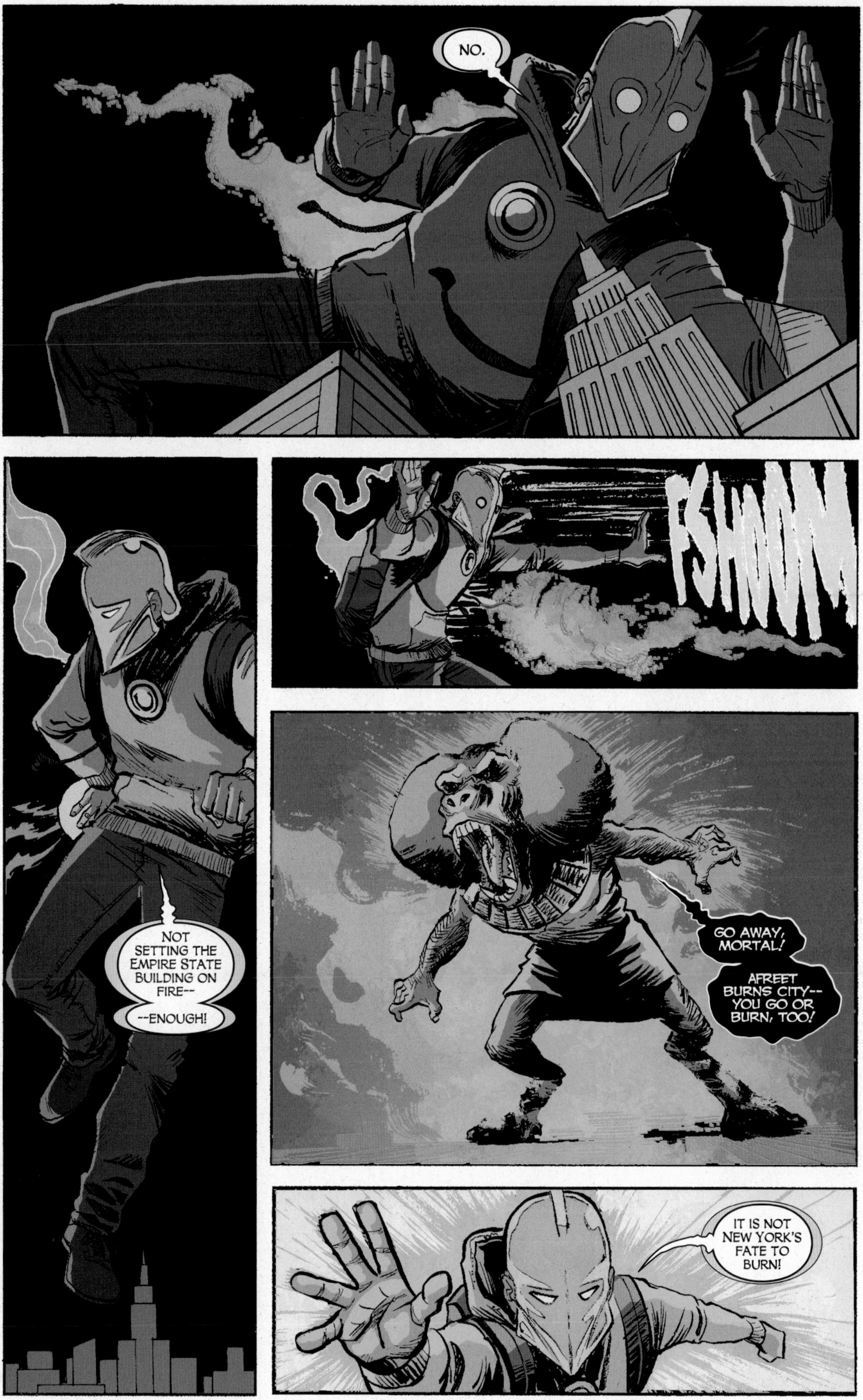
NO.
NOT SETTING THE EMPIRE STATE BUILDING ON FIRE--
--ENOUGH!
FSHOOM
GO AWAY, MORTAL!
AFREET BURNS CITY-- YOU GO OR BURN, TOO!
IT IS NOT NEW YORK'S FATE TO BURN!

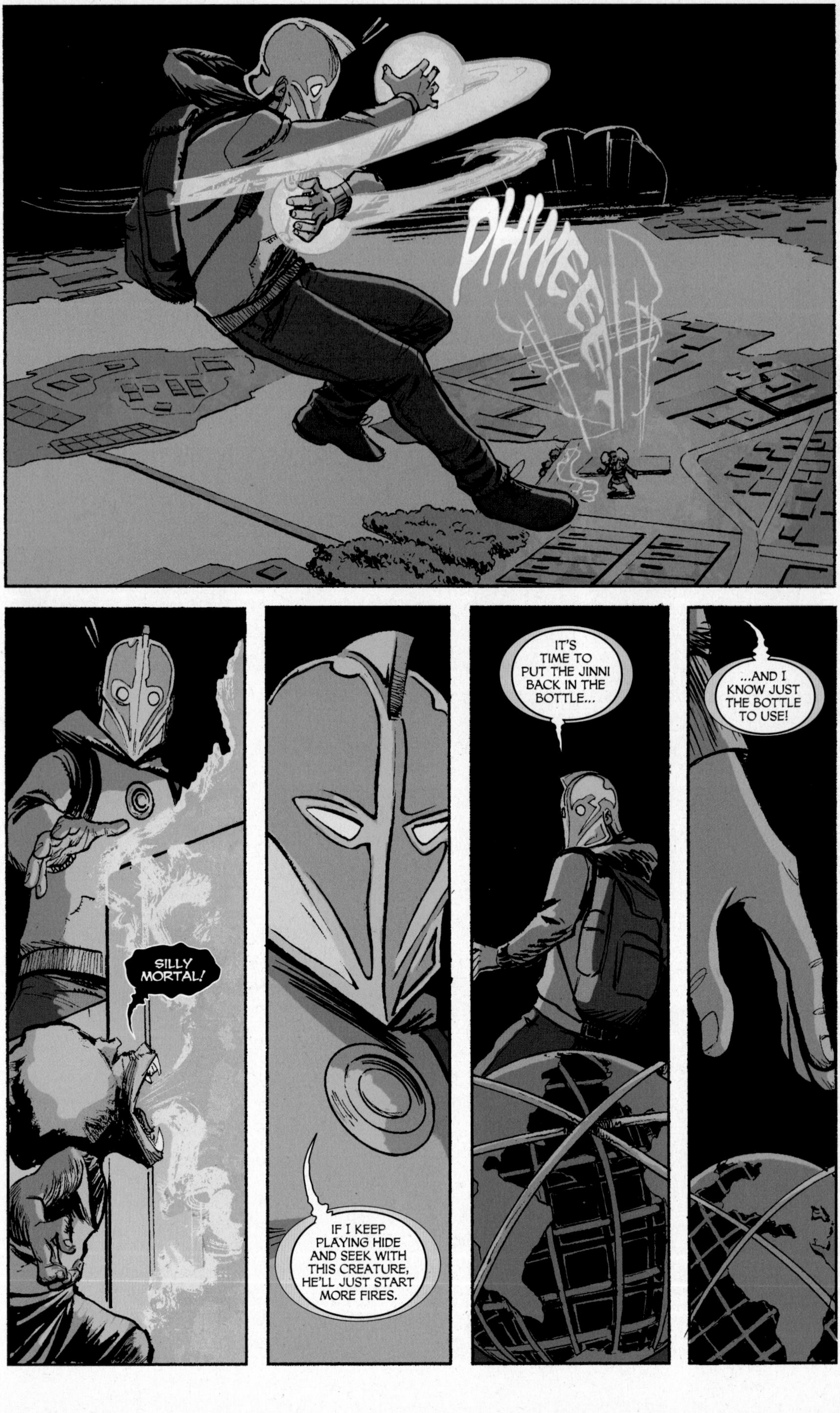
PHWEEE
SILLY MORTAL!
IF I KEEP PLAYING HIDE AND SEEK WITH THIS CREATURE, HE'LL JUST START MORE FIRES.
IT'S TIME TO PUT THE JINNI BACK IN THE BOTTLE...
...AND I KNOW JUST THE BOTTLE TO USE!

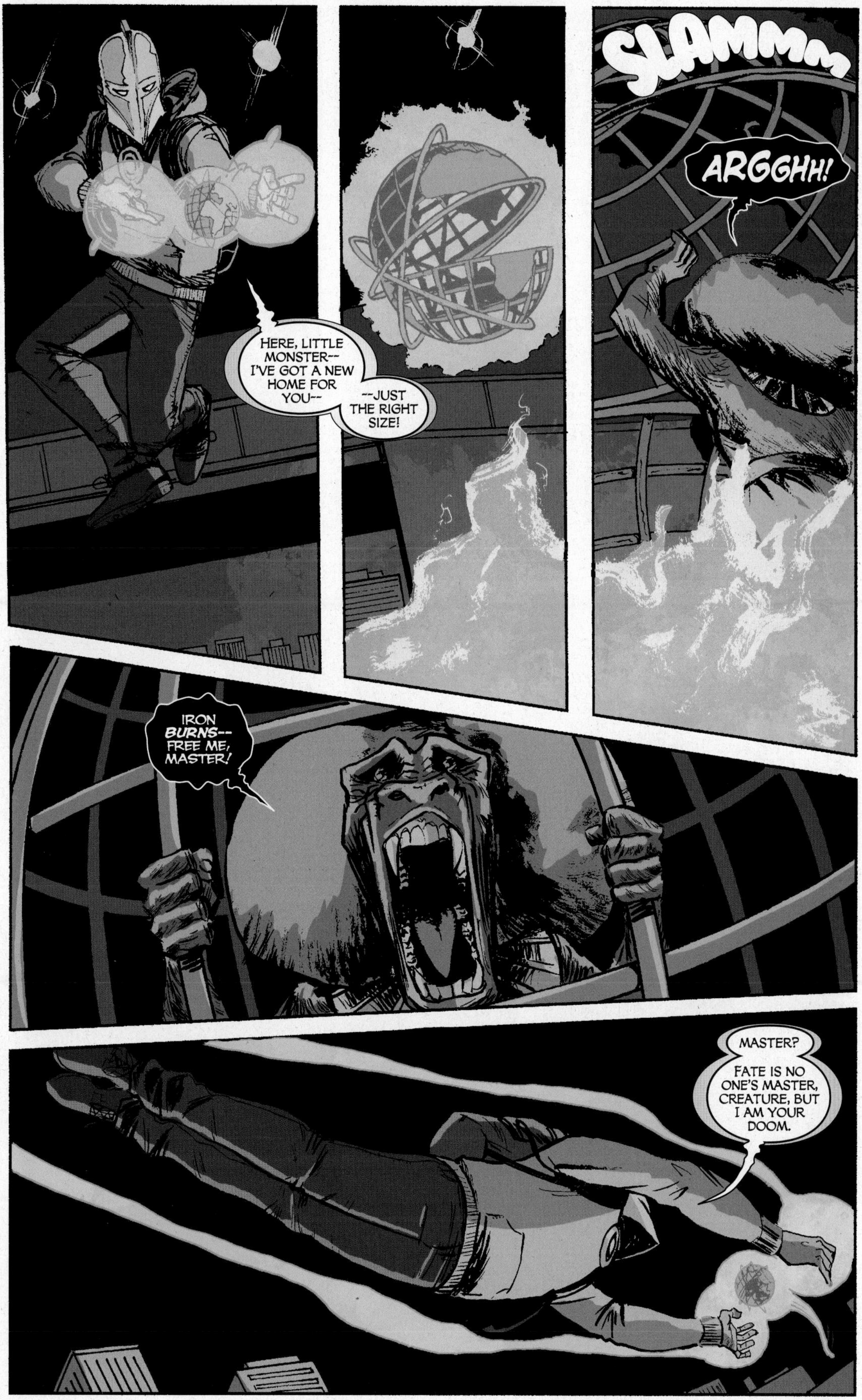
HERE, LITTLE MONSTER-- I'VE GOT A NEW HOME FOR YOU--
--JUST THE RIGHT SIZE!
SLAMMM
ARGGHH!
IRON BURNS-- FREE ME, MASTER!
MASTER?
FATE IS NO ONE'S MASTER, CREATURE, BUT I AM YOUR DOOM.

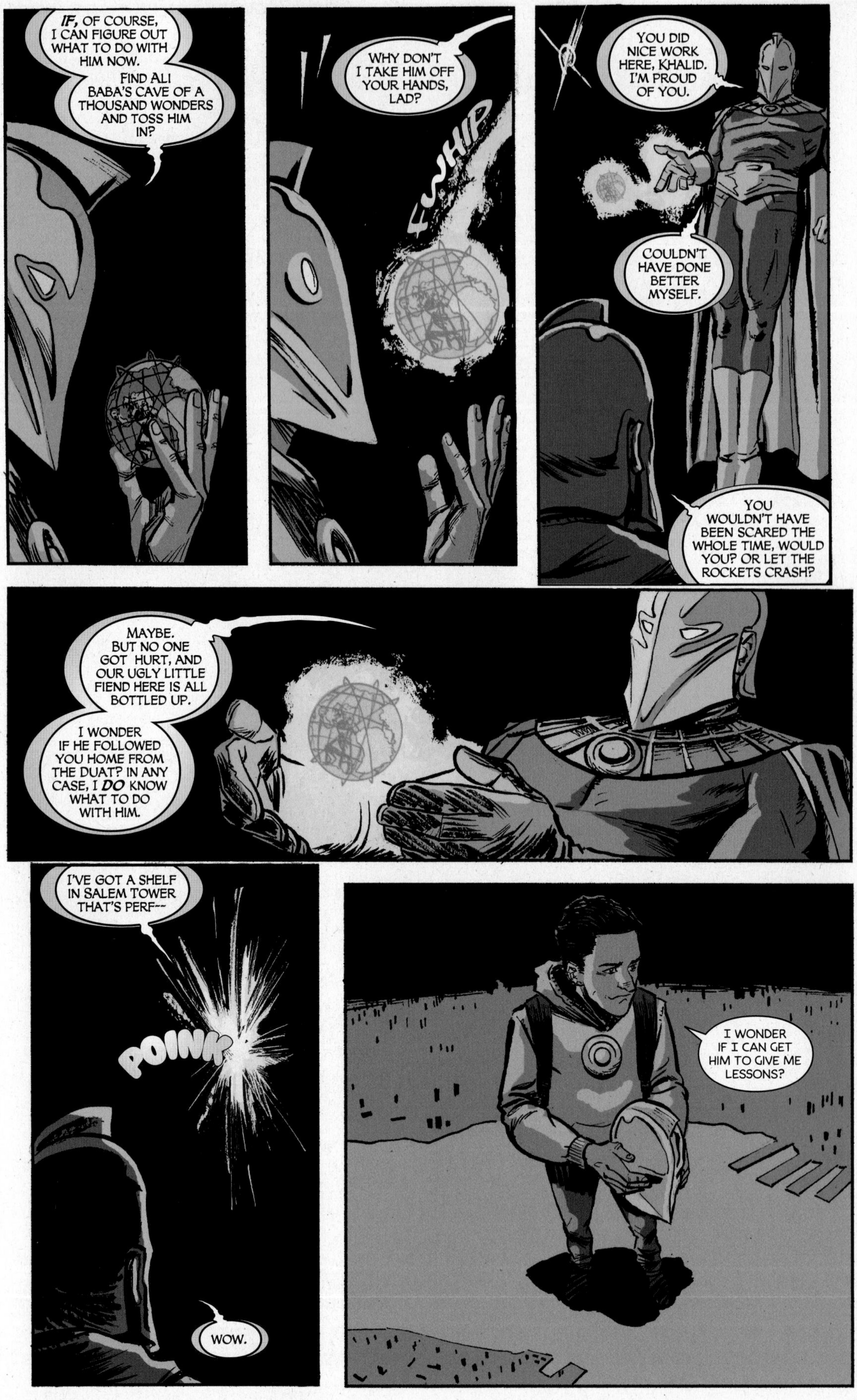

IF, OF COURSE, I CAN FIGURE OUT WHAT TO DO WITH HIM NOW.
FIND ALI BABA'S CAVE OF A THOUSAND WONDERS AND TOSS HIM IN?
WHY DON'T I TAKE HIM OFF YOUR HANDS, LAD?
FWHIP
YOU DID NICE WORK HERE, KHALID. I'M PROUD OF YOU.
COULDN'T HAVE DONE BETTER MYSELF.
YOU WOULDN'T HAVE BEEN SCARED THE WHOLE TIME, WOULD YOU? OR LET THE ROCKETS CRASH?
MAYBE. BUT NO ONE GOT HURT, AND OUR UGLY LITTLE FIEND HERE IS ALL BOTTLED UP.
I WONDER IF HE FOLLOWED YOU HOME FROM THE DUAT? IN ANY CASE, I ***DO*** KNOW WHAT TO DO WITH HIM.
I'VE GOT A SHELF IN SALEM TOWER THAT'S PERF--
POINK
WOW.
I WONDER IF I CAN GET HIM TO GIVE ME LESSONS?

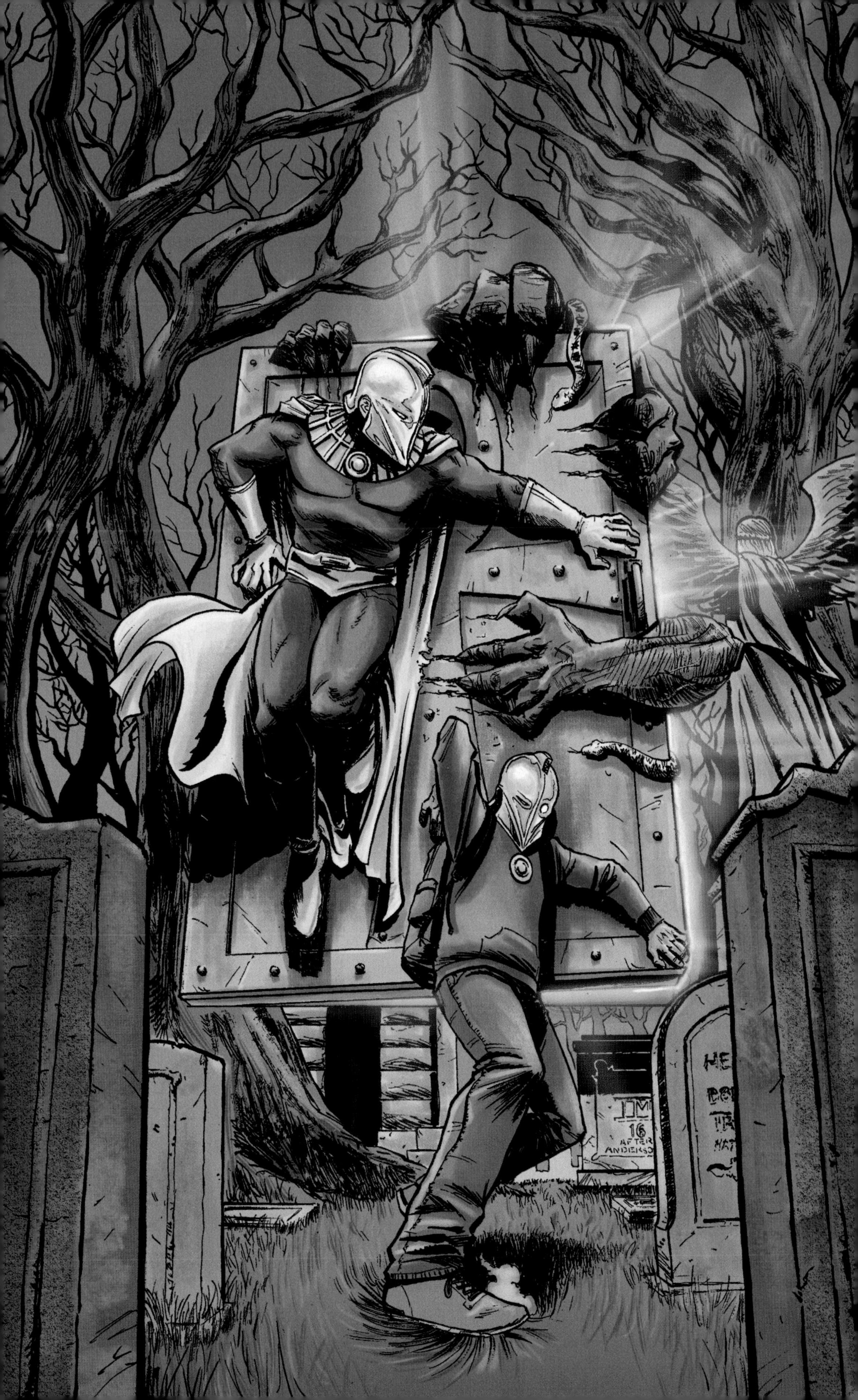
16
AFTER

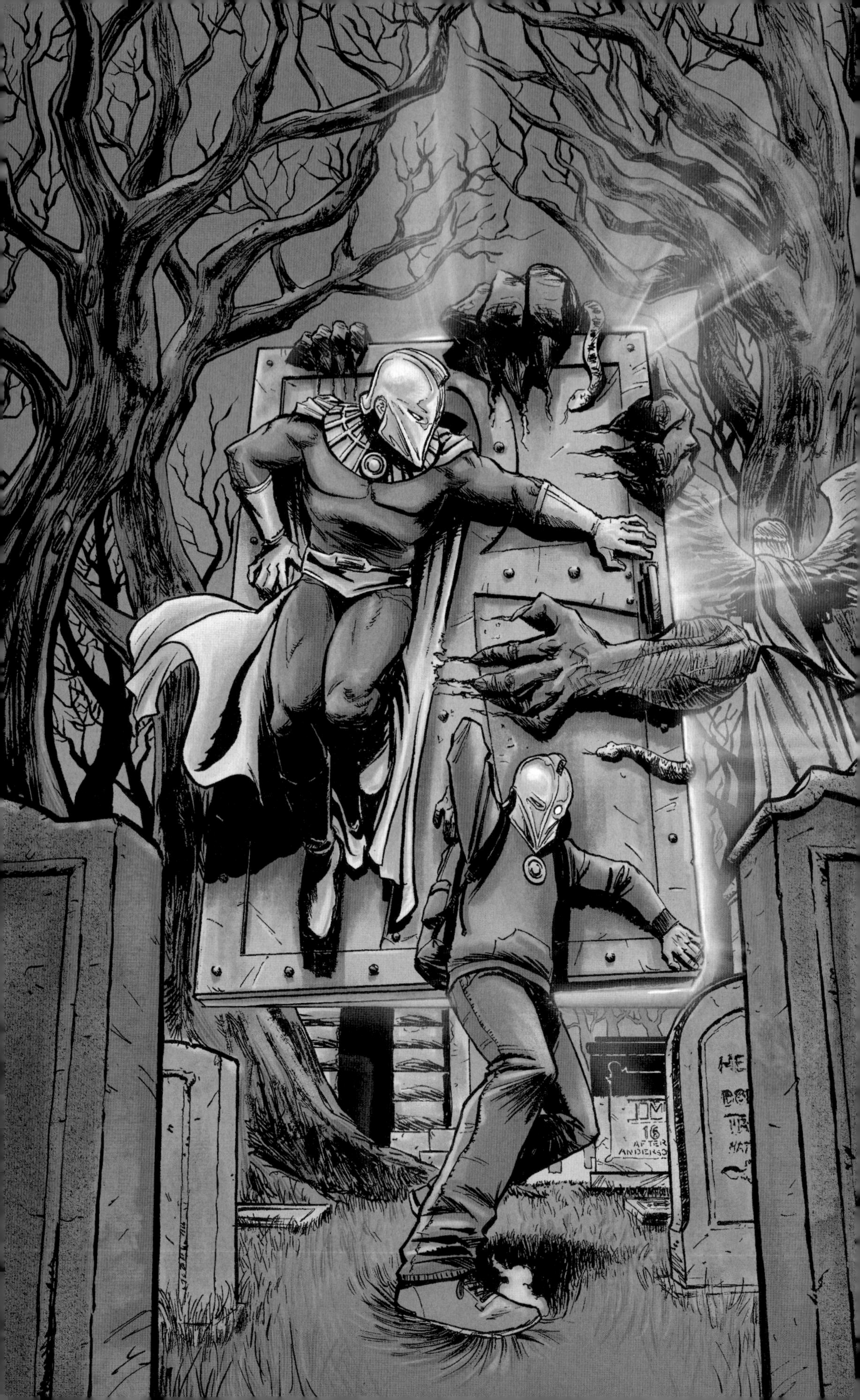

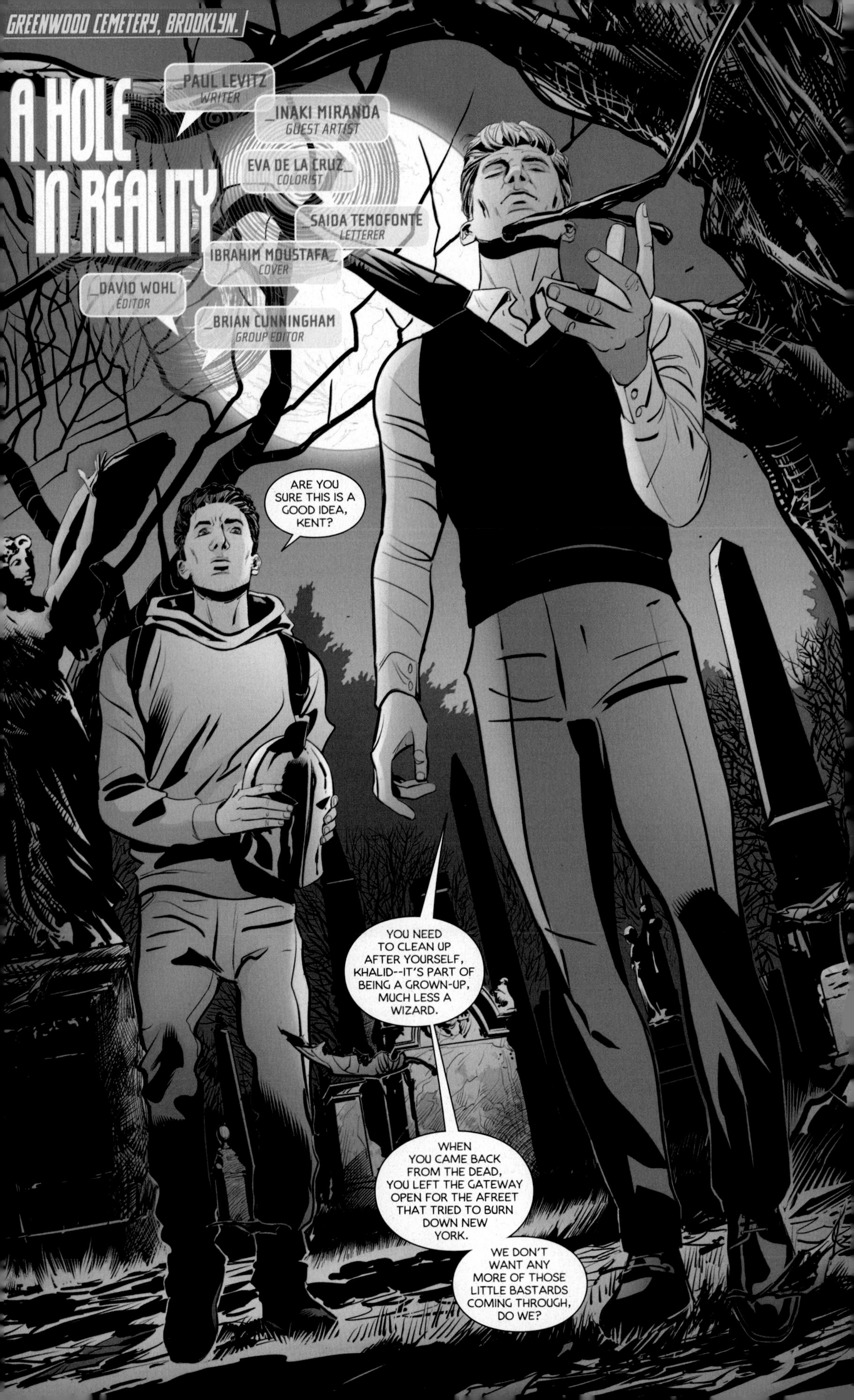
GREENWOOD CEMETERY, BROOKLYN.
A HOLE IN REALITY
_PAUL LEVITZ WRITER
_INAKI MIRANDA GUEST ARTIST
EVA DE LA CRUZ_ COLORIST
_SAIDA TEMOFONTE LETTERER
IBRAHIM MOUSTAFA_ COVER
_DAVID WOHL EDITOR
_BRIAN CUNNINGHAM GROUP EDITOR
ARE YOU SURE THIS IS A GOOD IDEA, KENT?
YOU NEED TO CLEAN UP AFTER YOURSELF, KHALID--IT'S PART OF BEING A GROWN-UP, MUCH LESS A WIZARD.
WHEN YOU CAME BACK FROM THE DEAD, YOU LEFT THE GATEWAY OPEN FOR THE AFREET THAT TRIED TO BURN DOWN NEW YORK.
WE DON'T WANT ANY MORE OF THOSE LITTLE BASTARDS COMING THROUGH, DO WE?

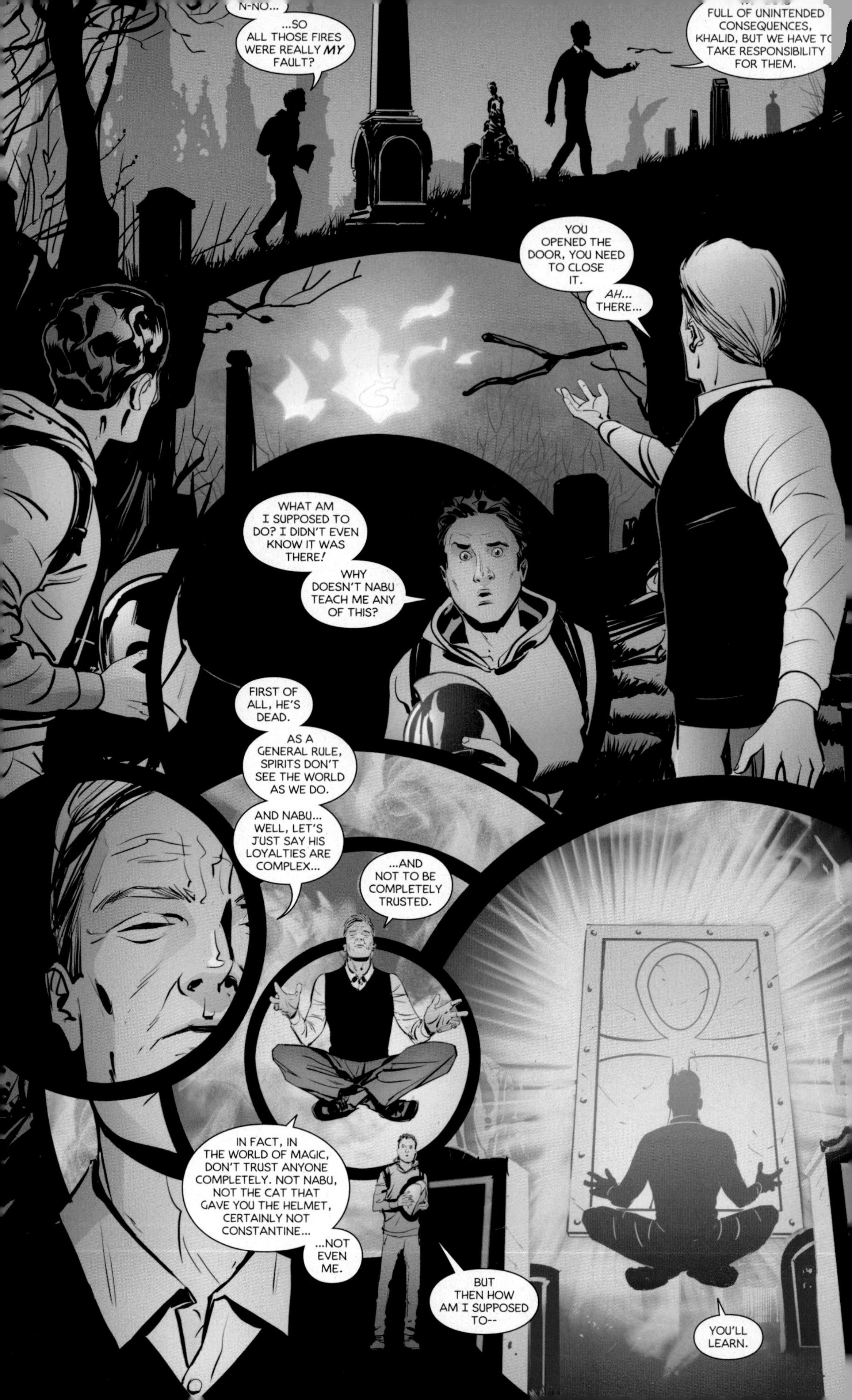
N-NO...
...SO ALL THOSE FIRES WERE REALLY *MY* FAULT?
FULL OF UNINTENDED CONSEQUENCES, KHALID, BUT WE HAVE TO TAKE RESPONSIBILITY FOR THEM.
YOU OPENED THE DOOR, YOU NEED TO CLOSE IT.
AH... THERE...
WHAT AM I SUPPOSED TO DO? I DIDN'T EVEN KNOW IT WAS THERE*!*
WHY DOESN'T NABU TEACH ME ANY OF THIS?
FIRST OF ALL, HE'S DEAD.
AS A GENERAL RULE, SPIRITS DON'T SEE THE WORLD AS WE DO.
AND NABU... WELL, LET'S JUST SAY HIS LOYALTIES ARE COMPLEX...
...AND NOT TO BE COMPLETELY TRUSTED.
IN FACT, IN THE WORLD OF MAGIC, DON'T TRUST ANYONE COMPLETELY. NOT NABU, NOT THE CAT THAT GAVE YOU THE HELMET, CERTAINLY NOT CONSTANTINE...
...NOT EVEN ME.
BUT THEN HOW AM I SUPPOSED TO--
YOU'LL LEARN.

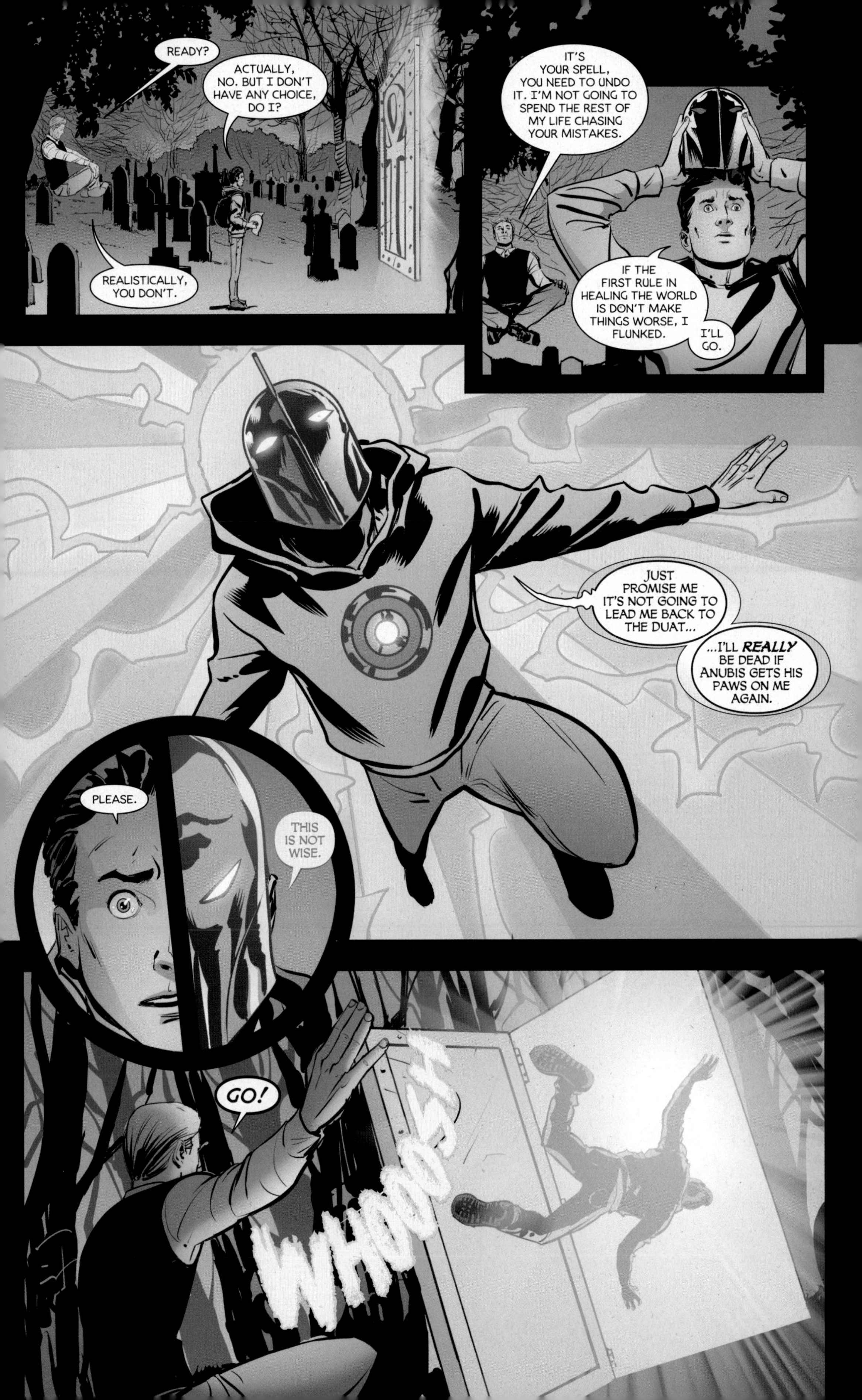
READY?
ACTUALLY, NO. BUT I DON'T HAVE ANY CHOICE, DO I?
REALISTICALLY, YOU DON'T.
IT'S YOUR SPELL, YOU NEED TO UNDO IT. I'M NOT GOING TO SPEND THE REST OF MY LIFE CHASING YOUR MISTAKES.
IF THE FIRST RULE IN HEALING THE WORLD IS DON'T MAKE THINGS WORSE, I FLUNKED.
I'LL GO.
JUST PROMISE ME IT'S NOT GOING TO LEAD ME BACK TO THE DUAT...
...I'LL REALLY BE DEAD IF ANUBIS GETS HIS PAWS ON ME AGAIN.
PLEASE.
THIS IS NOT WISE.
GO!
WHOOSH

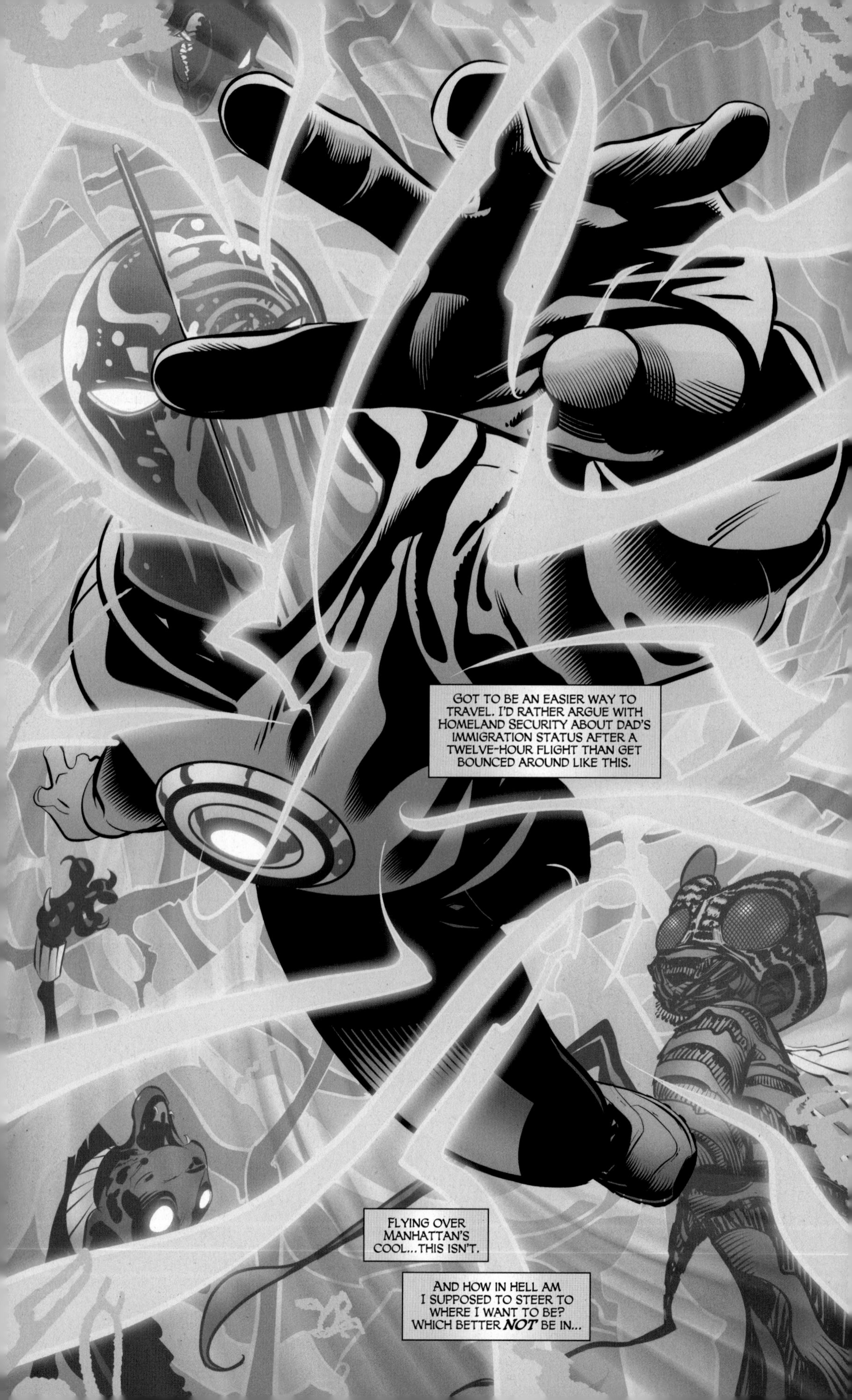
GOT TO BE AN EASIER WAY TO TRAVEL. I'D RATHER ARGUE WITH HOMELAND SECURITY ABOUT DAD'S IMMIGRATION STATUS AFTER A TWELVE-HOUR FLIGHT THAN GET BOUNCED AROUND LIKE THIS.
FLYING OVER MANHATTAN'S COOL...THIS ISN'T.
AND HOW IN HELL AM I SUPPOSED TO STEER TO WHERE I WANT TO BE? WHICH BETTER ***NOT*** BE IN...

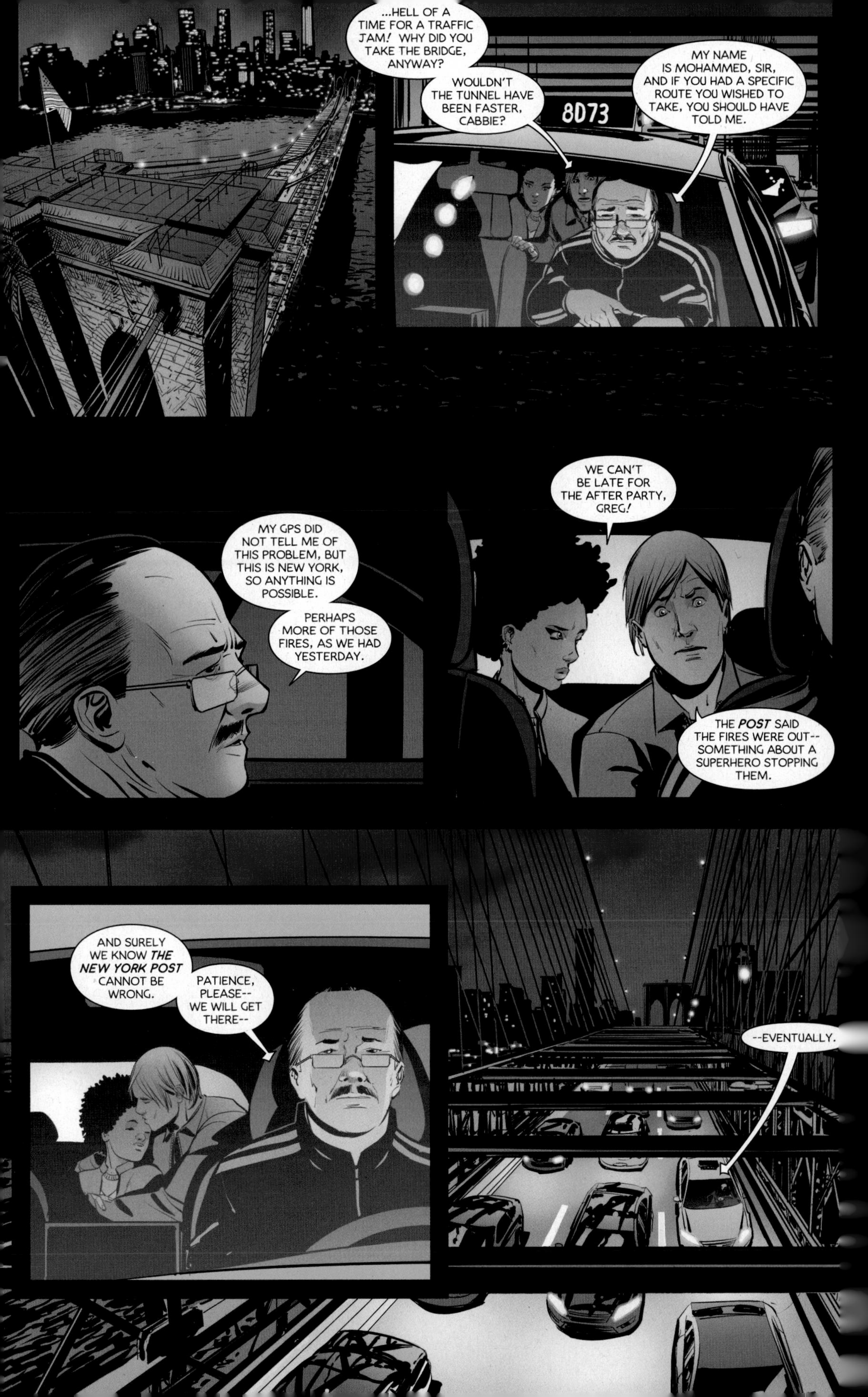
...HELL OF A TIME FOR A TRAFFIC JAM! WHY DID YOU TAKE THE BRIDGE, ANYWAY?
WOULDN'T THE TUNNEL HAVE BEEN FASTER, CABBIE?
8D73
MY NAME IS MOHAMMED, SIR, AND IF YOU HAD A SPECIFIC ROUTE YOU WISHED TO TAKE, YOU SHOULD HAVE TOLD ME.
MY GPS DID NOT TELL ME OF THIS PROBLEM, BUT THIS IS NEW YORK, SO ANYTHING IS POSSIBLE.
PERHAPS MORE OF THOSE FIRES, AS WE HAD YESTERDAY.
WE CAN'T BE LATE FOR THE AFTER PARTY, GREG!
THE *POST* SAID THE FIRES WERE OUT-- SOMETHING ABOUT A SUPERHERO STOPPING THEM.
AND SURELY WE KNOW ***THE NEW YORK POST*** CANNOT BE WRONG.
PATIENCE, PLEASE-- WE WILL GET THERE--
--EVENTUALLY.

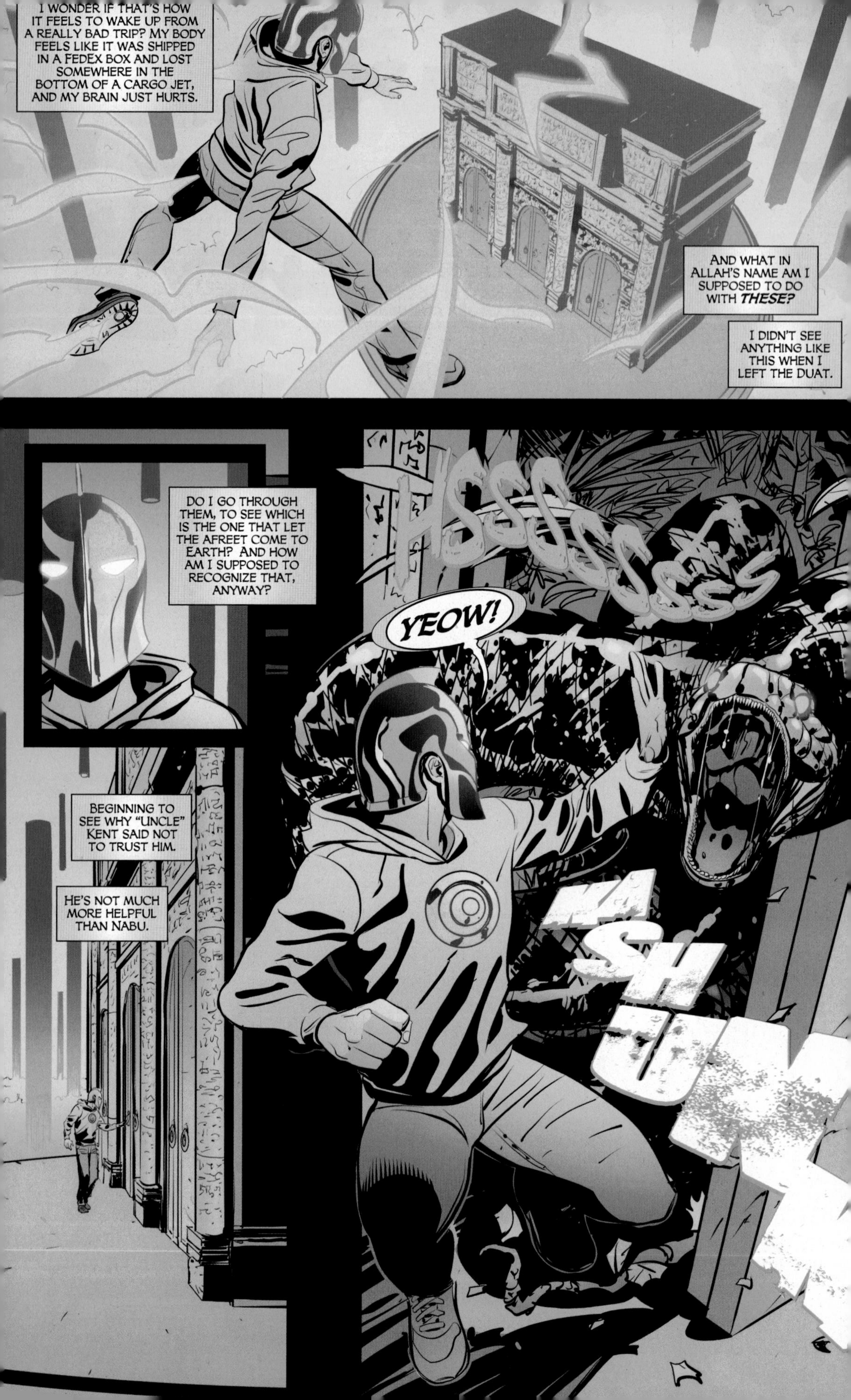
I WONDER IF THAT'S HOW IT FEELS TO WAKE UP FROM A REALLY BAD TRIP? MY BODY FEELS LIKE IT WAS SHIPPED IN A FEDEX BOX AND LOST SOMEWHERE IN THE BOTTOM OF A CARGO JET, AND MY BRAIN JUST HURTS.
AND WHAT IN ALLAH'S NAME AM I SUPPOSED TO DO WITH *THESE?*
I DIDN'T SEE ANYTHING LIKE THIS WHEN I LEFT THE DUAT.
DO I GO THROUGH THEM, TO SEE WHICH IS THE ONE THAT LET THE AFREET COME TO EARTH? AND HOW AM I SUPPOSED TO RECOGNIZE THAT, ANYWAY?
BEGINNING TO SEE WHY "UNCLE" KENT SAID NOT TO TRUST HIM.
HE'S NOT MUCH MORE HELPFUL THAN NABU.
HSSSSSSSS
YEOW!
KA SH UM

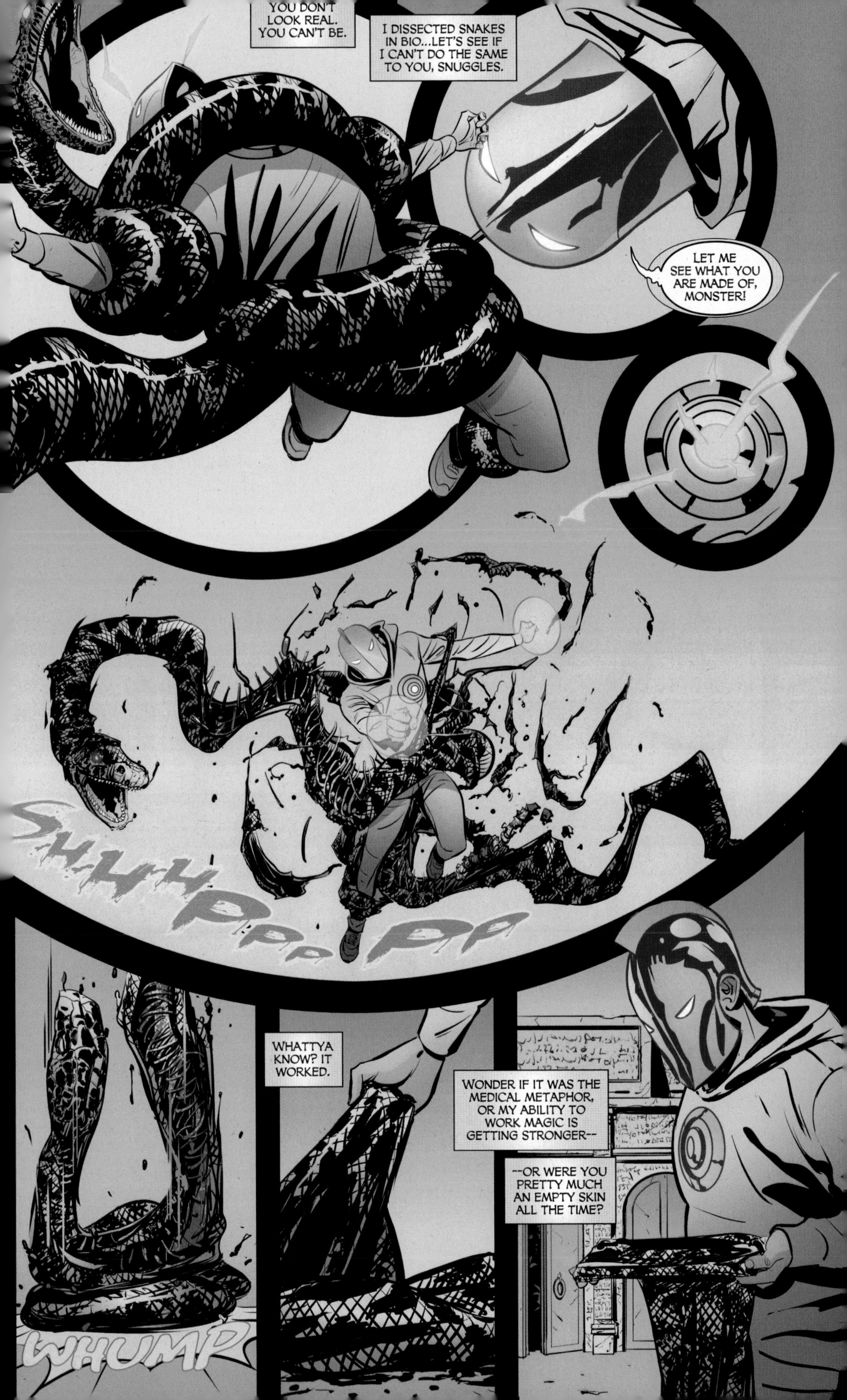
YOU DON'T LOOK REAL. YOU CAN'T BE.
I DISSECTED SNAKES IN BIO...LET'S SEE IF I CAN'T DO THE SAME TO YOU, SNUGGLES.
LET ME SEE WHAT YOU ARE MADE OF, MONSTER!
SHHHHPPPPPP
WHUMP
WHATTYA KNOW? IT WORKED.
WONDER IF IT WAS THE MEDICAL METAPHOR, OR MY ABILITY TO WORK MAGIC IS GETTING STRONGER--
--OR WERE YOU PRETTY MUCH AN EMPTY SKIN ALL THE TIME?

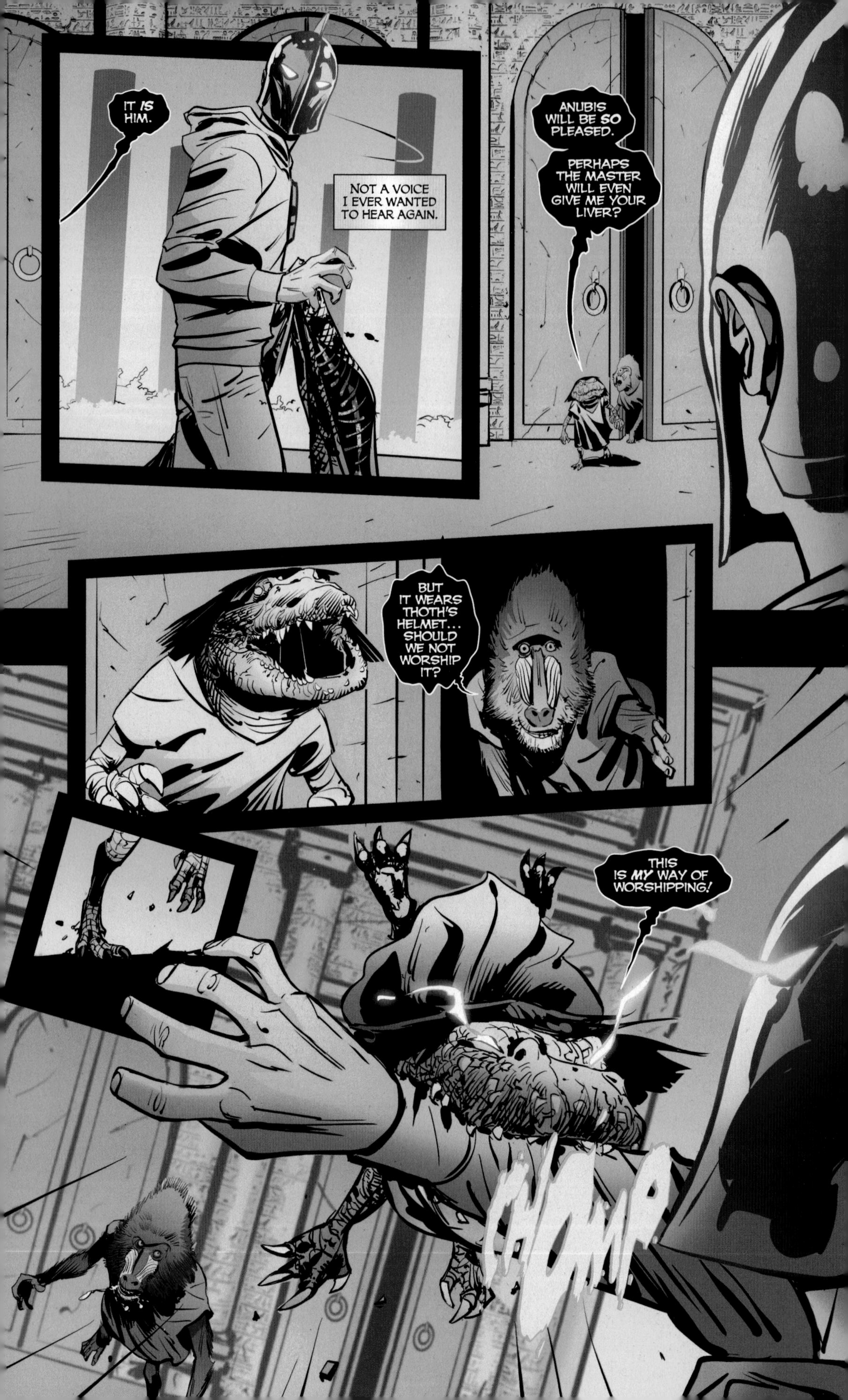
IT IS HIM.
NOT A VOICE I EVER WANTED TO HEAR AGAIN.
ANUBIS WILL BE SO PLEASED.
PERHAPS THE MASTER WILL EVEN GIVE ME YOUR LIVER?
BUT IT WEARS THOTH'S HELMET... SHOULD WE NOT WORSHIP IT?
THIS IS MY WAY OF WORSHIPPING!
CHOMP

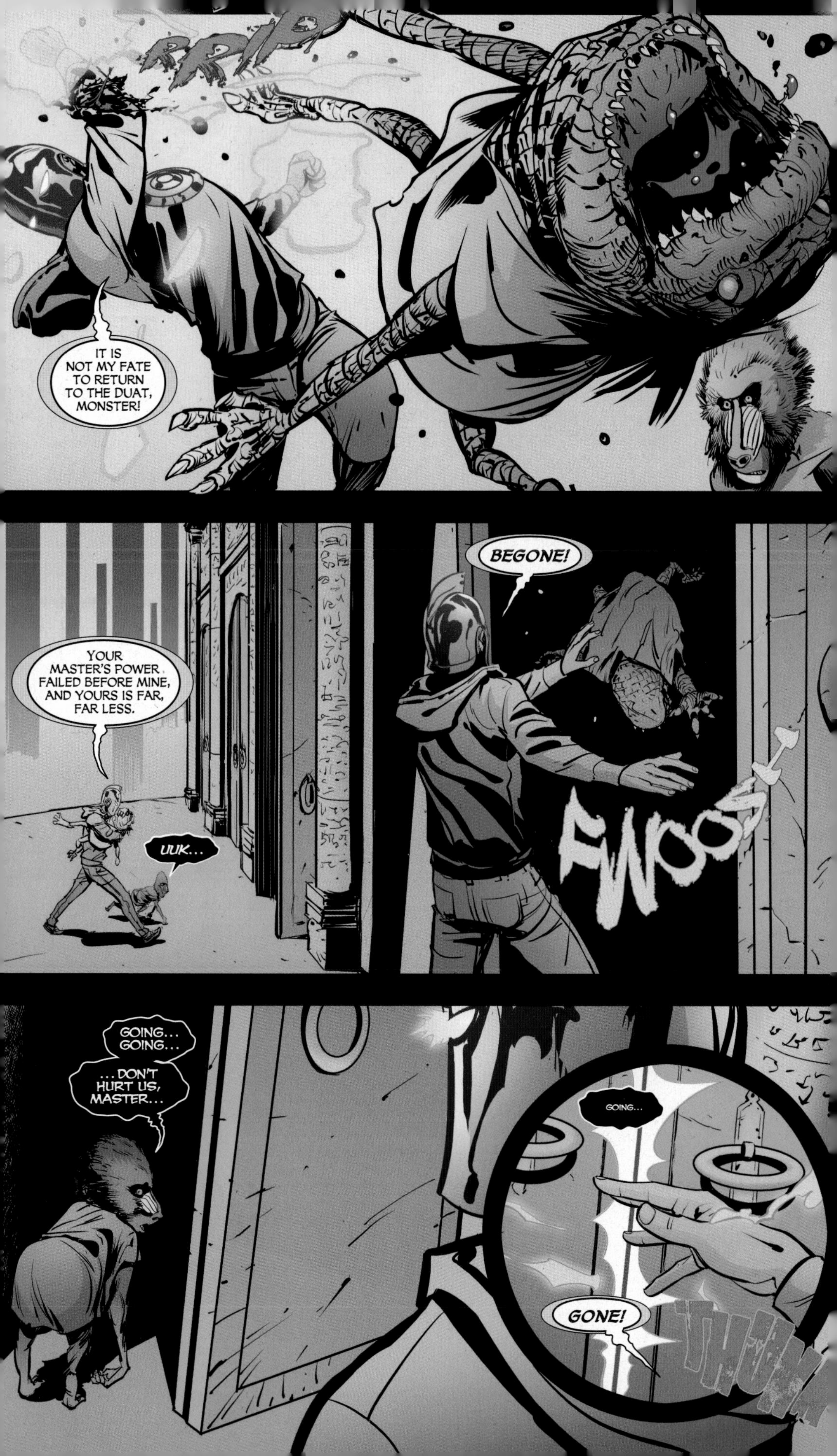
RRIP
IT IS NOT MY FATE TO RETURN TO THE DUAT, MONSTER!
YOUR MASTER'S POWER FAILED BEFORE MINE, AND YOURS IS FAR, FAR LESS.
UUK...
BEGONE!
FWOOSH
GOING... GOING...
...DON'T HURT US, MASTER...
GOING...
GONE!
THOOM

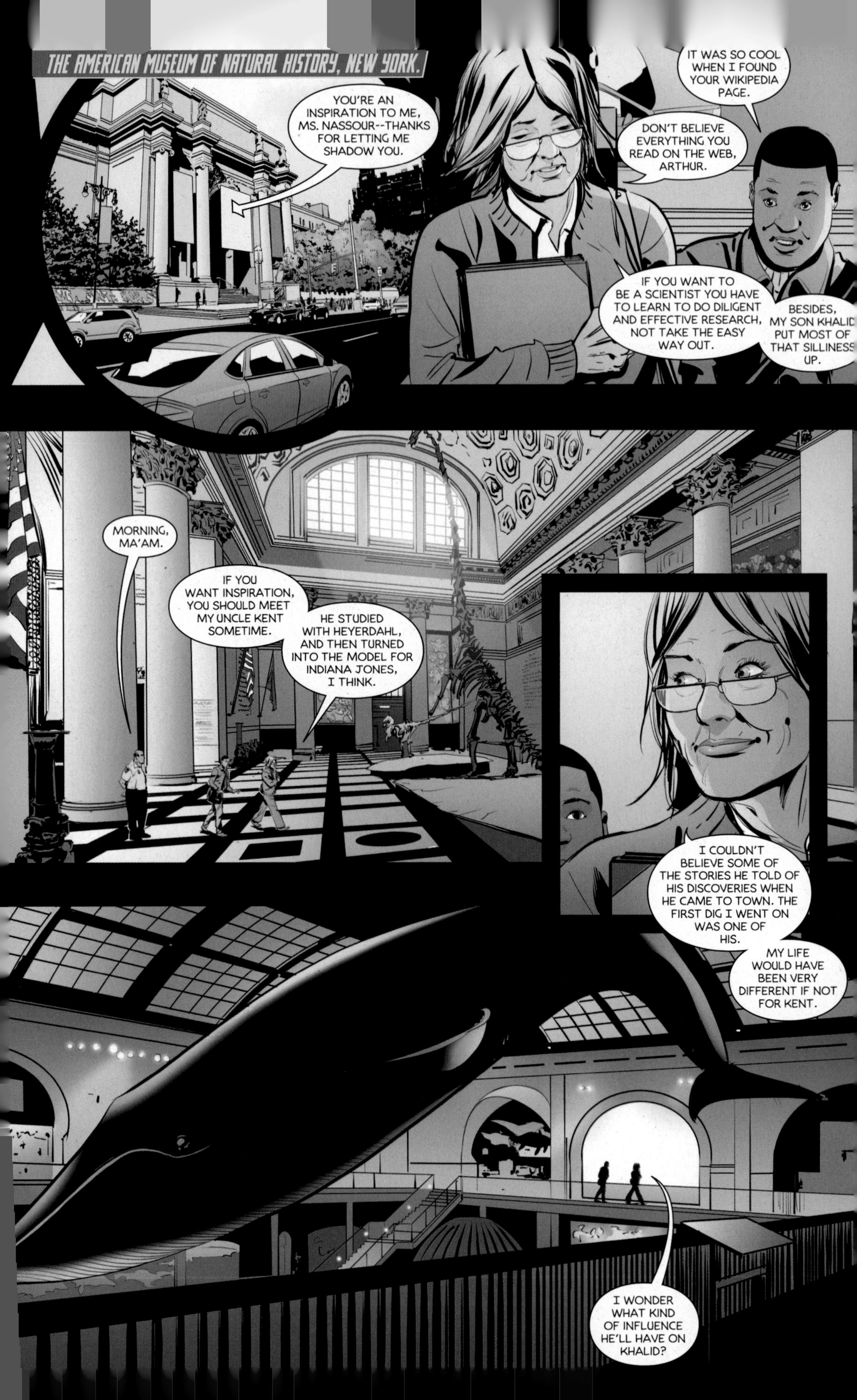
THE AMERICAN MUSEUM OF NATURAL HISTORY, NEW YORK.
YOU'RE AN INSPIRATION TO ME, MS. NASSOUR--THANKS FOR LETTING ME SHADOW YOU.
IT WAS SO COOL WHEN I FOUND YOUR WIKIPEDIA PAGE.
DON'T BELIEVE EVERYTHING YOU READ ON THE WEB, ARTHUR.
IF YOU WANT TO BE A SCIENTIST YOU HAVE TO LEARN TO DO DILIGENT AND EFFECTIVE RESEARCH, NOT TAKE THE EASY WAY OUT.
BESIDES, MY SON KHALID PUT MOST OF THAT SILLINESS UP.
MORNING, MA'AM.
IF YOU WANT INSPIRATION, YOU SHOULD MEET MY UNCLE KENT SOMETIME.
HE STUDIED WITH HEYERDAHL, AND THEN TURNED INTO THE MODEL FOR INDIANA JONES, I THINK.
I COULDN'T BELIEVE SOME OF THE STORIES HE TOLD OF HIS DISCOVERIES WHEN HE CAME TO TOWN. THE FIRST DIG I WENT ON WAS ONE OF HIS.
MY LIFE WOULD HAVE BEEN VERY DIFFERENT IF NOT FOR KENT.
I WONDER WHAT KIND OF INFLUENCE HE'LL HAVE ON KHALID?

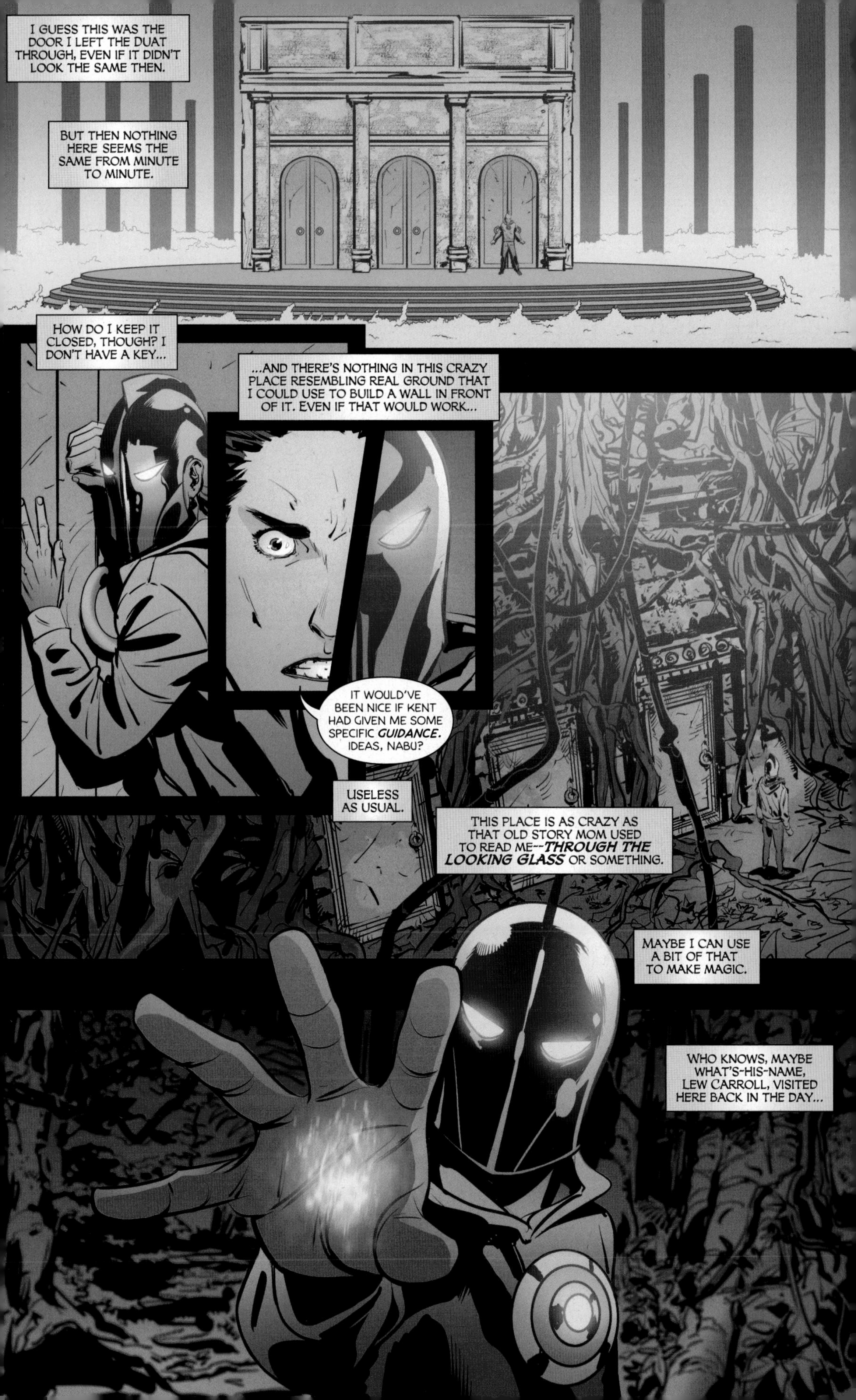
I GUESS THIS WAS THE DOOR I LEFT THE DUAT THROUGH, EVEN IF IT DIDN'T LOOK THE SAME THEN.
BUT THEN NOTHING HERE SEEMS THE SAME FROM MINUTE TO MINUTE.
HOW DO I KEEP IT CLOSED, THOUGH? I DON'T HAVE A KEY...
...AND THERE'S NOTHING IN THIS CRAZY PLACE RESEMBLING REAL GROUND THAT I COULD USE TO BUILD A WALL IN FRONT OF IT. EVEN IF THAT WOULD WORK...
IT WOULD'VE BEEN NICE IF KENT HAD GIVEN ME SOME SPECIFIC GUIDANCE. IDEAS, NABU?
USELESS AS USUAL.
THIS PLACE IS AS CRAZY AS THAT OLD STORY MOM USED TO READ ME--THROUGH THE LOOKING GLASS OR SOMETHING.
MAYBE I CAN USE A BIT OF THAT TO MAKE MAGIC.
WHO KNOWS, MAYBE WHAT'S-HIS-NAME, LEW CARROLL, VISITED HERE BACK IN THE DAY...

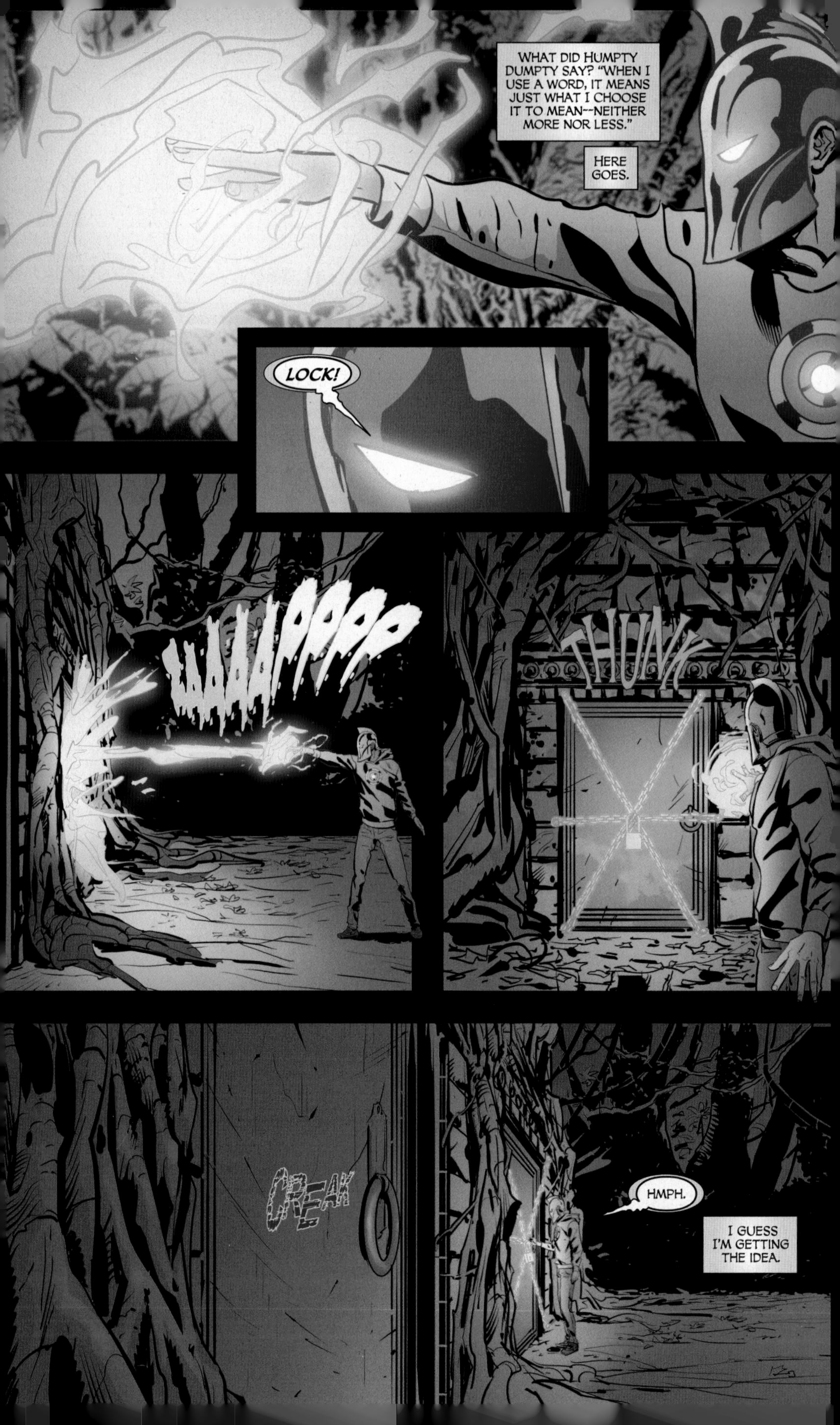
WHAT DID HUMPTY DUMPTY SAY? "WHEN I USE A WORD, IT MEANS JUST WHAT I CHOOSE IT TO MEAN--NEITHER MORE NOR LESS."
HERE GOES.
LOCK!
THUNK
CREAK
HMPH.
I GUESS I'M GETTING THE IDEA.

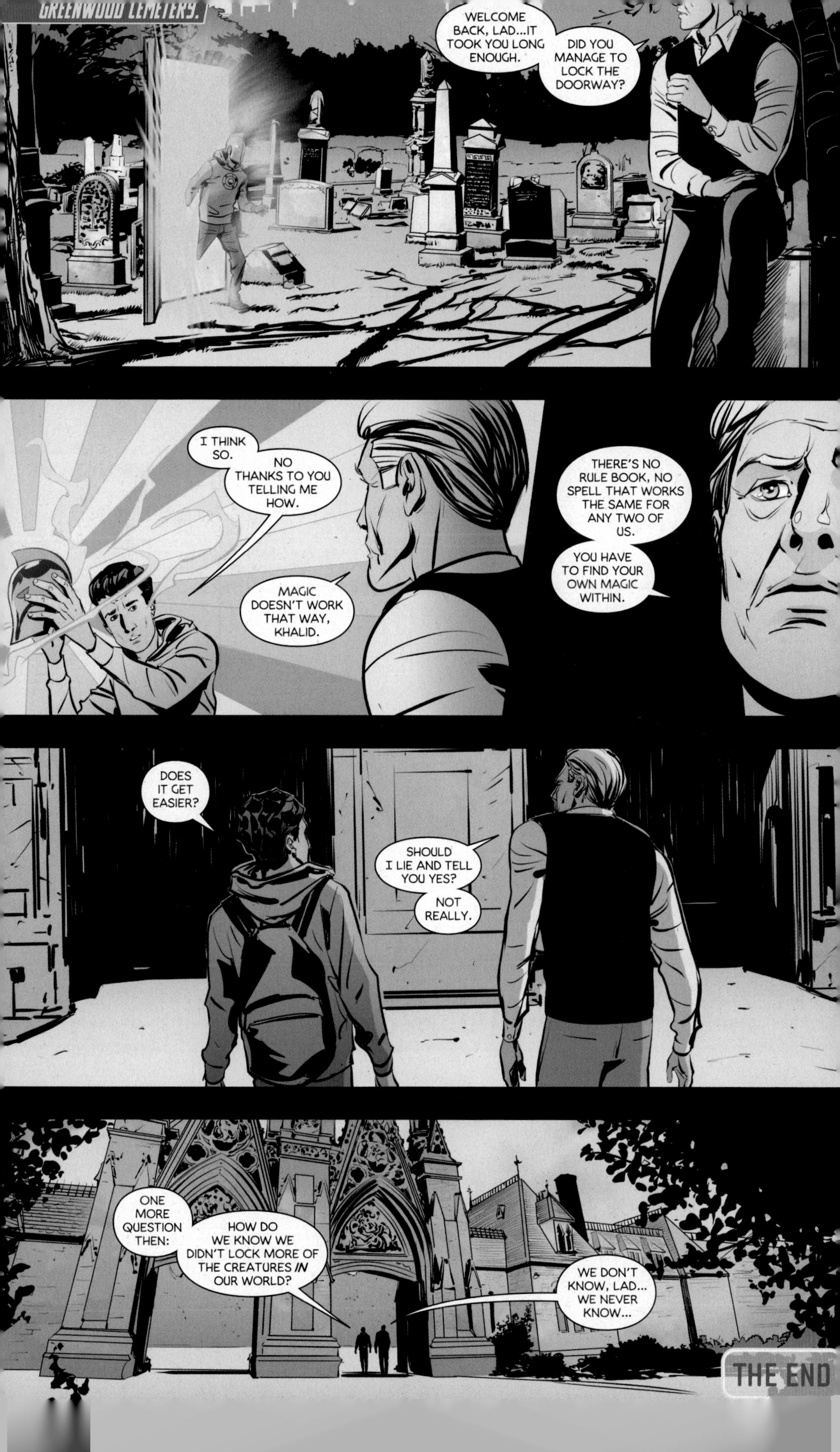

GREENWOOD CEMETERY.
WELCOME BACK, LAD...IT TOOK YOU LONG ENOUGH.
DID YOU MANAGE TO LOCK THE DOORWAY?
I THINK SO.
NO THANKS TO YOU TELLING ME HOW.
MAGIC DOESN'T WORK THAT WAY, KHALID.
THERE'S NO RULE BOOK, NO SPELL THAT WORKS THE SAME FOR ANY TWO OF US.
YOU HAVE TO FIND YOUR OWN MAGIC WITHIN.
DOES IT GET EASIER?
SHOULD I LIE AND TELL YOU YES?
NOT REALLY.
ONE MORE QUESTION THEN:
HOW DO WE KNOW WE DIDN'T LOCK MORE OF THE CREATURES *IN* OUR WORLD?
WE DON'T KNOW, LAD... WE NEVER KNOW...
THE END

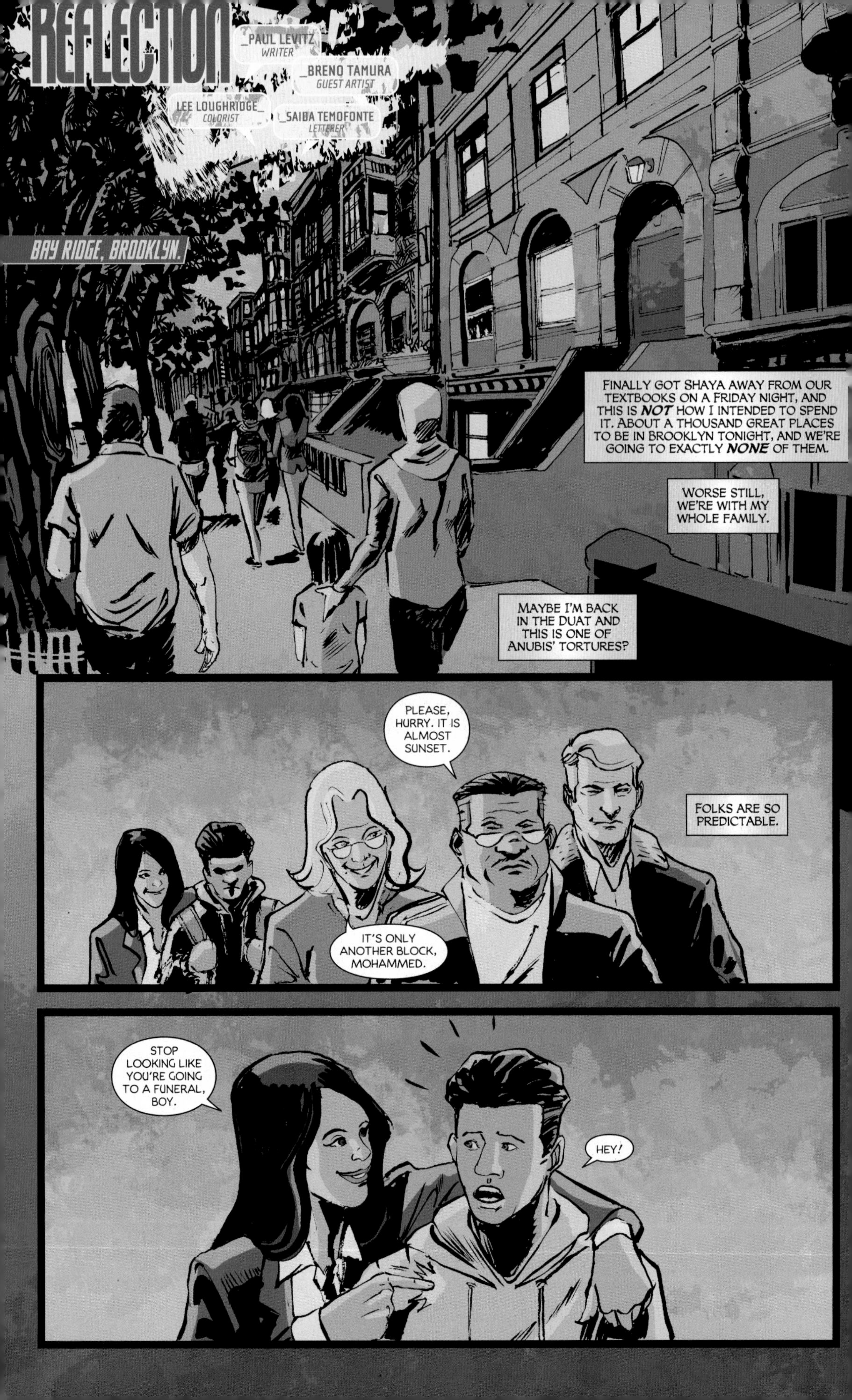
REFLECTION
_PAUL LEVITZ
WRITER
_BRENO TAMURA
GUEST ARTIST
LEE LOUGHRIDGE_
COLORIST
_SAIDA TEMOFONTE
LETTERER
BAY RIDGE, BROOKLYN.
FINALLY GOT SHAYA AWAY FROM OUR TEXTBOOKS ON A FRIDAY NIGHT, AND THIS IS NOT HOW I INTENDED TO SPEND IT. ABOUT A THOUSAND GREAT PLACES TO BE IN BROOKLYN TONIGHT, AND WE'RE GOING TO EXACTLY NONE OF THEM.
WORSE STILL, WE'RE WITH MY WHOLE FAMILY.
MAYBE I'M BACK IN THE DUAT AND THIS IS ONE OF ANUBIS' TORTURES?
PLEASE, HURRY. IT IS ALMOST SUNSET.
FOLKS ARE SO PREDICTABLE.
IT'S ONLY ANOTHER BLOCK, MOHAMMED.
STOP LOOKING LIKE YOU'RE GOING TO A FUNERAL, BOY.
HEY!

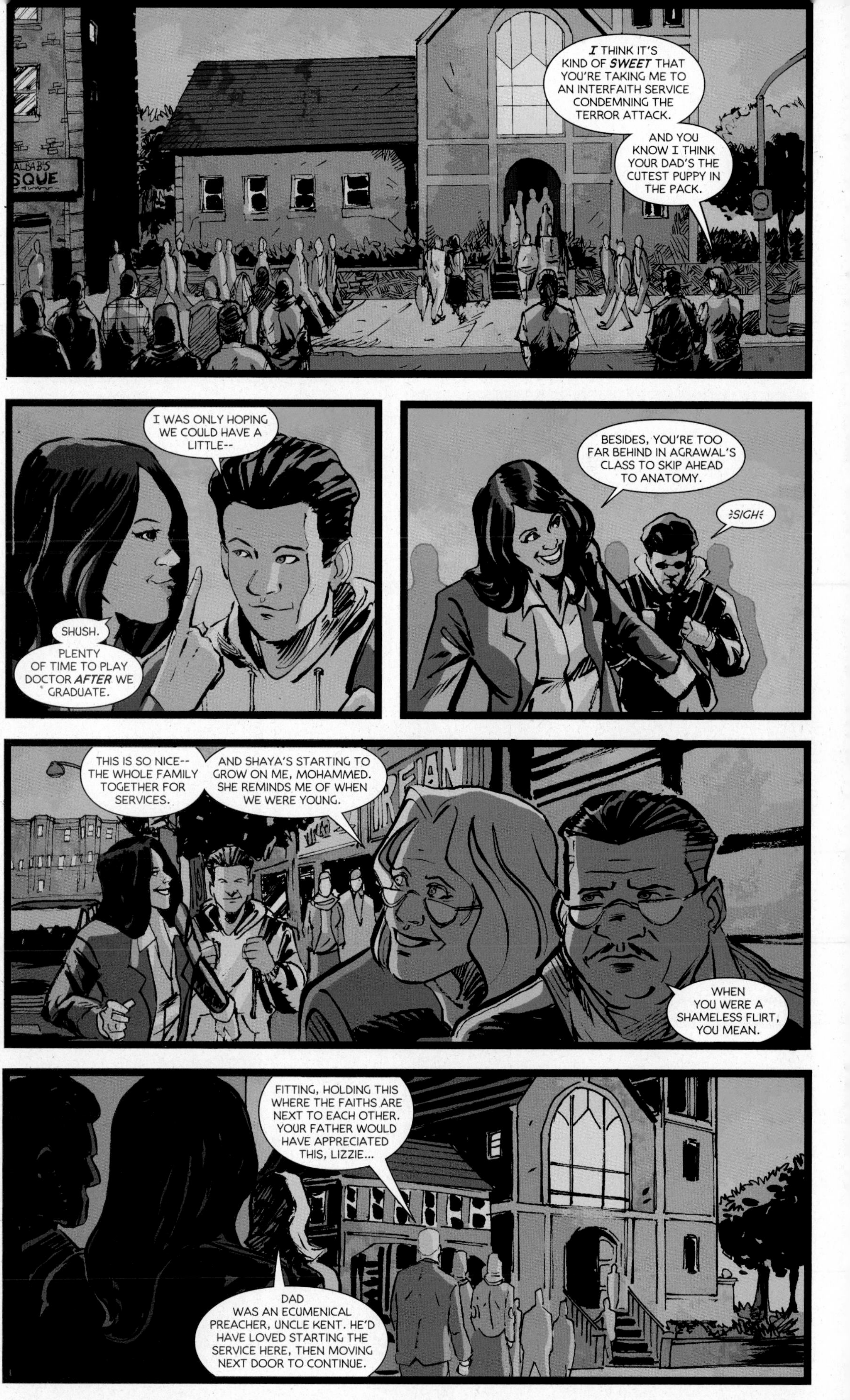
I THINK IT'S KIND OF SWEET THAT YOU'RE TAKING ME TO AN INTERFAITH SERVICE CONDEMNING THE TERROR ATTACK.
AND YOU KNOW I THINK YOUR DAD'S THE CUTEST PUPPY IN THE PACK.
I WAS ONLY HOPING WE COULD HAVE A LITTLE--
SHUSH.
PLENTY OF TIME TO PLAY DOCTOR AFTER WE GRADUATE.
BESIDES, YOU'RE TOO FAR BEHIND IN AGRAWAL'S CLASS TO SKIP AHEAD TO ANATOMY.
SIGH
THIS IS SO NICE-- THE WHOLE FAMILY TOGETHER FOR SERVICES.
AND SHAYA'S STARTING TO GROW ON ME, MOHAMMED. SHE REMINDS ME OF WHEN WE WERE YOUNG.
WHEN YOU WERE A SHAMELESS FLIRT, YOU MEAN.
FITTING, HOLDING THIS WHERE THE FAITHS ARE NEXT TO EACH OTHER. YOUR FATHER WOULD HAVE APPRECIATED THIS, LIZZIE...
DAD WAS AN ECUMENICAL PREACHER, UNCLE KENT. HE'D HAVE LOVED STARTING THE SERVICE HERE, THEN MOVING NEXT DOOR TO CONTINUE.

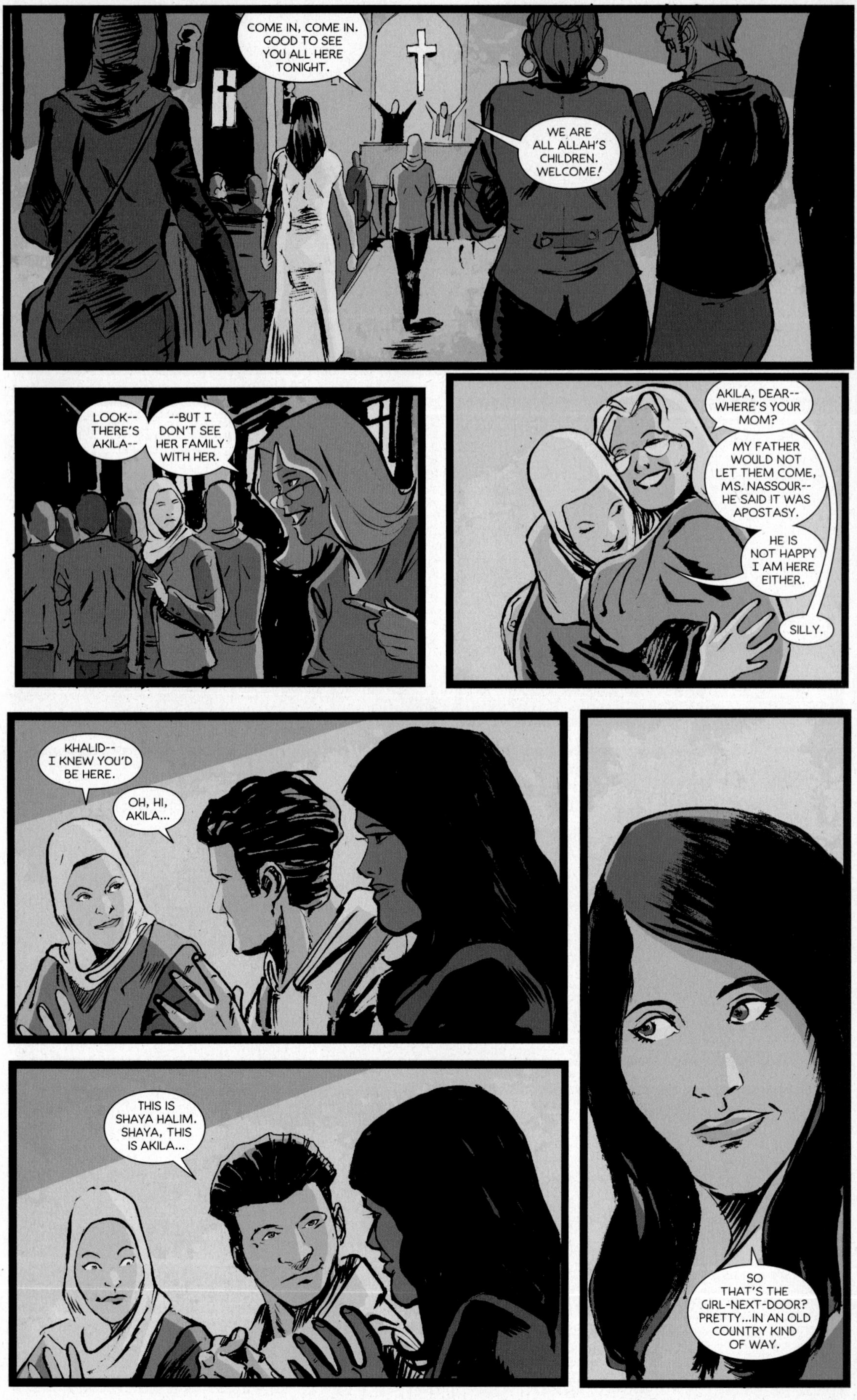
COME IN, COME IN. GOOD TO SEE YOU ALL HERE TONIGHT.
WE ARE ALL ALLAH'S CHILDREN. WELCOME!
LOOK-- THERE'S AKILA--
--BUT I DON'T SEE HER FAMILY WITH HER.
AKILA, DEAR-- WHERE'S YOUR MOM?
MY FATHER WOULD NOT LET THEM COME, MS. NASSOUR-- HE SAID IT WAS APOSTASY.
HE IS NOT HAPPY I AM HERE EITHER.
SILLY.
KHALID-- I KNEW YOU'D BE HERE.
OH, HI, AKILA...
THIS IS SHAYA HALIM. SHAYA, THIS IS AKILA...
SO THAT'S THE GIRL-NEXT-DOOR? PRETTY...IN AN OLD COUNTRY KIND OF WAY.

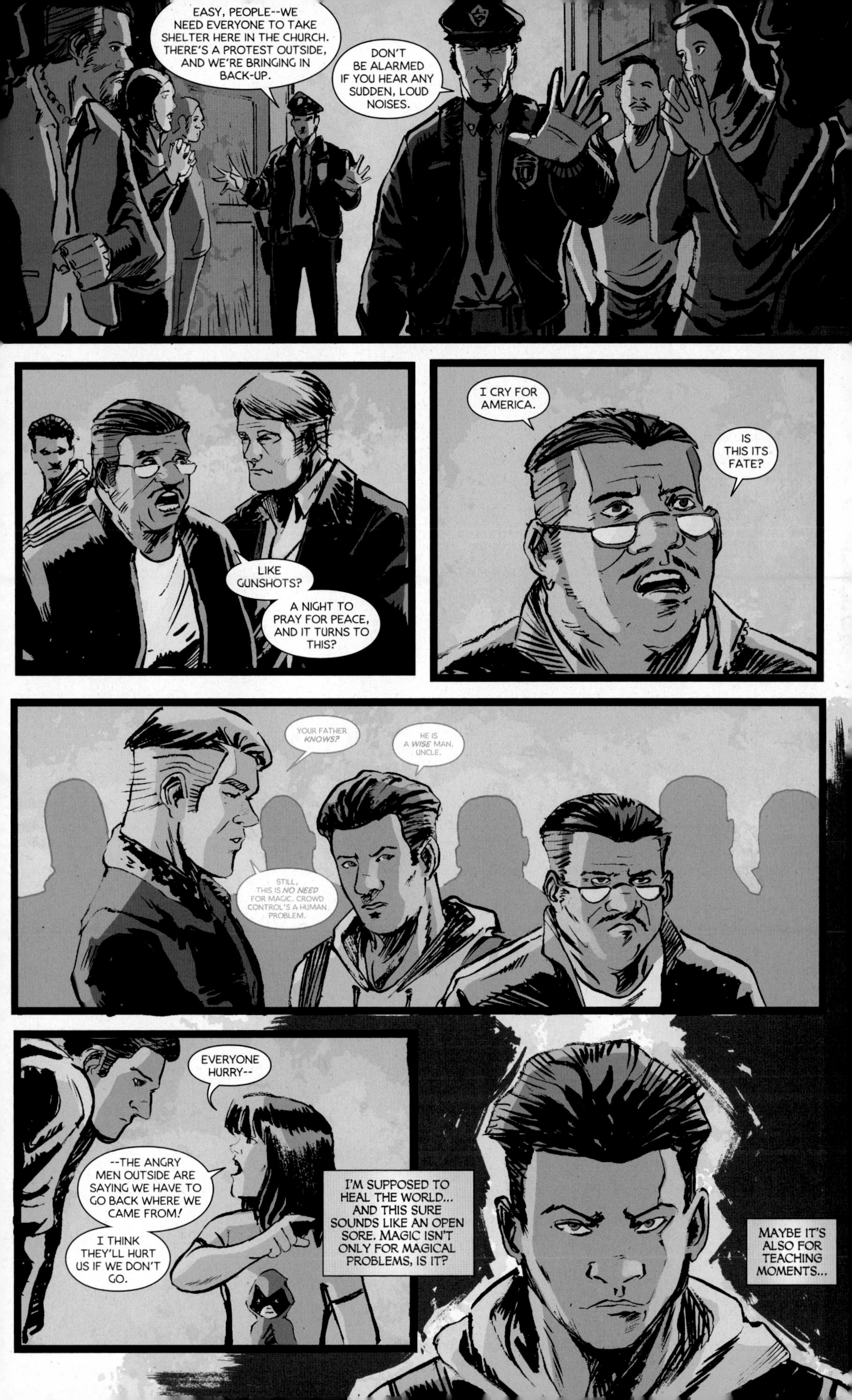
EASY, PEOPLE--WE NEED EVERYONE TO TAKE SHELTER HERE IN THE CHURCH. THERE'S A PROTEST OUTSIDE, AND WE'RE BRINGING IN BACK-UP.
DON'T BE ALARMED IF YOU HEAR ANY SUDDEN, LOUD NOISES.
LIKE GUNSHOTS?
A NIGHT TO PRAY FOR PEACE, AND IT TURNS TO THIS?
I CRY FOR AMERICA.
IS THIS ITS FATE?
YOUR FATHER *KNOWS?*
HE IS A *WISE* MAN, UNCLE.
STILL, THIS IS *NO NEED* FOR MAGIC. CROWD CONTROL'S A HUMAN PROBLEM.
EVERYONE HURRY--
--THE ANGRY MEN OUTSIDE ARE SAYING WE HAVE TO GO BACK WHERE WE CAME FROM*!*
I THINK THEY'LL HURT US IF WE DON'T GO.
I'M SUPPOSED TO HEAL THE WORLD... AND THIS SURE SOUNDS LIKE AN OPEN SORE. MAGIC ISN'T ONLY FOR MAGICAL PROBLEMS, IS IT?
MAYBE IT'S ALSO FOR TEACHING MOMENTS...

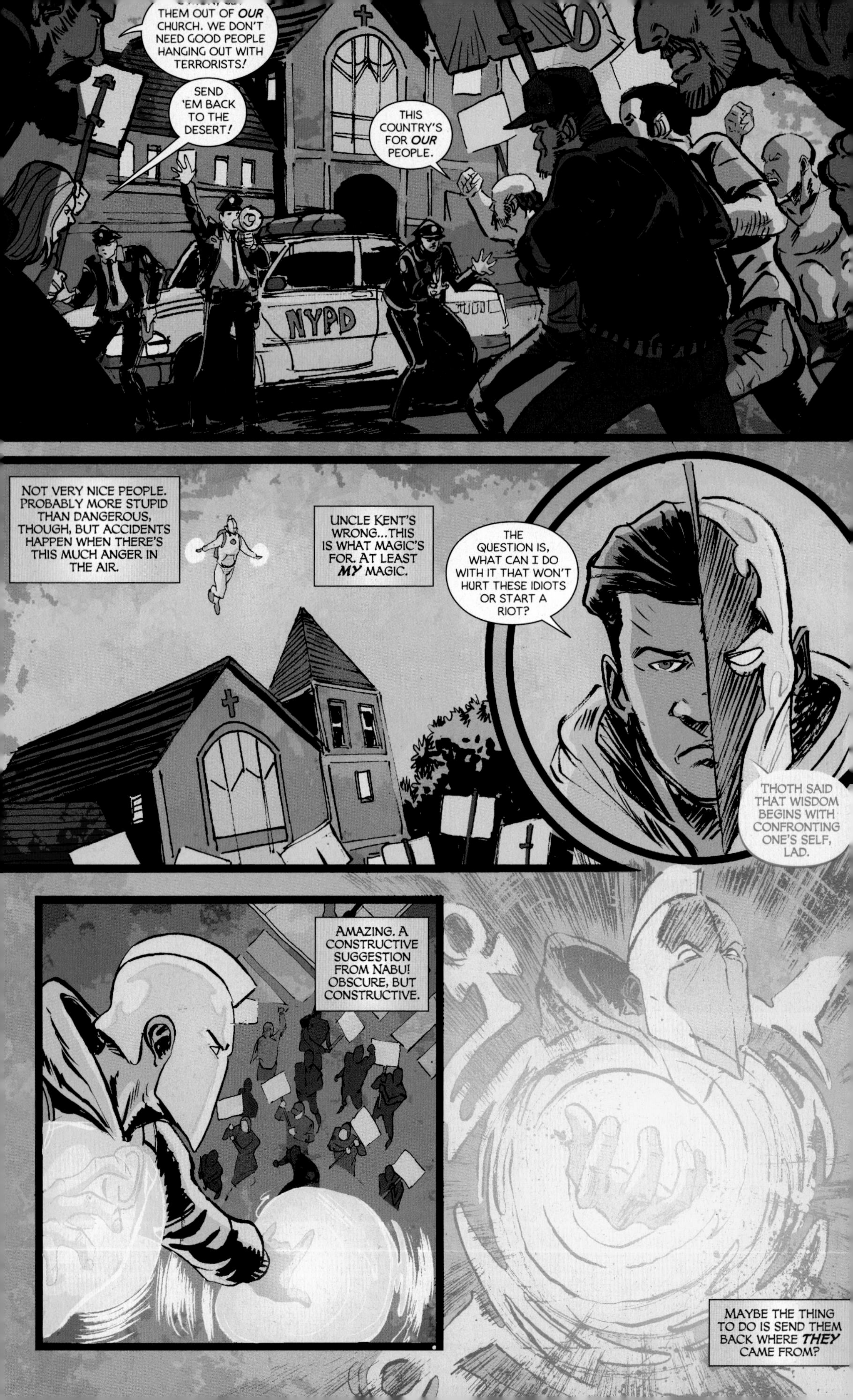
THEM OUT OF OUR CHURCH. WE DON'T NEED GOOD PEOPLE HANGING OUT WITH TERRORISTS!
SEND 'EM BACK TO THE DESERT!
THIS COUNTRY'S FOR OUR PEOPLE.
NOT VERY NICE PEOPLE. PROBABLY MORE STUPID THAN DANGEROUS, THOUGH, BUT ACCIDENTS HAPPEN WHEN THERE'S THIS MUCH ANGER IN THE AIR.
UNCLE KENT'S WRONG...THIS IS WHAT MAGIC'S FOR. AT LEAST MY MAGIC.
THE QUESTION IS, WHAT CAN I DO WITH IT THAT WON'T HURT THESE IDIOTS OR START A RIOT?
THOTH SAID THAT WISDOM BEGINS WITH CONFRONTING ONE'S SELF, LAD.
AMAZING. A CONSTRUCTIVE SUGGESTION FROM NABU! OBSCURE, BUT CONSTRUCTIVE.
MAYBE THE THING TO DO IS SEND THEM BACK WHERE THEY CAME FROM?

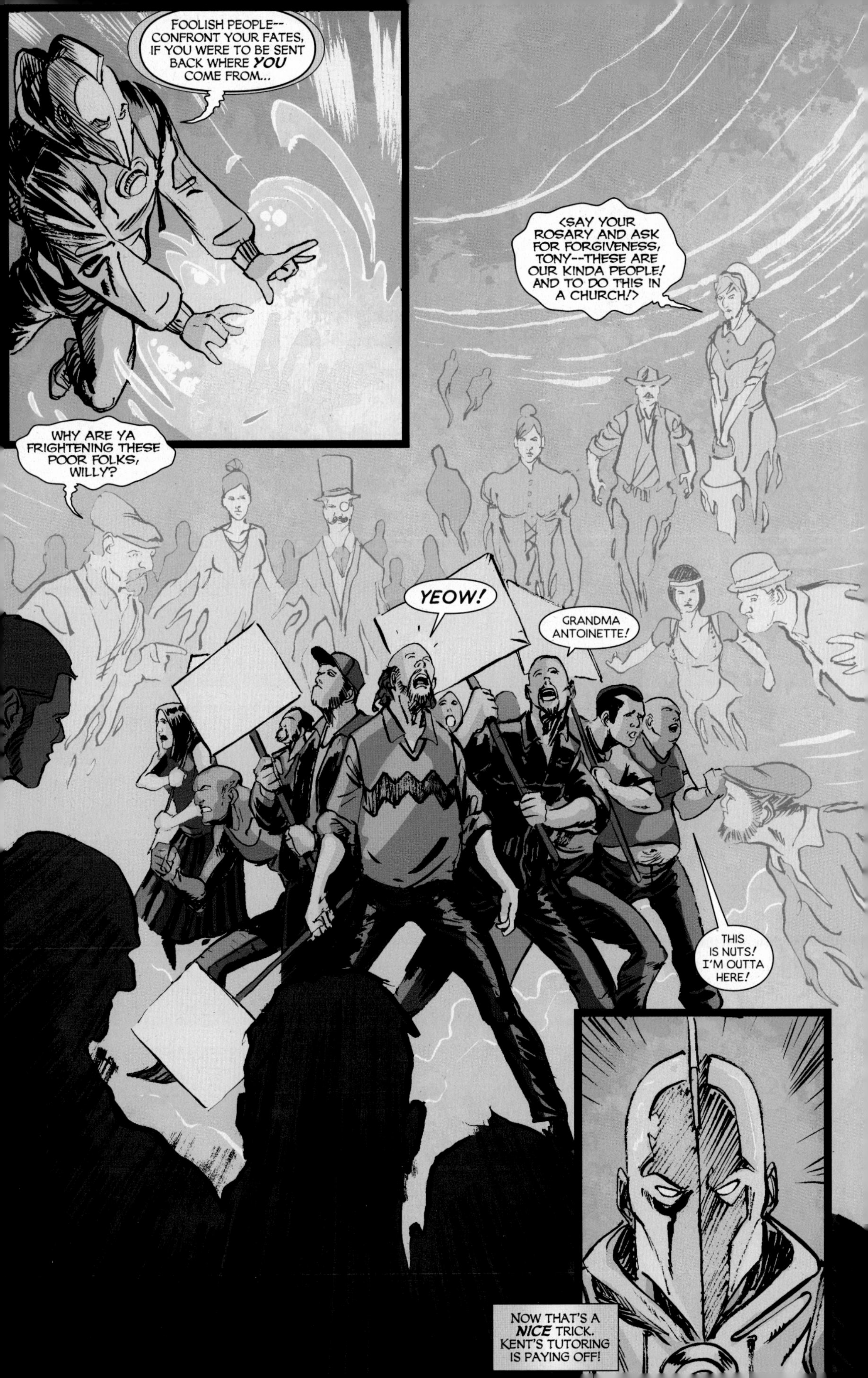
FOOLISH PEOPLE-- CONFRONT YOUR FATES, IF YOU WERE TO BE SENT BACK WHERE *YOU* COME FROM...
<SAY YOUR ROSARY AND ASK FOR FORGIVENESS, TONY--THESE ARE OUR KINDA PEOPLE! AND TO DO THIS IN A CHURCH!>
WHY ARE YA FRIGHTENING THESE POOR FOLKS, WILLY?
YEOW!
GRANDMA ANTOINETTE!
THIS IS NUTS! I'M OUTTA HERE!
NOW THAT'S A *NICE* TRICK. KENT'S TUTORING IS PAYING OFF!

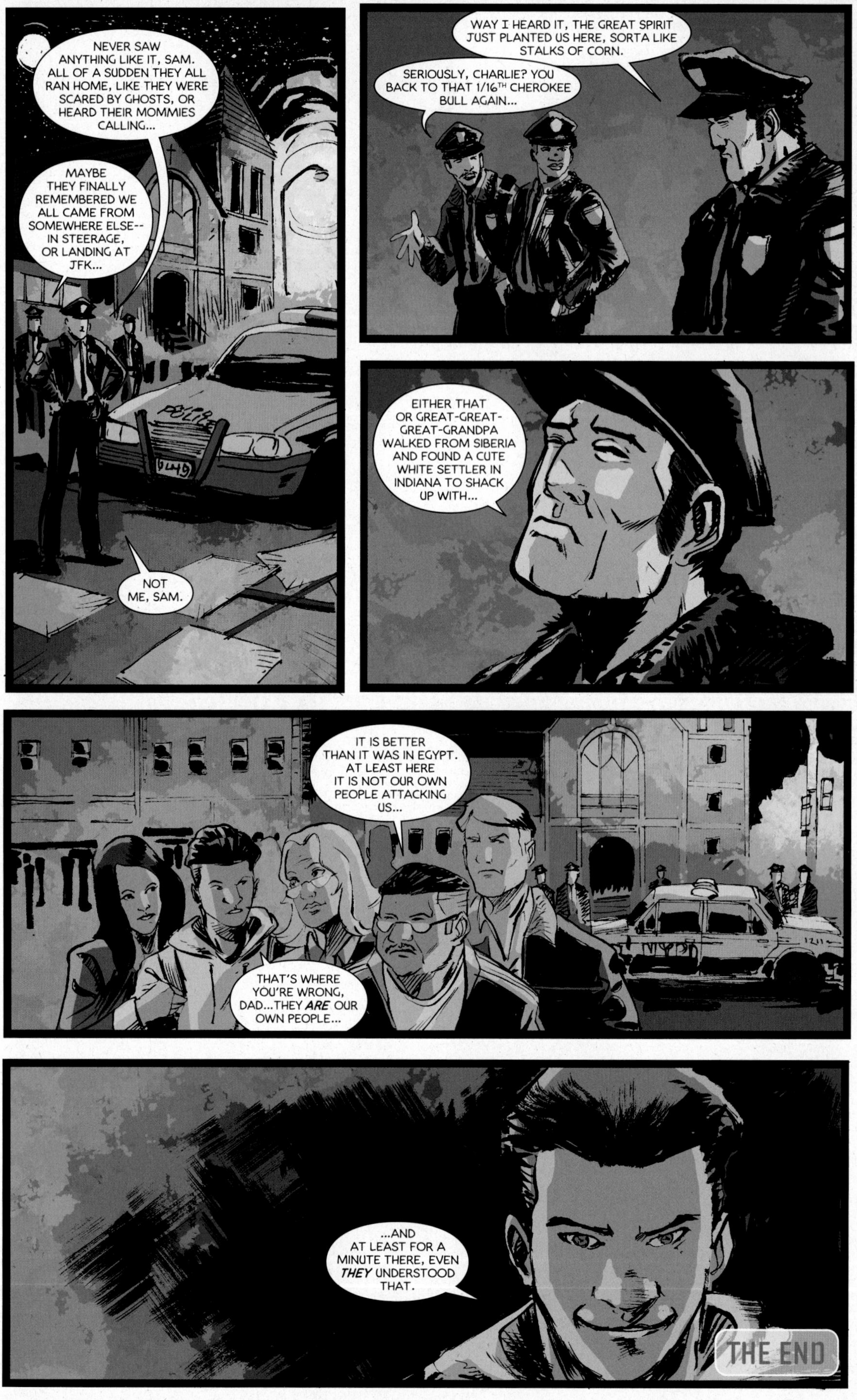
NEVER SAW ANYTHING LIKE IT, SAM. ALL OF A SUDDEN THEY ALL RAN HOME, LIKE THEY WERE SCARED BY GHOSTS, OR HEARD THEIR MOMMIES CALLING...
MAYBE THEY FINALLY REMEMBERED WE ALL CAME FROM SOMEWHERE ELSE-- IN STEERAGE, OR LANDING AT JFK...
NOT ME, SAM.
POLICE
WAY I HEARD IT, THE GREAT SPIRIT JUST PLANTED US HERE, SORTA LIKE STALKS OF CORN.
SERIOUSLY, CHARLIE? YOU BACK TO THAT 1/16TH CHEROKEE BULL AGAIN...
EITHER THAT OR GREAT-GREAT-GREAT-GRANDPA WALKED FROM SIBERIA AND FOUND A CUTE WHITE SETTLER IN INDIANA TO SHACK UP WITH...
IT IS BETTER THAN IT WAS IN EGYPT. AT LEAST HERE IT IS NOT OUR OWN PEOPLE ATTACKING US...
THAT'S WHERE YOU'RE WRONG, DAD...THEY *ARE* OUR OWN PEOPLE...
...AND AT LEAST FOR A MINUTE THERE, EVEN *THEY* UNDERSTOOD THAT.
THE END

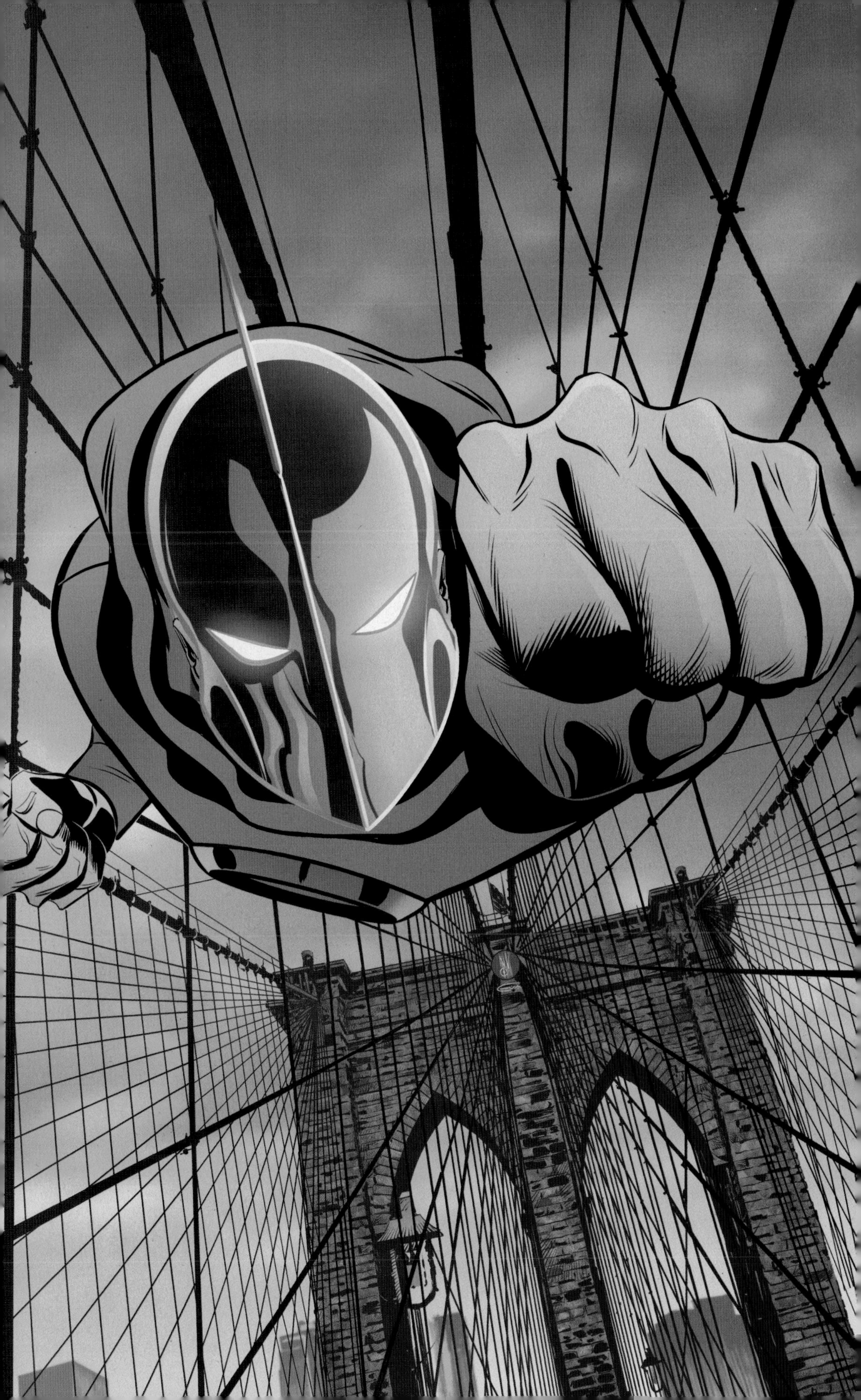

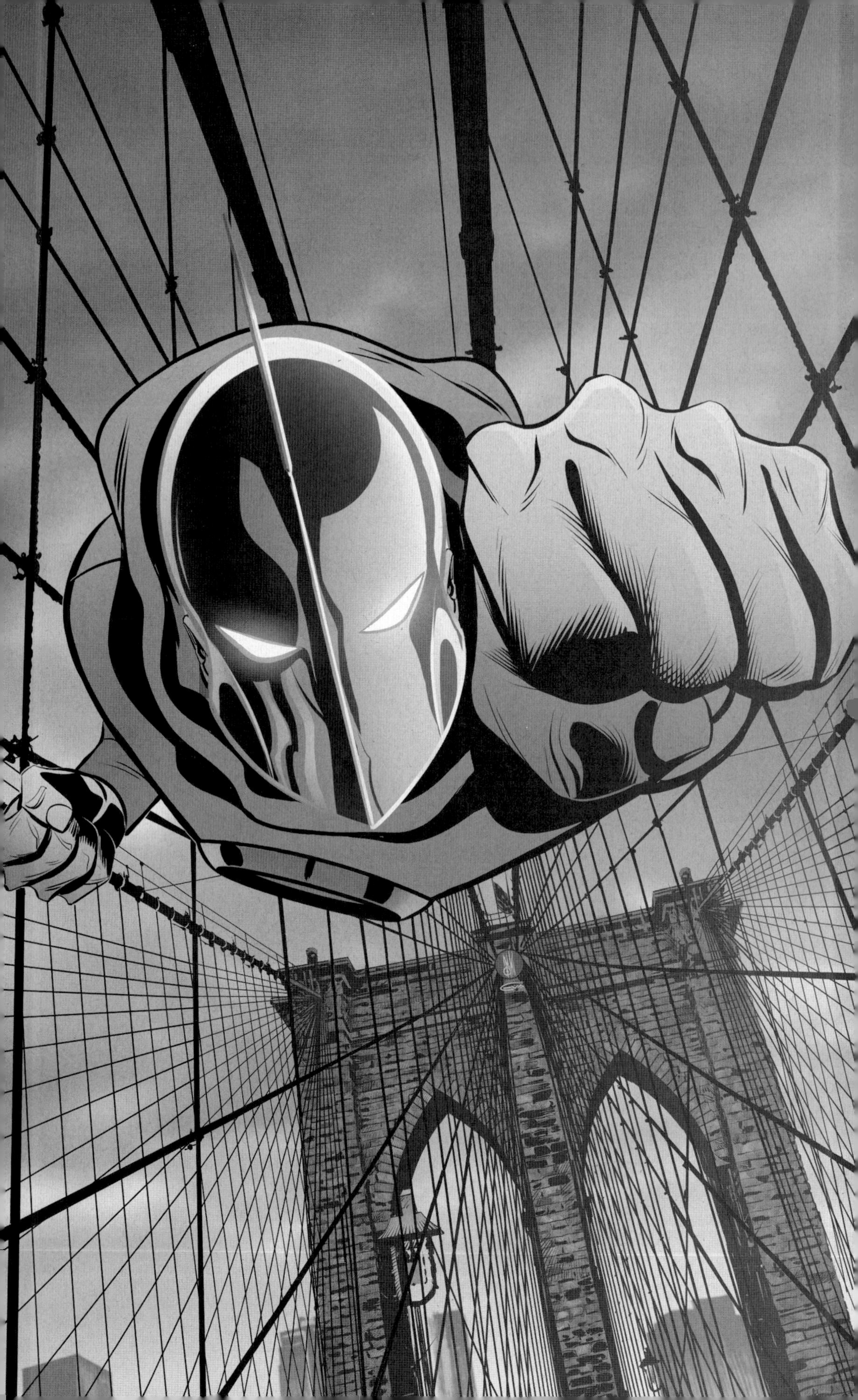

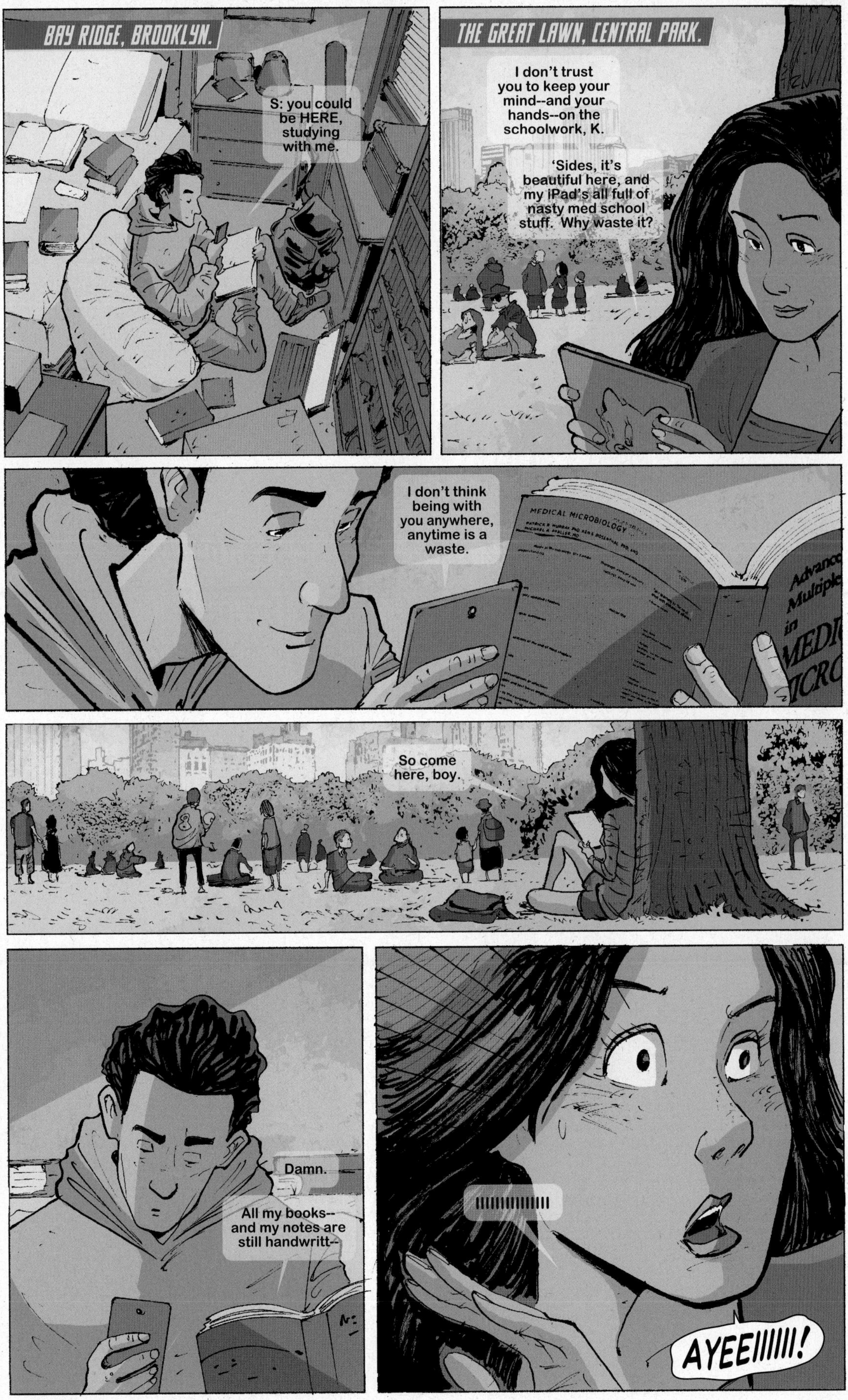
BAY RIDGE, BROOKLYN.
S: you could be HERE, studying with me.
THE GREAT LAWN, CENTRAL PARK.
I don't trust you to keep your mind--and your hands--on the schoolwork, K.
'Sides, it's beautiful here, and my iPad's all full of nasty med school stuff. Why waste it?
I don't think being with you anywhere, anytime is a waste.
MEDICAL MICROBIOLOGY
So come here, boy.
Damn.
All my books--and my notes are still handwritt--
IIIIIIIIIIIII
AYEEIIIIIII!

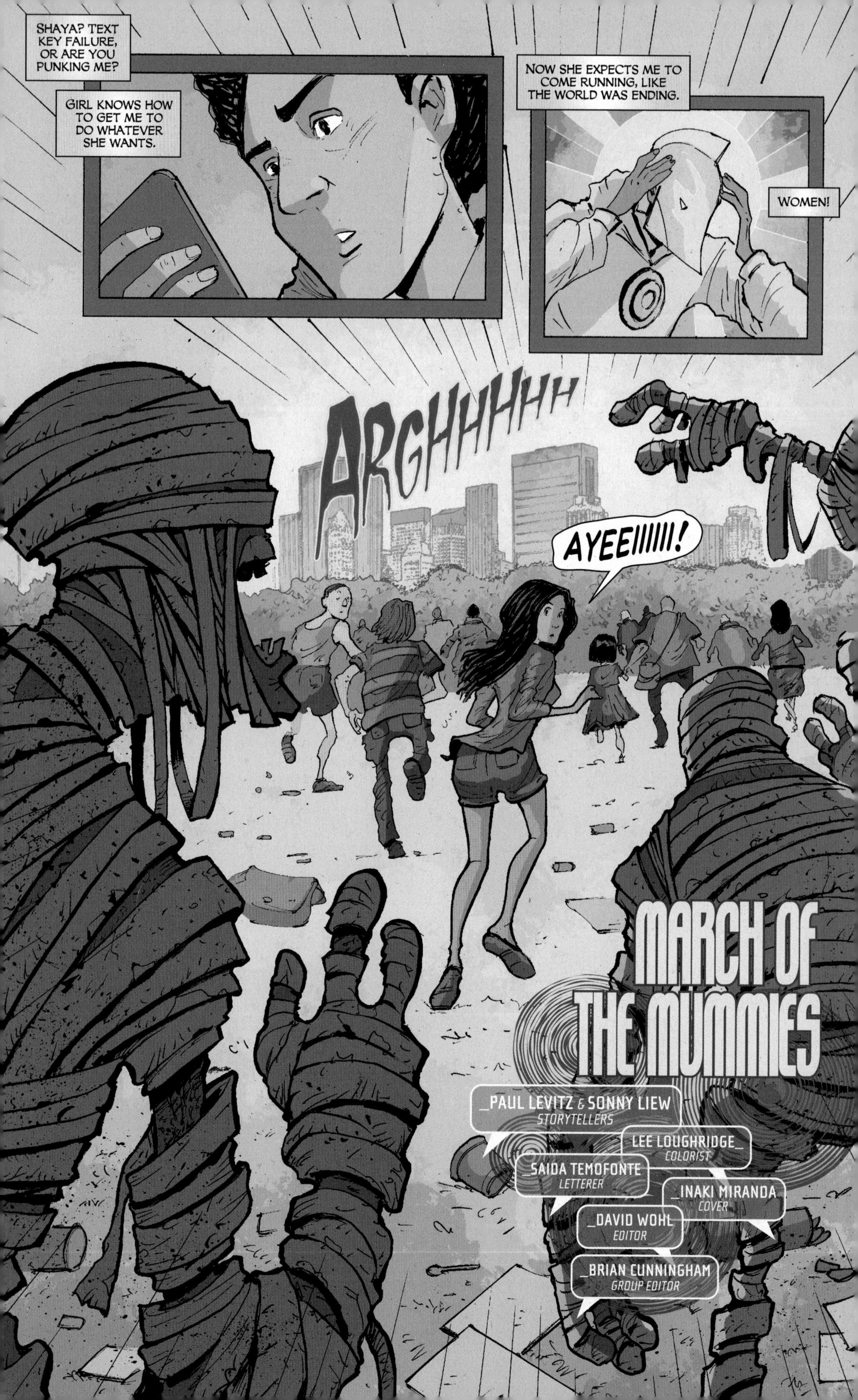
SHAYA? TEXT KEY FAILURE, OR ARE YOU PUNKING ME?
GIRL KNOWS HOW TO GET ME TO DO WHATEVER SHE WANTS.
NOW SHE EXPECTS ME TO COME RUNNING, LIKE THE WORLD WAS ENDING.
WOMEN!
ARGHHHHH
AYEEIIIIII!
MARCH OF THE MUMMIES
_PAUL LEVITZ & SONNY LIEW STORYTELLERS
LEE LOUGHRIDGE_ COLORIST
_SAIDA TEMOFONTE LETTERER
_INAKI MIRANDA COVER
_DAVID WOHL EDITOR
_BRIAN CUNNINGHAM GROUP EDITOR

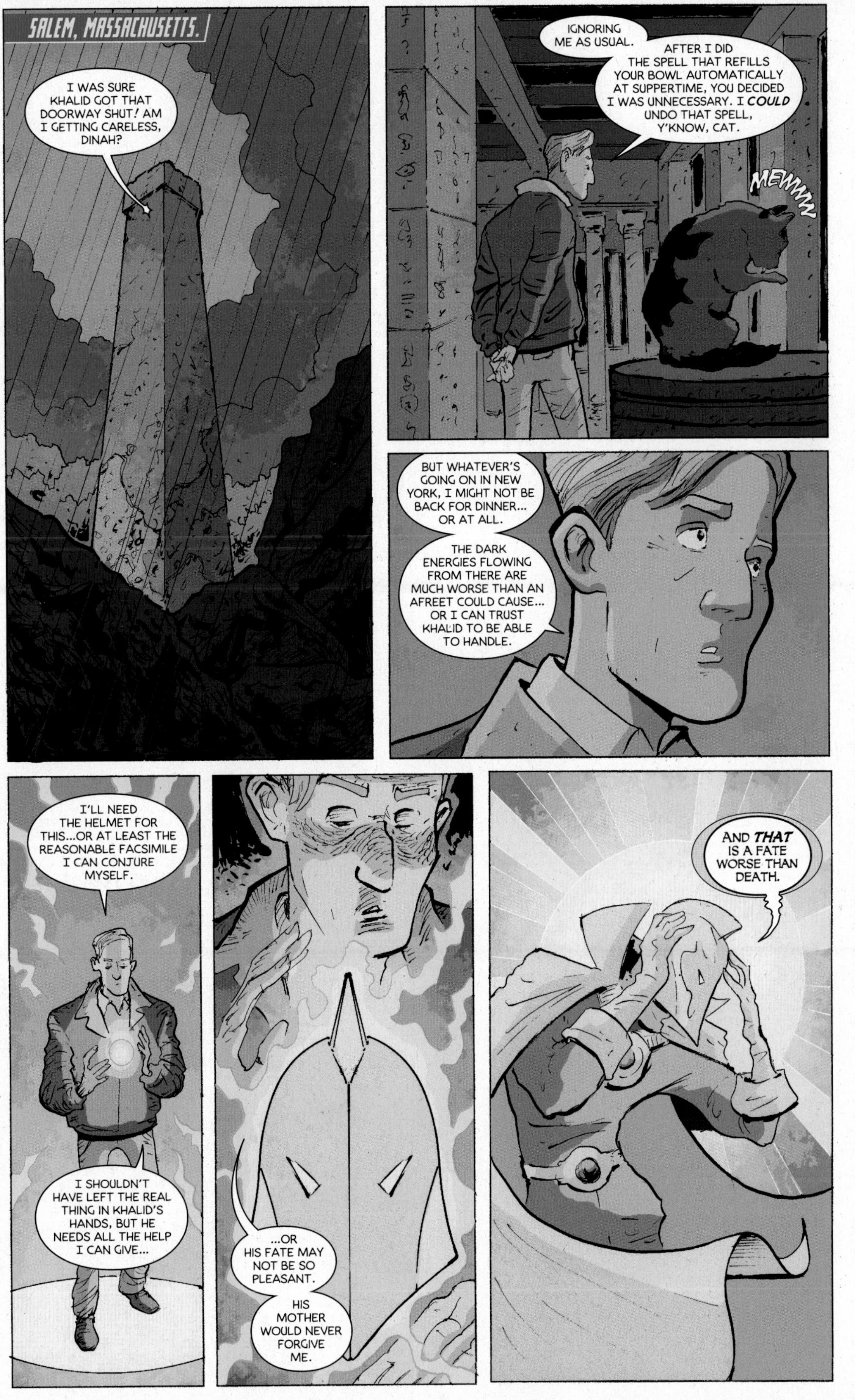
SALEM, MASSACHUSETTS.
I WAS SURE KHALID GOT THAT DOORWAY SHUT! AM I GETTING CARELESS, DINAH?
IGNORING ME AS USUAL.
AFTER I DID THE SPELL THAT REFILLS YOUR BOWL AUTOMATICALLY AT SUPPERTIME, YOU DECIDED I WAS UNNECESSARY. I COULD UNDO THAT SPELL, Y'KNOW, CAT.
MEWWWW
BUT WHATEVER'S GOING ON IN NEW YORK, I MIGHT NOT BE BACK FOR DINNER... OR AT ALL.
THE DARK ENERGIES FLOWING FROM THERE ARE MUCH WORSE THAN AN AFREET COULD CAUSE... OR I CAN TRUST KHALID TO BE ABLE TO HANDLE.
I'LL NEED THE HELMET FOR THIS...OR AT LEAST THE REASONABLE FACSIMILE I CAN CONJURE MYSELF.
I SHOULDN'T HAVE LEFT THE REAL THING IN KHALID'S HANDS, BUT HE NEEDS ALL THE HELP I CAN GIVE...
...OR HIS FATE MAY NOT BE SO PLEASANT.
HIS MOTHER WOULD NEVER FORGIVE ME.
AND THAT IS A FATE WORSE THAN DEATH.

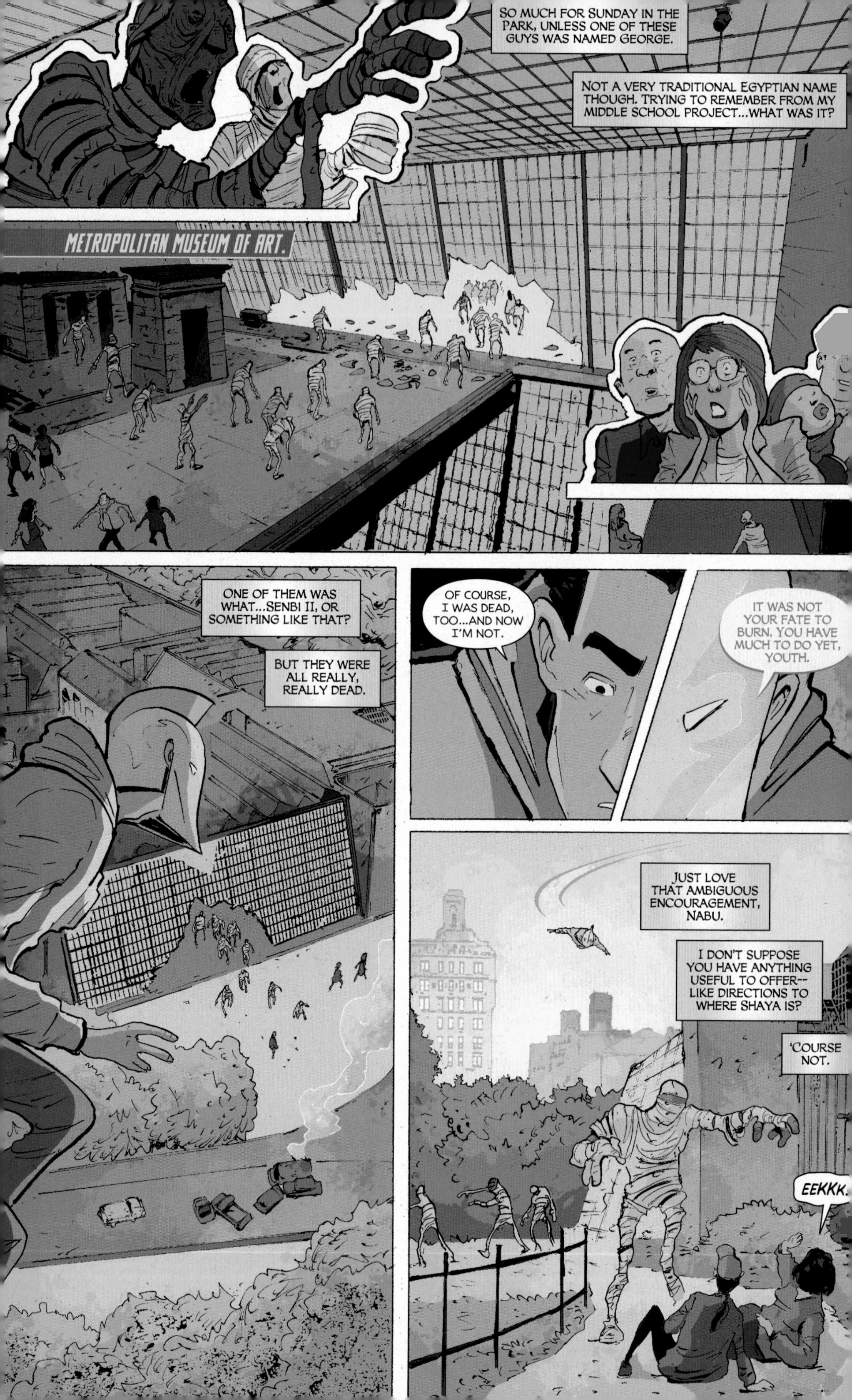
SO MUCH FOR SUNDAY IN THE PARK, UNLESS ONE OF THESE GUYS WAS NAMED GEORGE.
NOT A VERY TRADITIONAL EGYPTIAN NAME THOUGH. TRYING TO REMEMBER FROM MY MIDDLE SCHOOL PROJECT...WHAT WAS IT?
METROPOLITAN MUSEUM OF ART.
ONE OF THEM WAS WHAT...SENBI II, OR SOMETHING LIKE THAT?
BUT THEY WERE ALL REALLY, REALLY DEAD.
OF COURSE, I WAS DEAD, TOO...AND NOW I'M NOT.
IT WAS NOT YOUR FATE TO BURN. YOU HAVE MUCH TO DO YET, YOUTH.
JUST LOVE THAT AMBIGUOUS ENCOURAGEMENT, NABU.
I DON'T SUPPOSE YOU HAVE ANYTHING USEFUL TO OFFER-- LIKE DIRECTIONS TO WHERE SHAYA IS?
'COURSE NOT.
EEKKK.

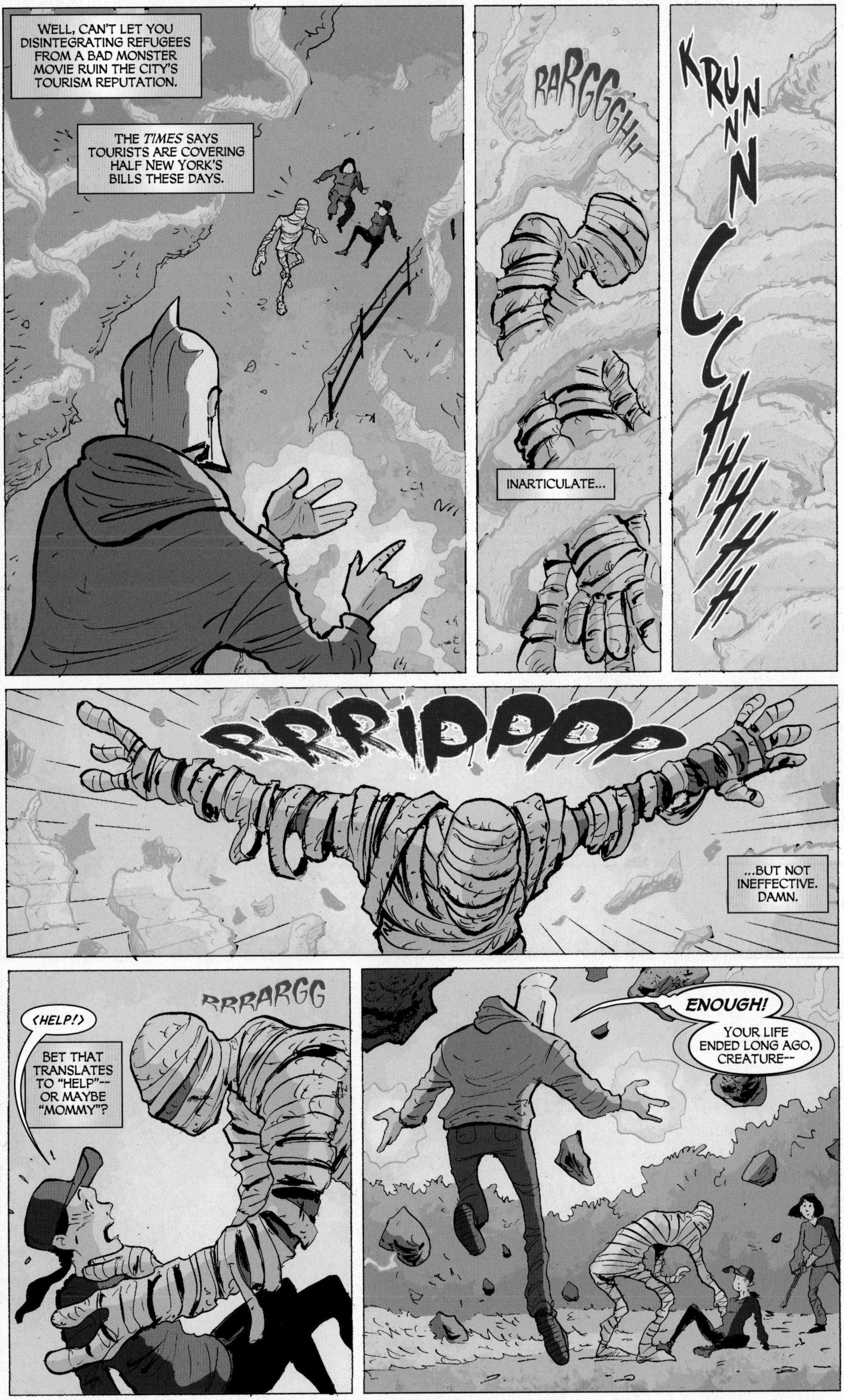
WELL, CAN'T LET YOU DISINTEGRATING REFUGEES FROM A BAD MONSTER MOVIE RUIN THE CITY'S TOURISM REPUTATION.
THE *TIMES* SAYS TOURISTS ARE COVERING HALF NEW YORK'S BILLS THESE DAYS.
RARGGGHH
INARTICULATE...
KRUNNNCHHHHHH
RRRIPPPPP
...BUT NOT INEFFECTIVE. DAMN.
RRRARGG
‹HELP!›
BET THAT TRANSLATES TO "HELP"--OR MAYBE "MOMMY"?
ENOUGH!
YOUR LIFE ENDED LONG AGO, CREATURE--

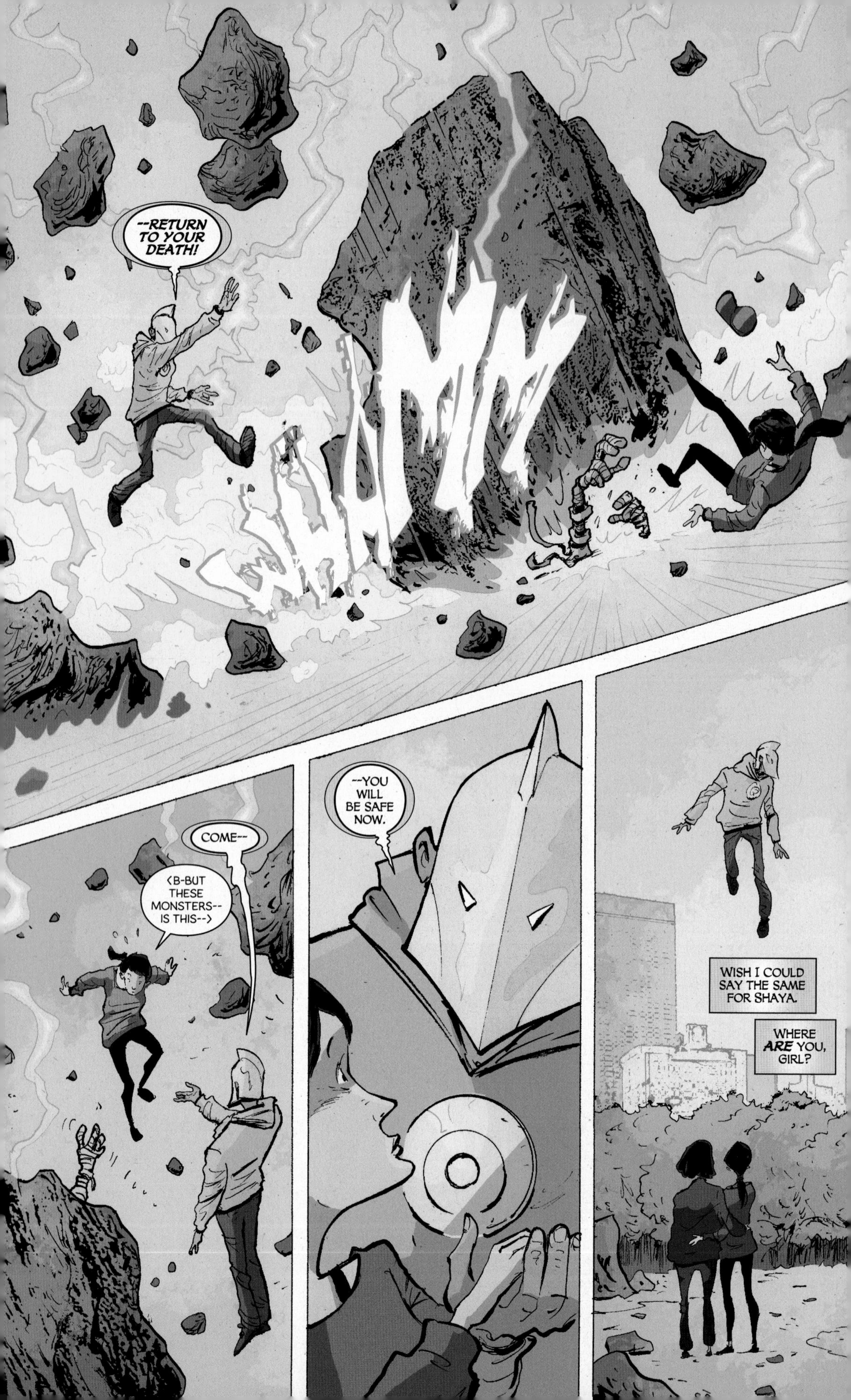
--RETURN TO YOUR DEATH!
WHAMM
COME--
<B-BUT THESE MONSTERS-- IS THIS-->
--YOU WILL BE SAFE NOW.
WISH I COULD SAY THE SAME FOR SHAYA.
WHERE ARE YOU, GIRL?

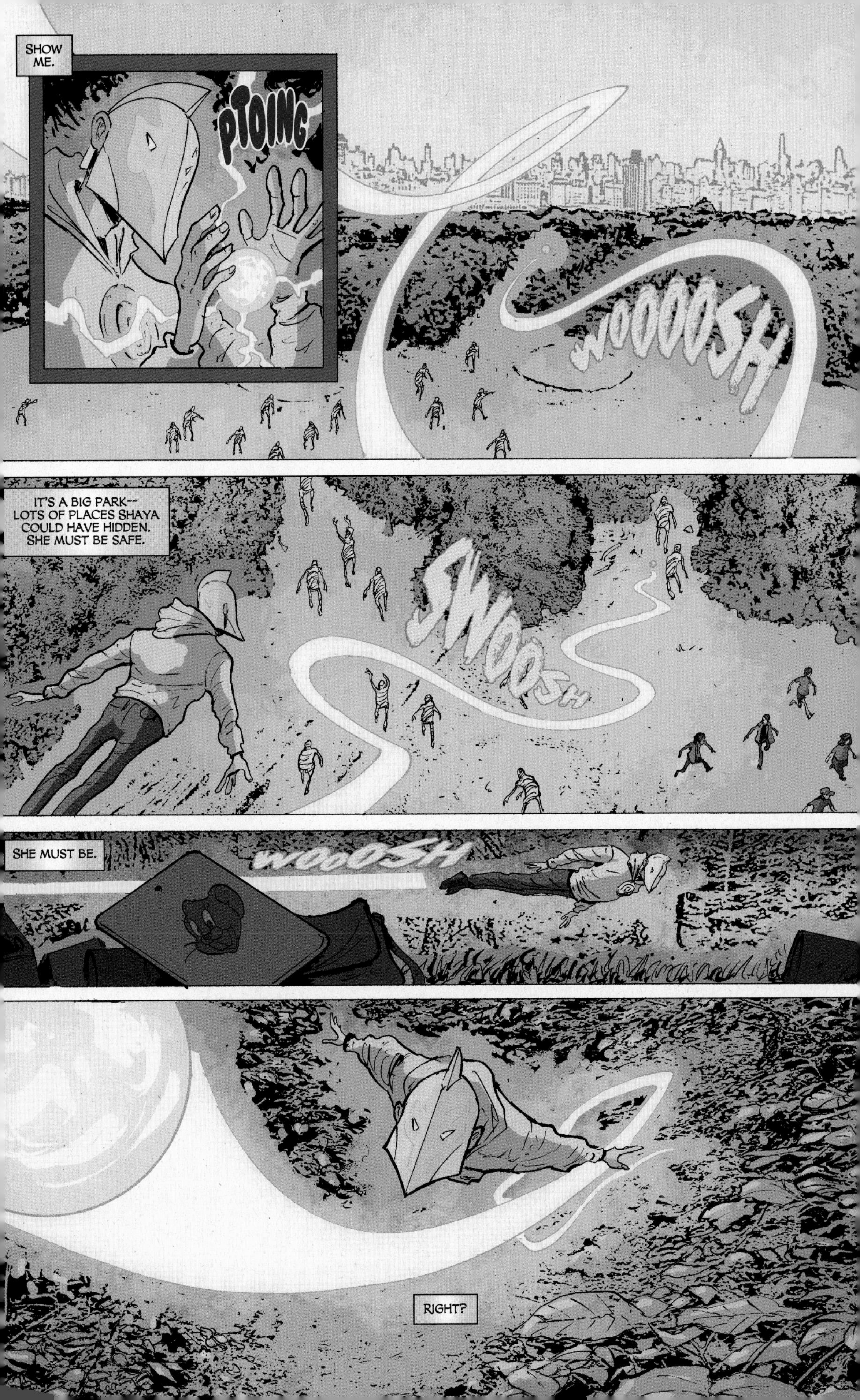
SHOW ME.
PTOING
WOOOOSH
IT'S A BIG PARK-- LOTS OF PLACES SHAYA COULD HAVE HIDDEN. SHE MUST BE SAFE.
SWOOOSH
SHE MUST BE.
WOOOSH
RIGHT?

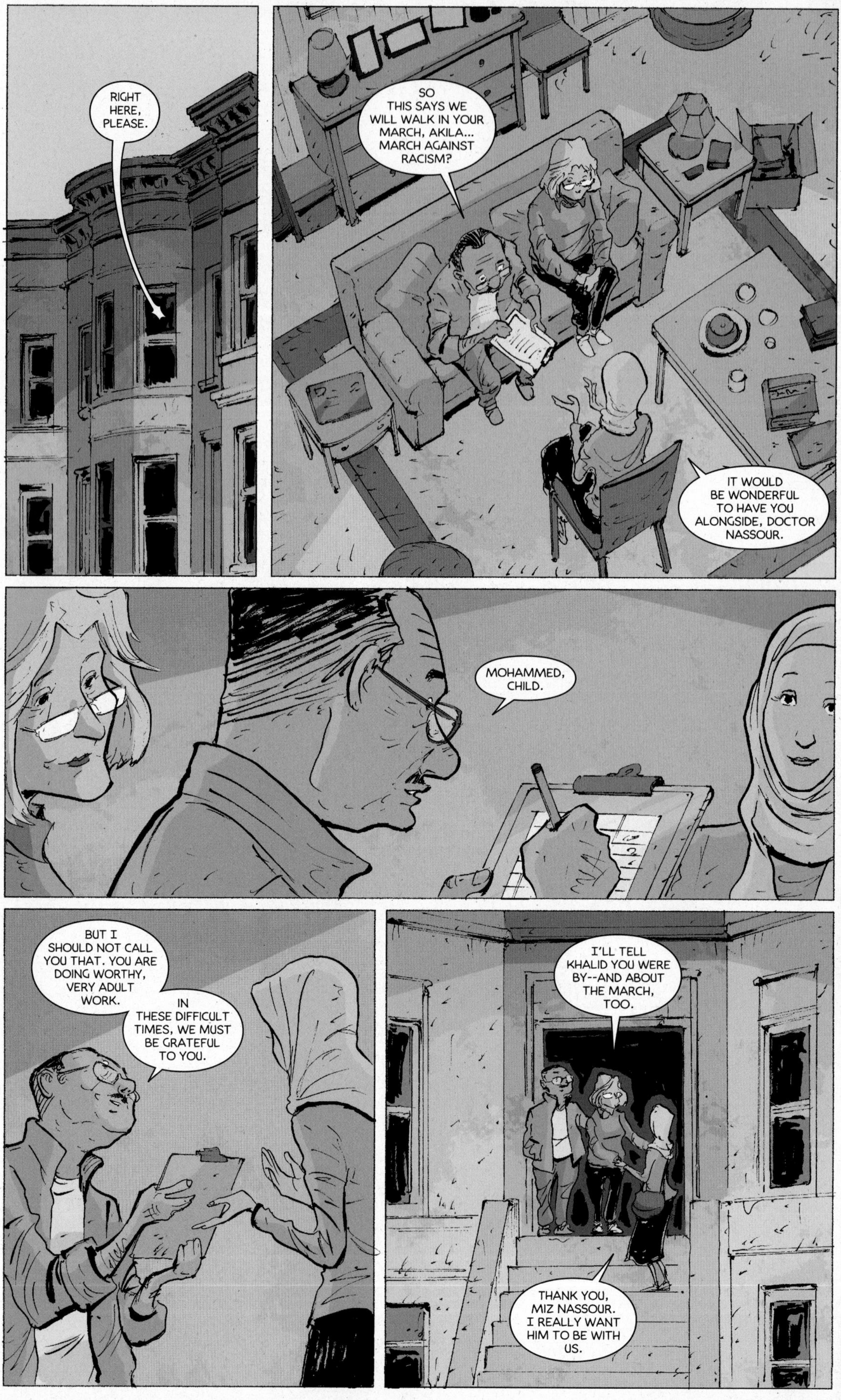
RIGHT HERE, PLEASE.
SO THIS SAYS WE WILL WALK IN YOUR MARCH, AKILA... MARCH AGAINST RACISM?
IT WOULD BE WONDERFUL TO HAVE YOU ALONGSIDE, DOCTOR NASSOUR.
MOHAMMED, CHILD.
BUT I SHOULD NOT CALL YOU THAT. YOU ARE DOING WORTHY, VERY ADULT WORK.
IN THESE DIFFICULT TIMES, WE MUST BE GRATEFUL TO YOU.
I'LL TELL KHALID YOU WERE BY--AND ABOUT THE MARCH, TOO.
THANK YOU, MIZ NASSOUR. I REALLY WANT HIM TO BE WITH US.

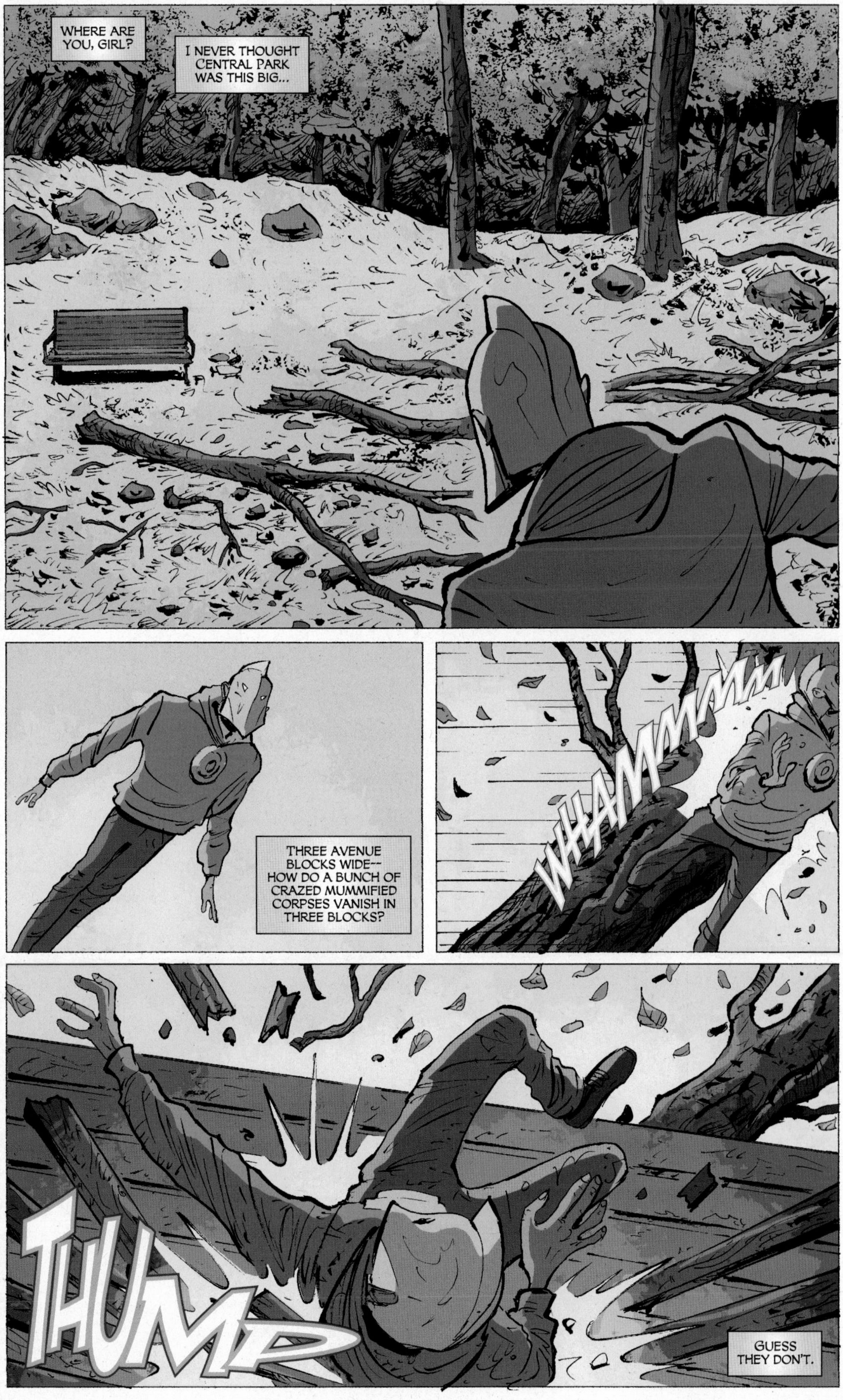
WHERE ARE YOU, GIRL?
I NEVER THOUGHT CENTRAL PARK WAS THIS BIG...
THREE AVENUE BLOCKS WIDE-- HOW DO A BUNCH OF CRAZED MUMMIFIED CORPSES VANISH IN THREE BLOCKS?
WHAMMMMM
THUMP
GUESS THEY DON'T.

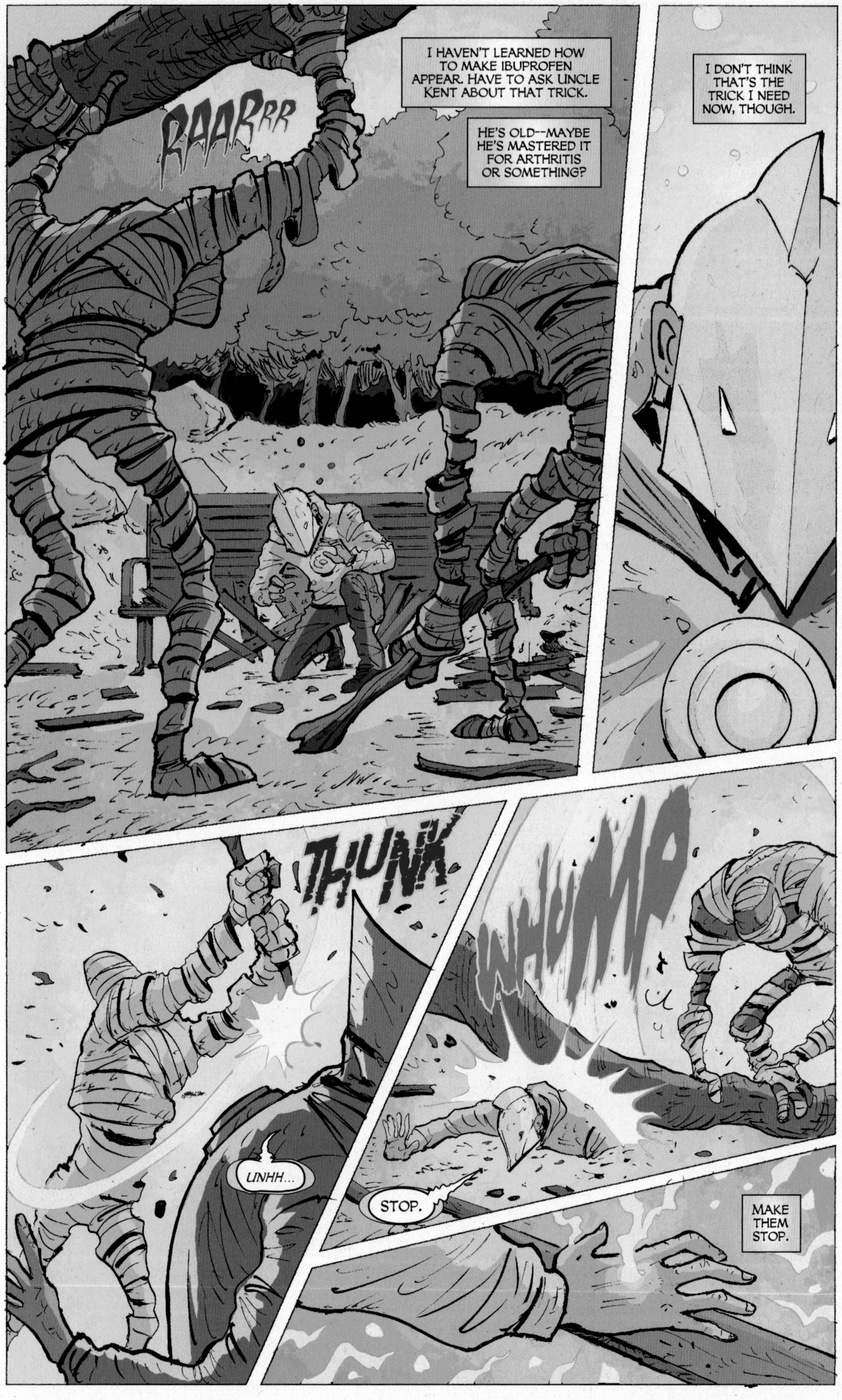

RAARRR
I HAVEN'T LEARNED HOW TO MAKE IBUPROFEN APPEAR. HAVE TO ASK UNCLE KENT ABOUT THAT TRICK.
HE'S OLD--MAYBE HE'S MASTERED IT FOR ARTHRITIS OR SOMETHING?
I DON'T THINK THAT'S THE TRICK I NEED NOW, THOUGH.
THUNK
UNHH...
WHUMP
STOP.
MAKE THEM STOP.

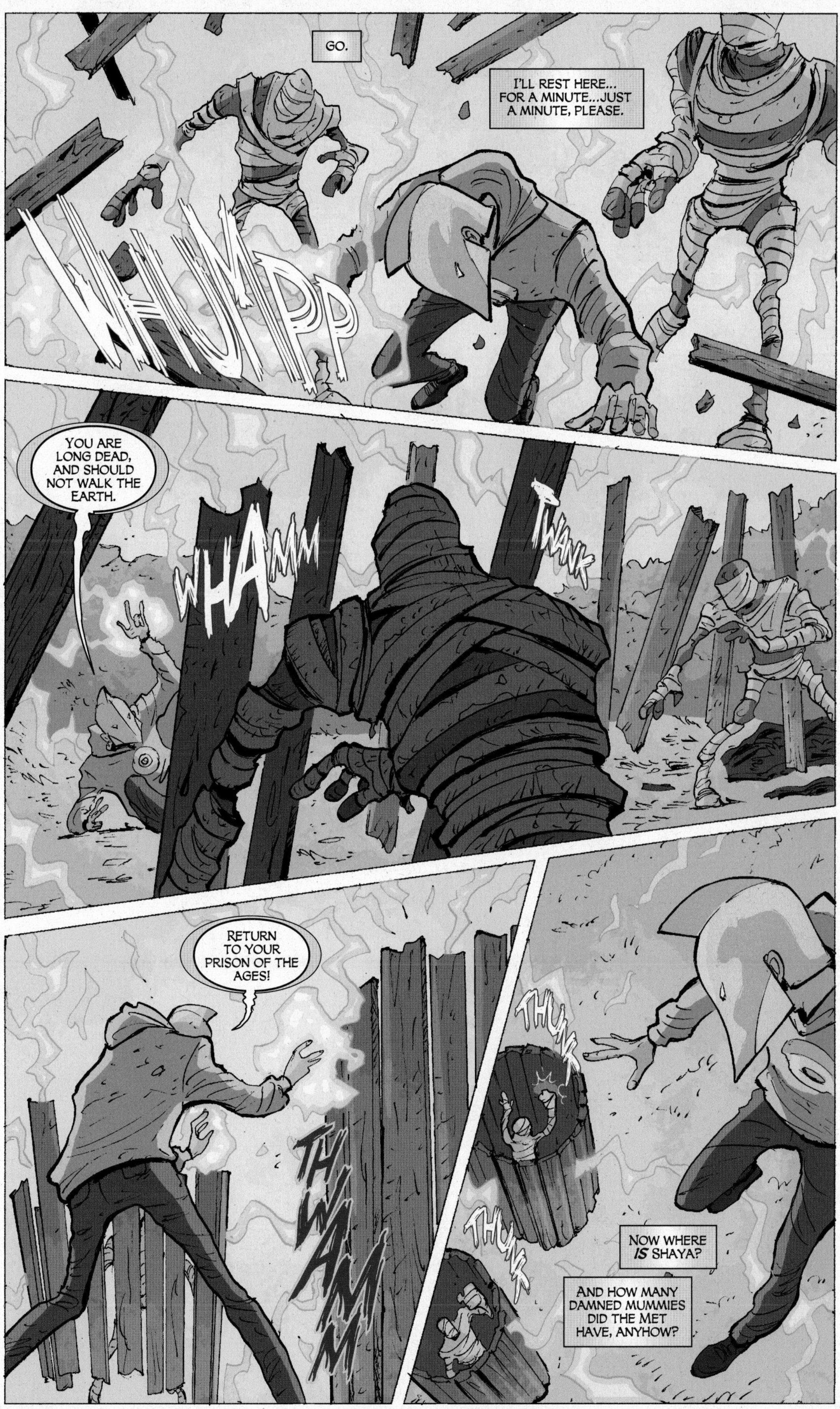
GO.
I'LL REST HERE... FOR A MINUTE...JUST A MINUTE, PLEASE.
WHUMPP
YOU ARE LONG DEAD, AND SHOULD NOT WALK THE EARTH.
WHAMMM
TWANK
RETURN TO YOUR PRISON OF THE AGES!
THWAMM
THUNK
THUNK
NOW WHERE *IS* SHAYA?
AND HOW MANY DAMNED MUMMIES DID THE MET HAVE, ANYHOW?

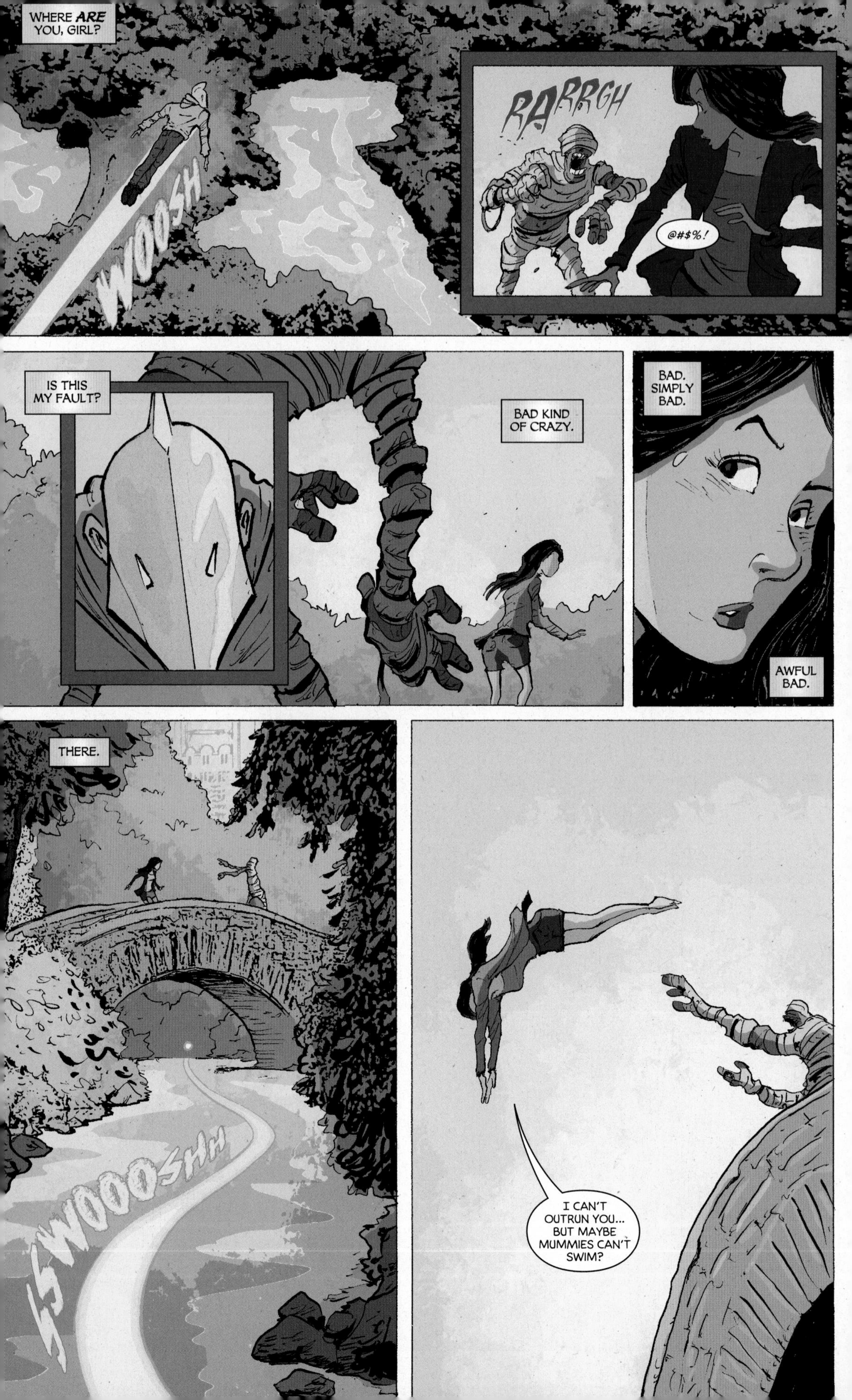
WHERE ARE YOU, GIRL?
WOOSH
RARRGH
@#$%!
IS THIS MY FAULT?
BAD KIND OF CRAZY.
BAD. SIMPLY BAD.
AWFUL BAD.
THERE.
SSWOOOSHH
I CAN'T OUTRUN YOU... BUT MAYBE MUMMIES CAN'T SWIM?

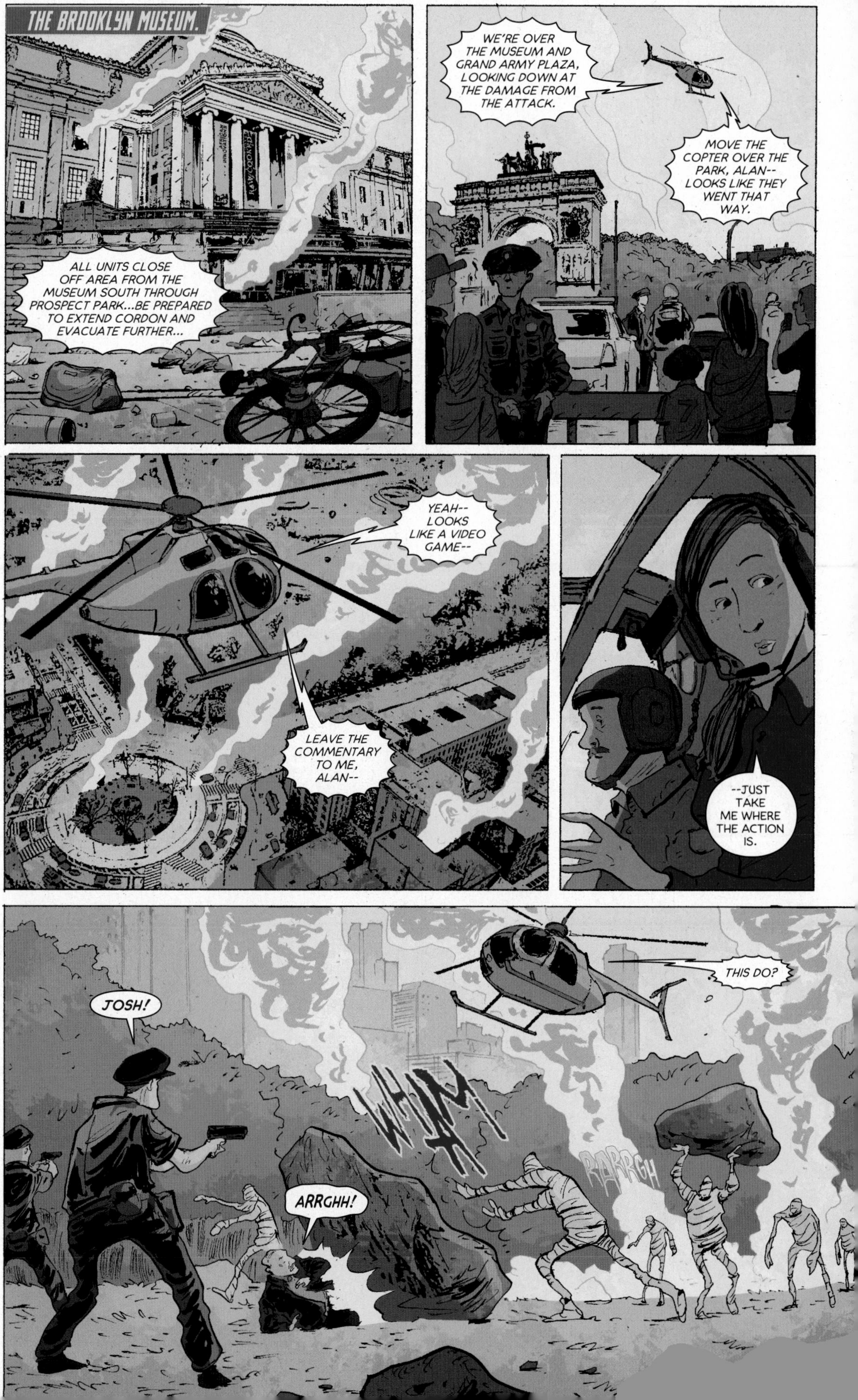
THE BROOKLYN MUSEUM.
ALL UNITS CLOSE OFF AREA FROM THE MUSEUM SOUTH THROUGH PROSPECT PARK...BE PREPARED TO EXTEND CORDON AND EVACUATE FURTHER...
WE'RE OVER THE MUSEUM AND GRAND ARMY PLAZA, LOOKING DOWN AT THE DAMAGE FROM THE ATTACK.
MOVE THE COPTER OVER THE PARK, ALAN-- LOOKS LIKE THEY WENT THAT WAY.
YEAH-- LOOKS LIKE A VIDEO GAME--
LEAVE THE COMMENTARY TO ME, ALAN--
--JUST TAKE ME WHERE THE ACTION IS.
THIS DO?
JOSH!
WHAM
RARRGH
ARRGHH!

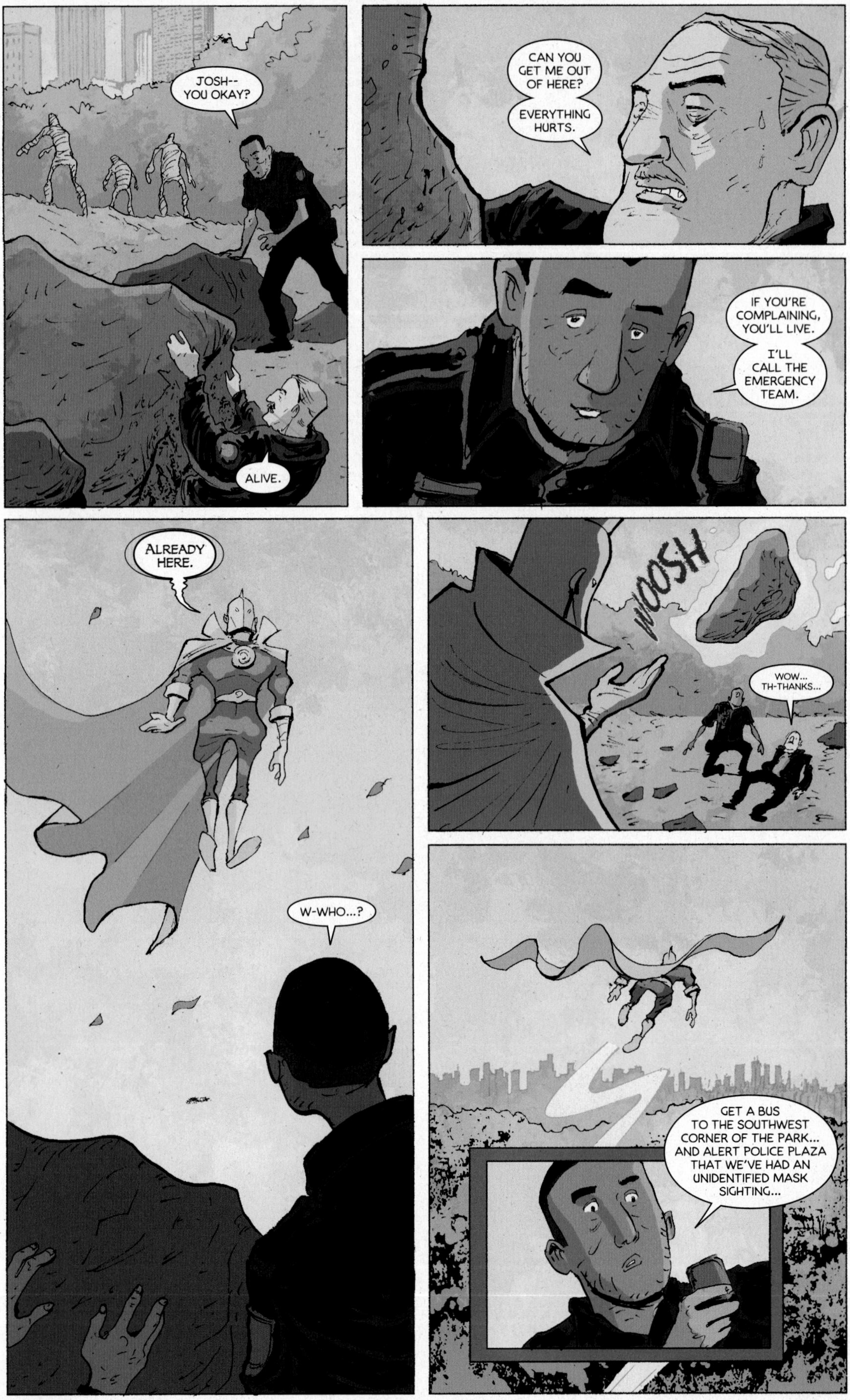
JOSH-- YOU OKAY?
ALIVE.
CAN YOU GET ME OUT OF HERE?
EVERYTHING HURTS.
IF YOU'RE COMPLAINING, YOU'LL LIVE.
I'LL CALL THE EMERGENCY TEAM.
ALREADY HERE.
W-WHO...?
WOOSH
WOW... TH-THANKS...
GET A BUS TO THE SOUTHWEST CORNER OF THE PARK... AND ALERT POLICE PLAZA THAT WE'VE HAD AN UNIDENTIFIED MASK SIGHTING...

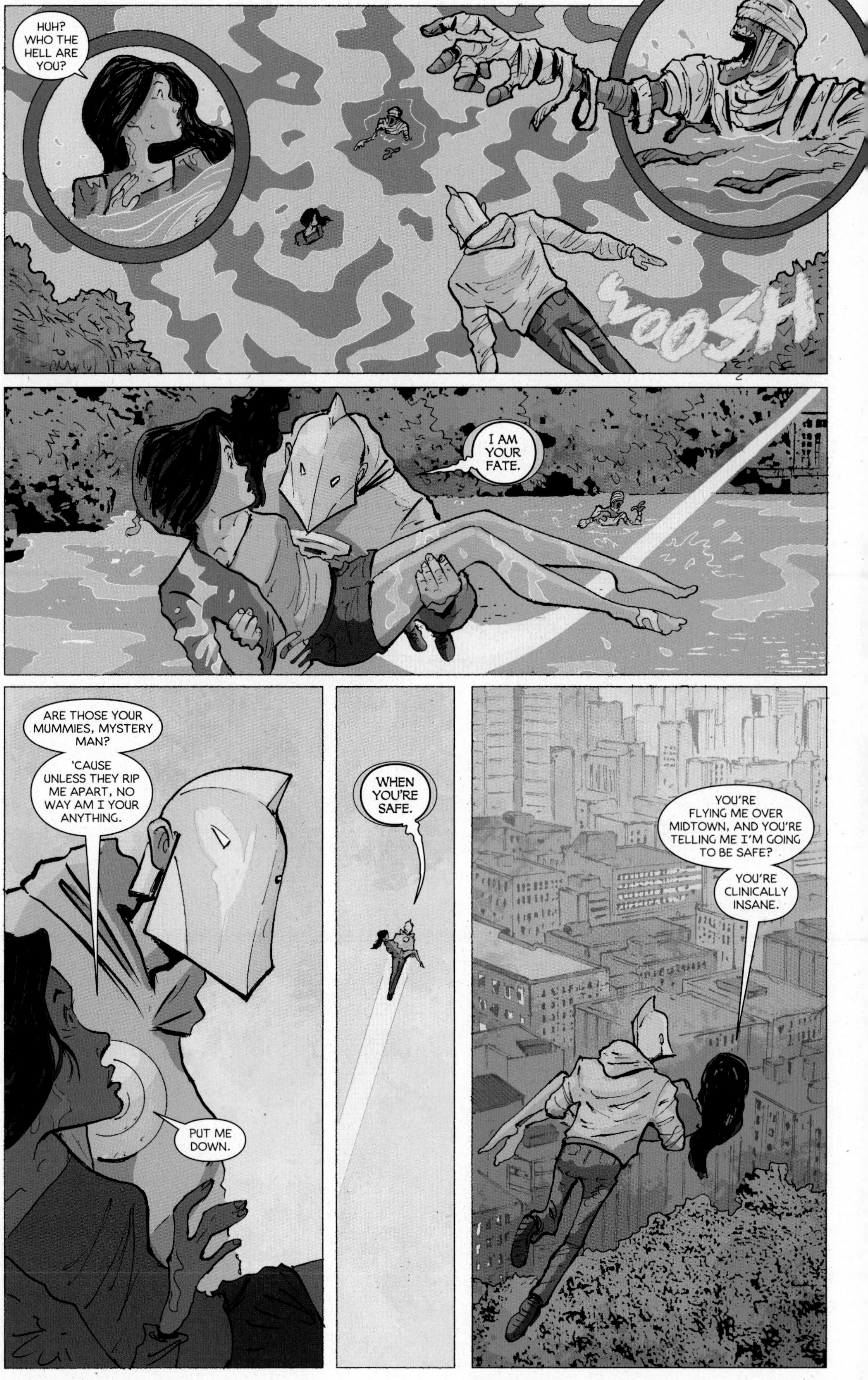
HUH? WHO THE HELL ARE YOU?
WOOSH
I AM YOUR FATE.
ARE THOSE YOUR MUMMIES, MYSTERY MAN?
'CAUSE UNLESS THEY RIP ME APART, NO WAY AM I YOUR ANYTHING.
PUT ME DOWN.
WHEN YOU'RE SAFE.
YOU'RE FLYING ME OVER MIDTOWN, AND YOU'RE TELLING ME I'M GOING TO BE SAFE?
YOU'RE CLINICALLY INSANE.

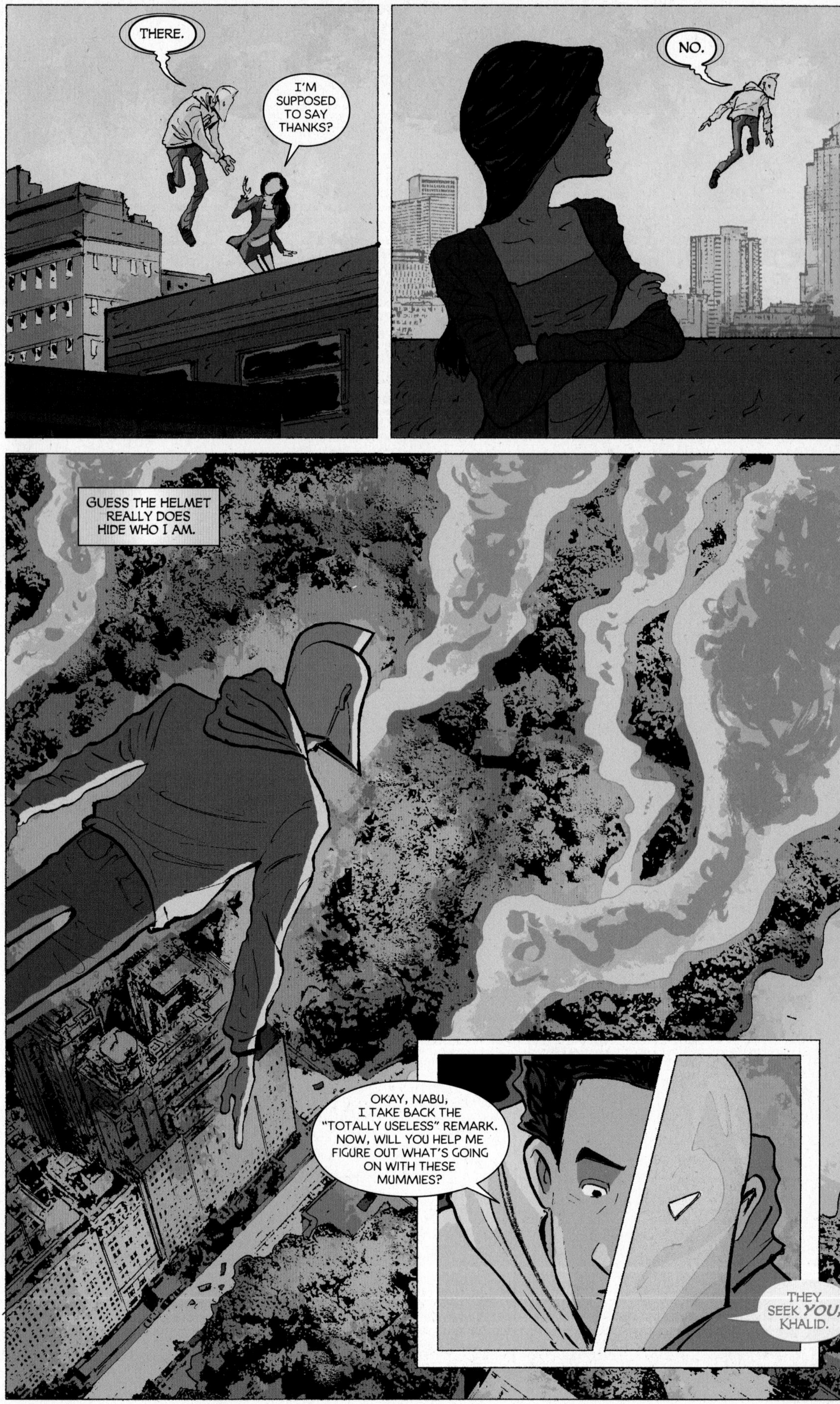
THERE.
I'M SUPPOSED TO SAY THANKS?
NO.
GUESS THE HELMET REALLY DOES HIDE WHO I AM.
OKAY, NABU, I TAKE BACK THE "TOTALLY USELESS" REMARK. NOW, WILL YOU HELP ME FIGURE OUT WHAT'S GOING ON WITH THESE MUMMIES?
THEY SEEK *YOU,* KHALID.

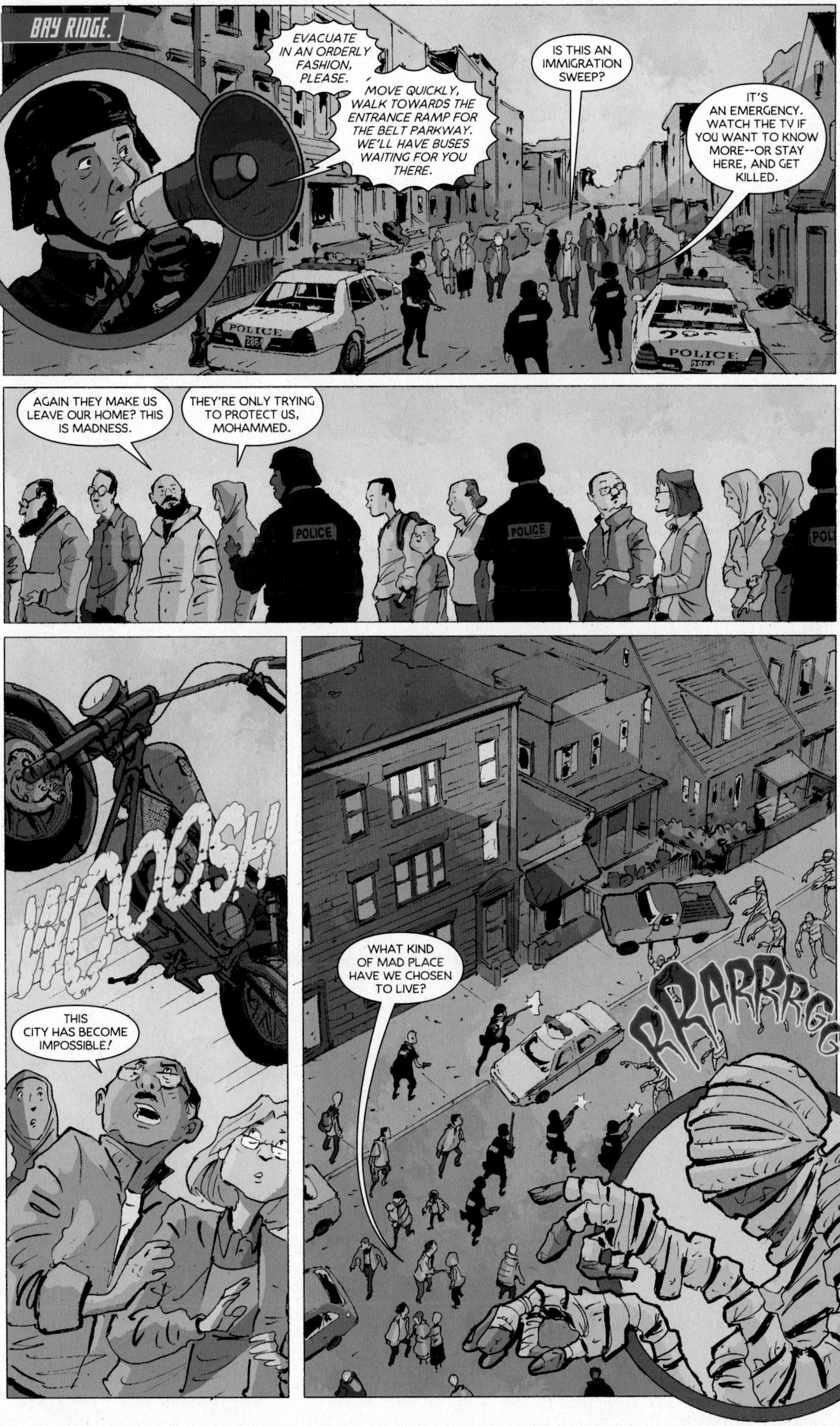
BAY RIDGE.
EVACUATE IN AN ORDERLY FASHION, PLEASE.
MOVE QUICKLY, WALK TOWARDS THE ENTRANCE RAMP FOR THE BELT PARKWAY. WE'LL HAVE BUSES WAITING FOR YOU THERE.
IS THIS AN IMMIGRATION SWEEP?
IT'S AN EMERGENCY. WATCH THE TV IF YOU WANT TO KNOW MORE--OR STAY HERE, AND GET KILLED.
POLICE
AGAIN THEY MAKE US LEAVE OUR HOME? THIS IS MADNESS.
THEY'RE ONLY TRYING TO PROTECT US, MOHAMMED.
POLICE
POLICE
WHOOOSH!
THIS CITY HAS BECOME IMPOSSIBLE!
WHAT KIND OF MAD PLACE HAVE WE CHOSEN TO LIVE?
RRARRRGG

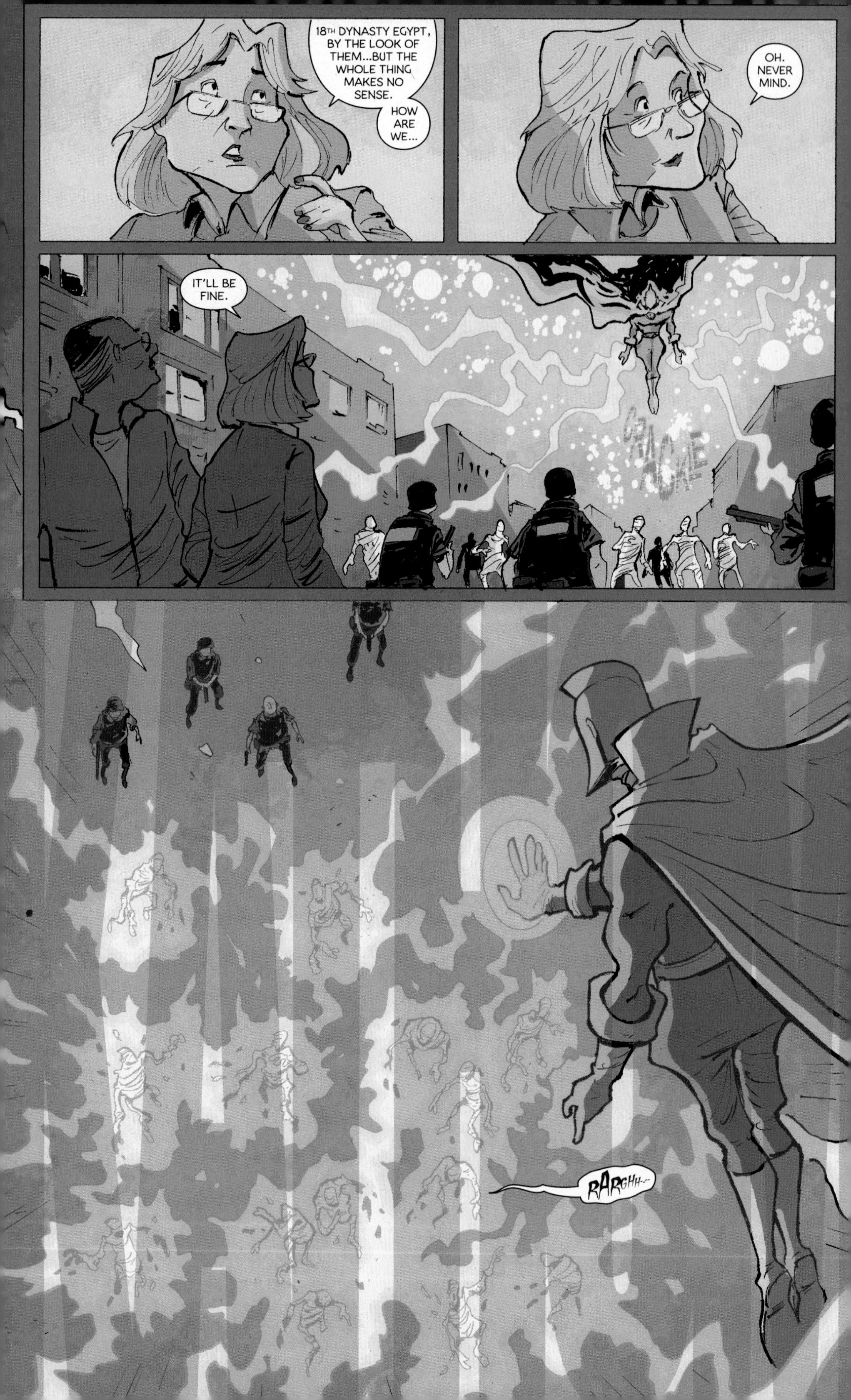
18TH DYNASTY EGYPT, BY THE LOOK OF THEM...BUT THE WHOLE THING MAKES NO SENSE.
HOW ARE WE...
OH. NEVER MIND.
IT'LL BE FINE.
RARGHH--

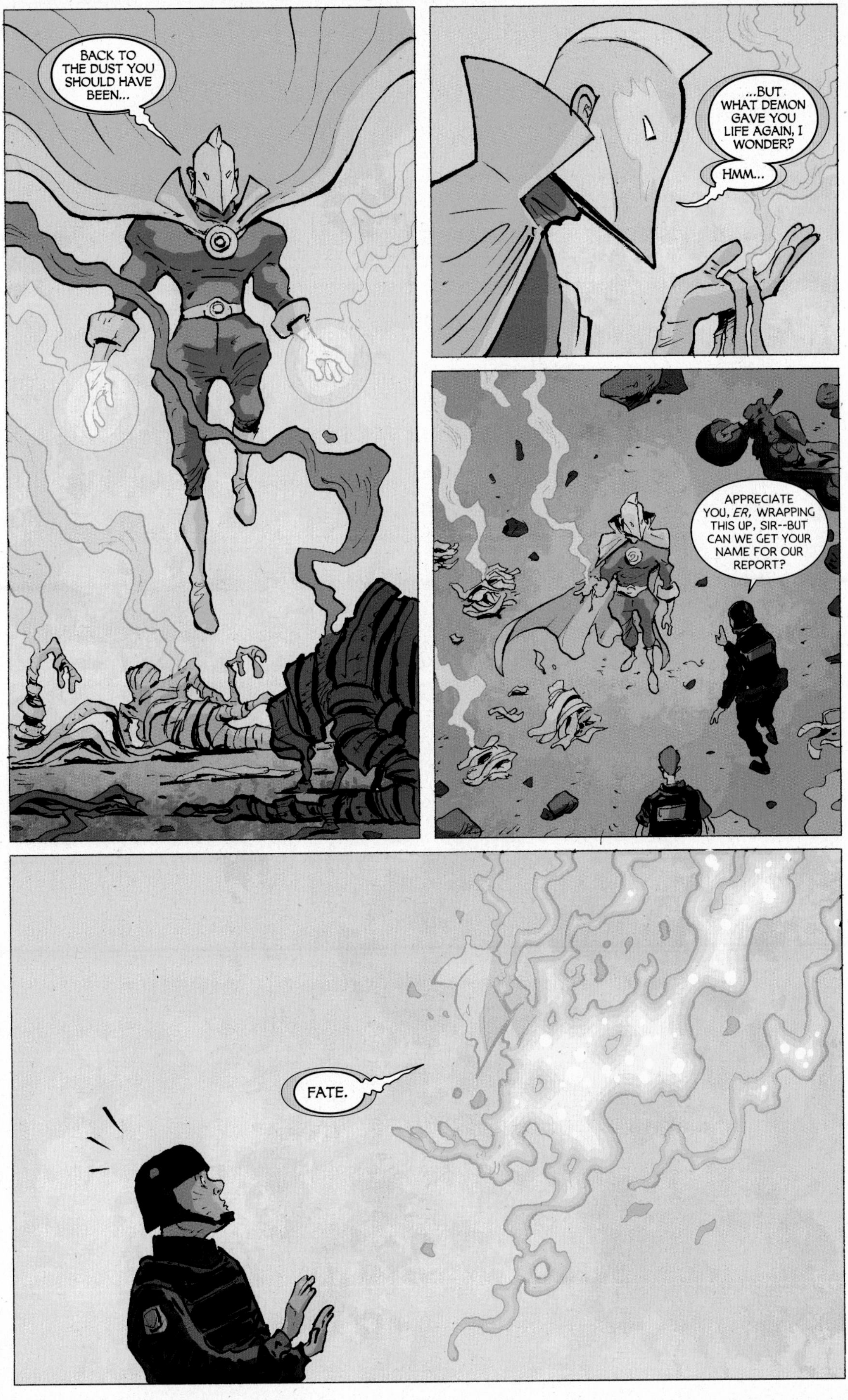
BACK TO THE DUST YOU SHOULD HAVE BEEN...
...BUT WHAT DEMON GAVE YOU LIFE AGAIN, I WONDER?
HMM...
APPRECIATE YOU, *ER,* WRAPPING THIS UP, SIR--BUT CAN WE GET YOUR NAME FOR OUR REPORT?
FATE.

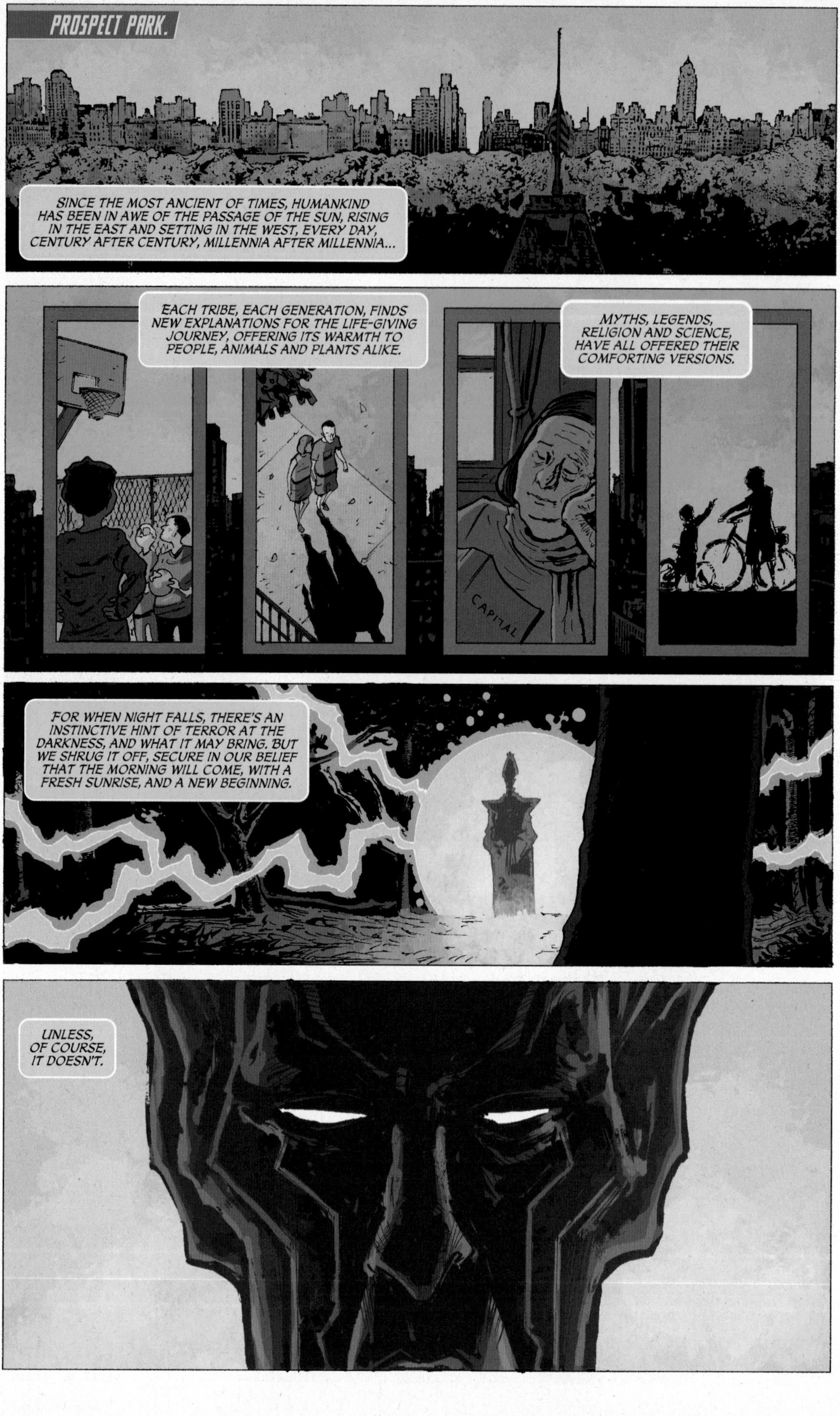
PROSPECT PARK.
SINCE THE MOST ANCIENT OF TIMES, HUMANKIND HAS BEEN IN AWE OF THE PASSAGE OF THE SUN, RISING IN THE EAST AND SETTING IN THE WEST, EVERY DAY, CENTURY AFTER CENTURY, MILLENNIA AFTER MILLENNIA...
EACH TRIBE, EACH GENERATION, FINDS NEW EXPLANATIONS FOR THE LIFE-GIVING JOURNEY, OFFERING ITS WARMTH TO PEOPLE, ANIMALS AND PLANTS ALIKE.
CAPITAL
MYTHS, LEGENDS, RELIGION AND SCIENCE, HAVE ALL OFFERED THEIR COMFORTING VERSIONS.
FOR WHEN NIGHT FALLS, THERE'S AN INSTINCTIVE HINT OF TERROR AT THE DARKNESS, AND WHAT IT MAY BRING. BUT WE SHRUG IT OFF, SECURE IN OUR BELIEF THAT THE MORNING WILL COME, WITH A FRESH SUNRISE, AND A NEW BEGINNING.
UNLESS, OF COURSE, IT DOESN'T.

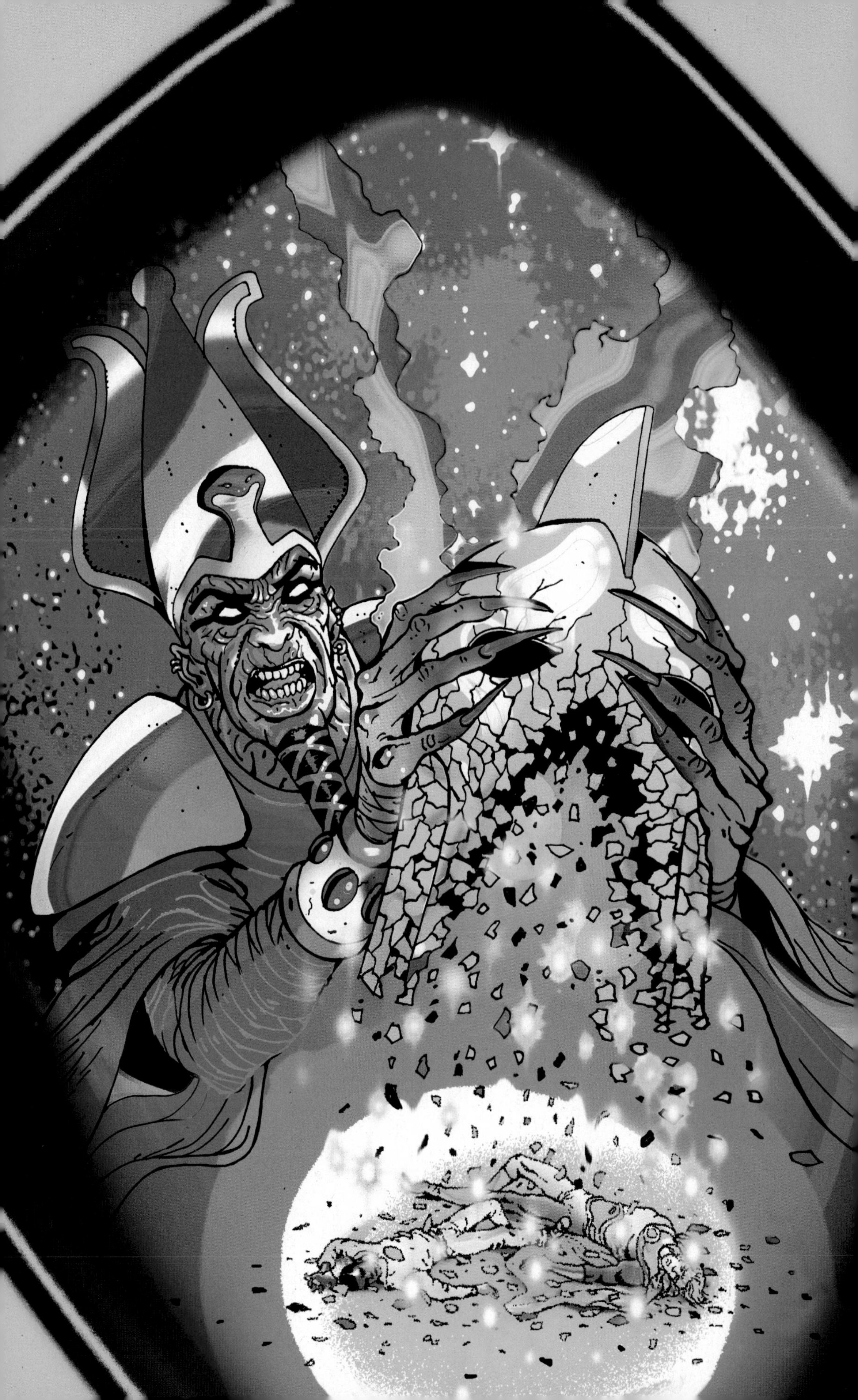

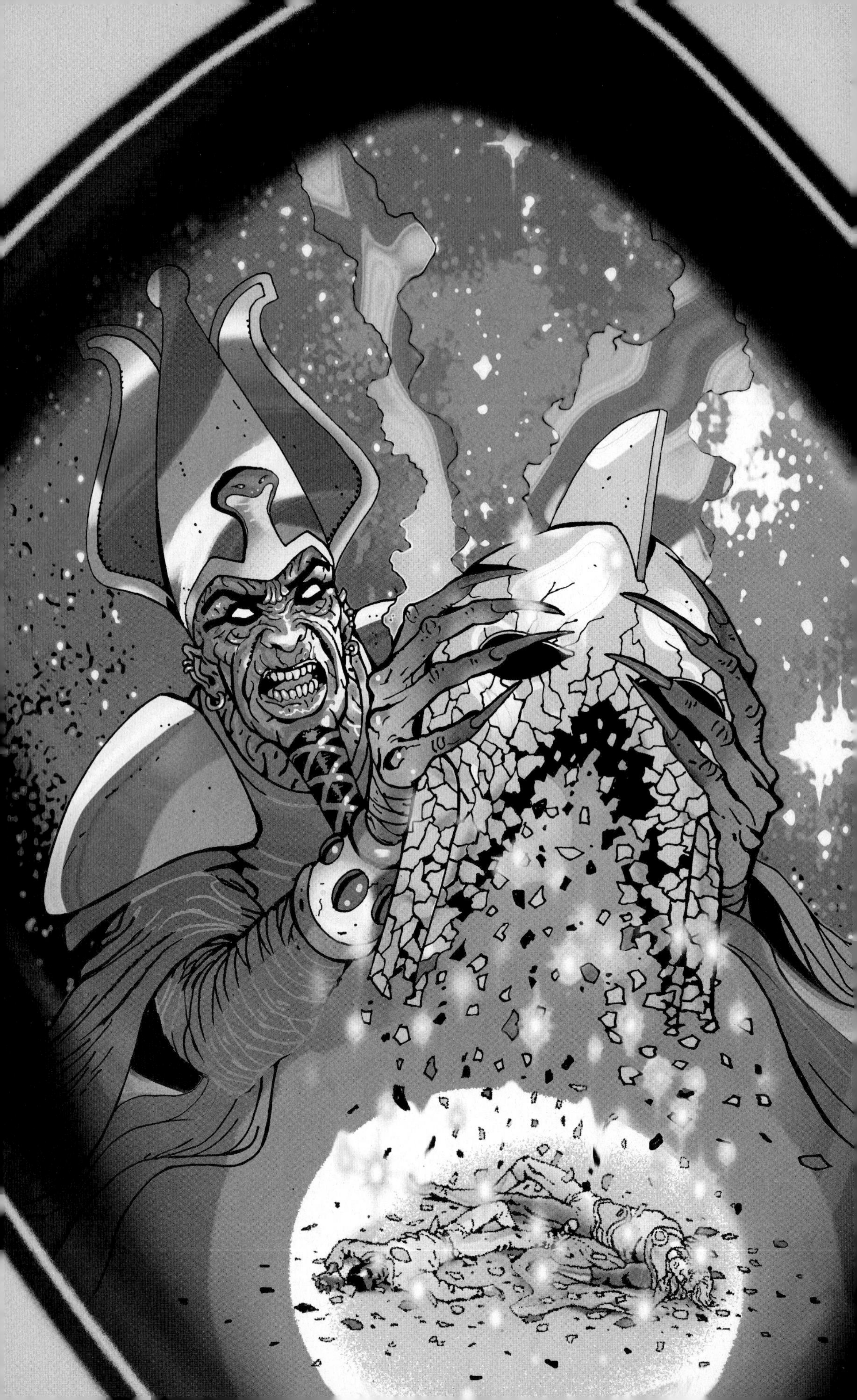

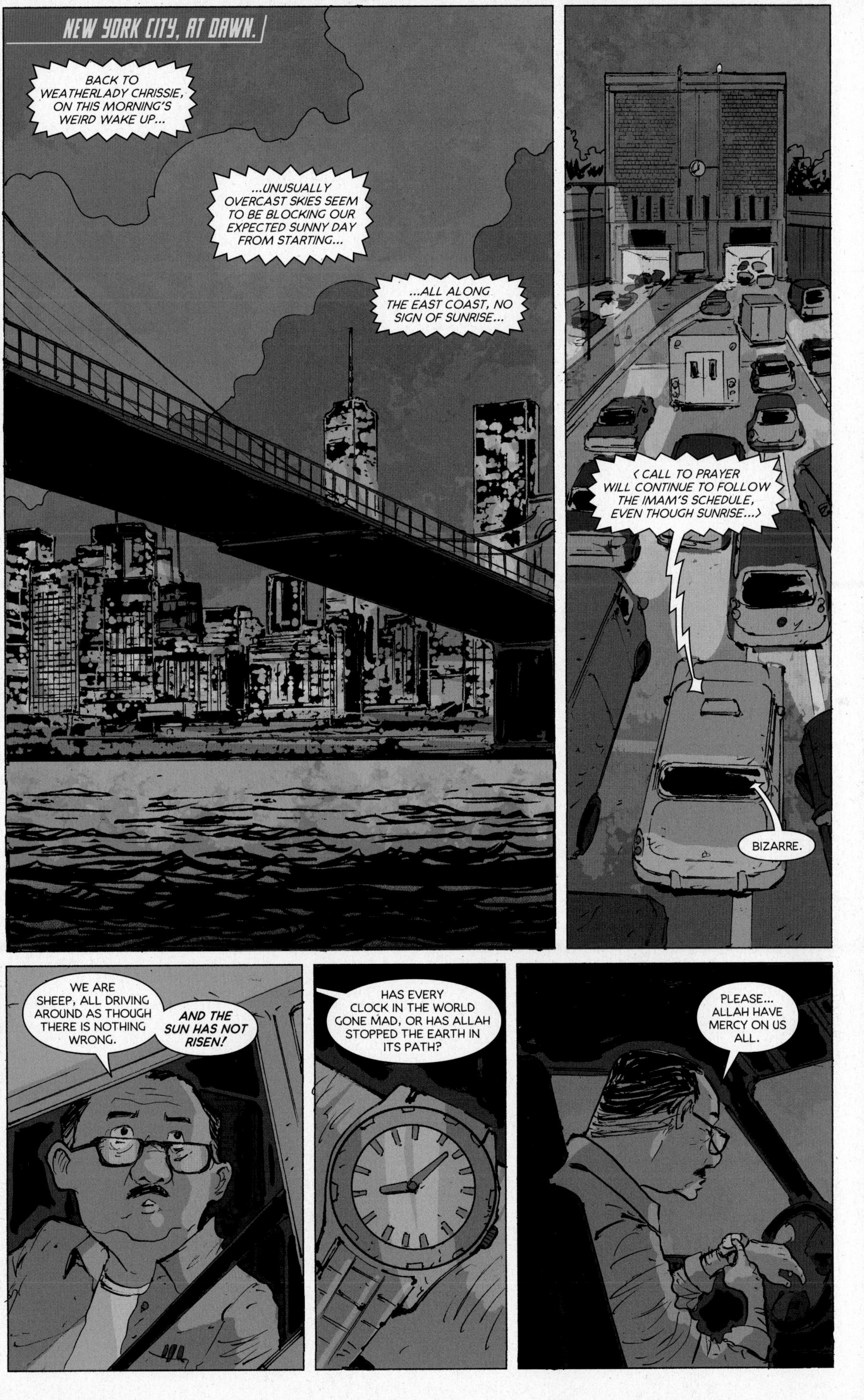
NEW YORK CITY, AT DAWN.
BACK TO WEATHERLADY CHRISSIE, ON THIS MORNING'S WEIRD WAKE UP...
...UNUSUALLY OVERCAST SKIES SEEM TO BE BLOCKING OUR EXPECTED SUNNY DAY FROM STARTING...
...ALL ALONG THE EAST COAST, NO SIGN OF SUNRISE...
< CALL TO PRAYER WILL CONTINUE TO FOLLOW THE IMAM'S SCHEDULE, EVEN THOUGH SUNRISE...>
BIZARRE.
WE ARE SHEEP, ALL DRIVING AROUND AS THOUGH THERE IS NOTHING WRONG.
AND THE SUN HAS NOT RISEN!
HAS EVERY CLOCK IN THE WORLD GONE MAD, OR HAS ALLAH STOPPED THE EARTH IN ITS PATH?
PLEASE... ALLAH HAVE MERCY ON US ALL.

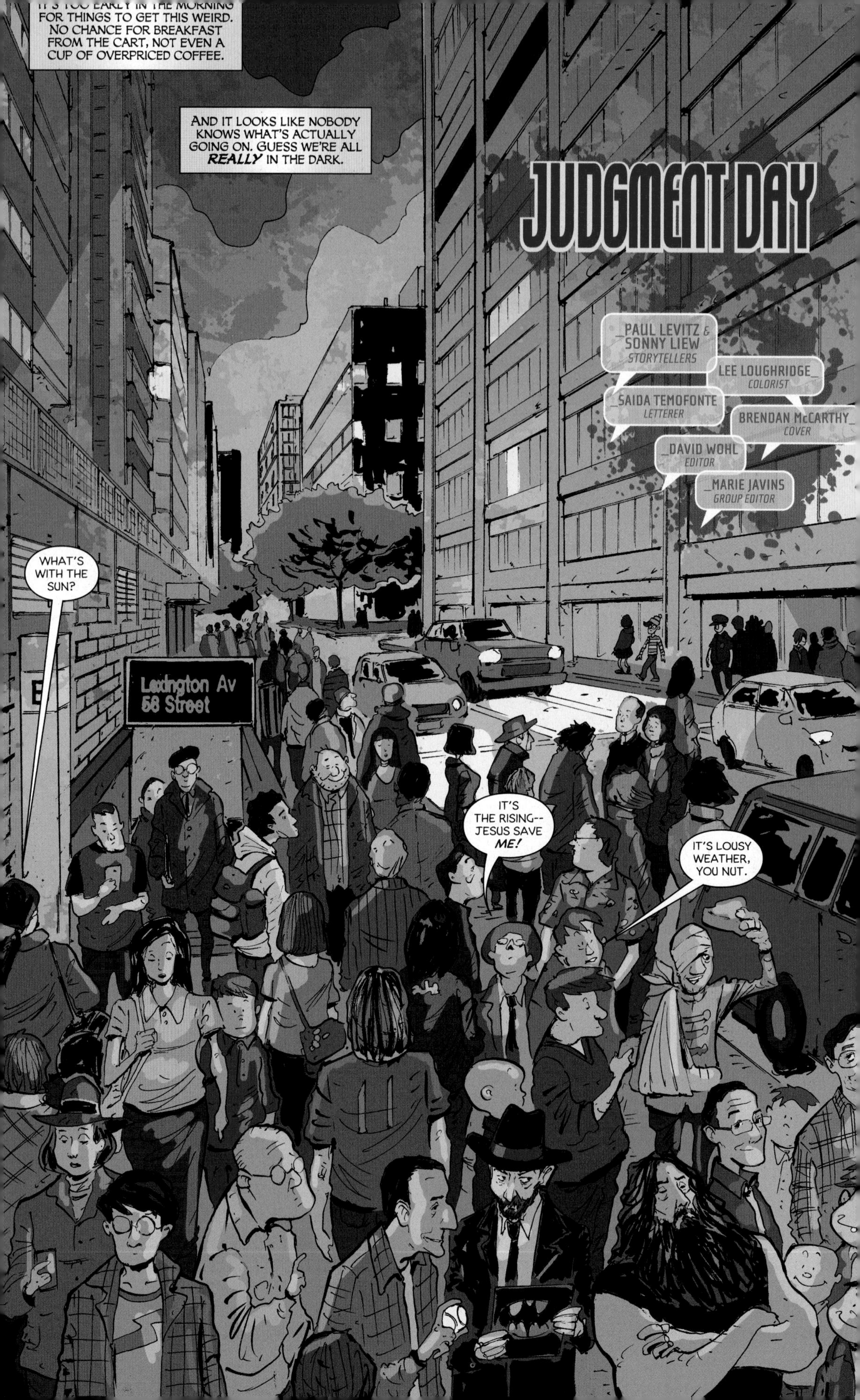
IT'S TOO EARLY IN THE MORNING FOR THINGS TO GET THIS WEIRD. NO CHANCE FOR BREAKFAST FROM THE CART, NOT EVEN A CUP OF OVERPRICED COFFEE.
AND IT LOOKS LIKE NOBODY KNOWS WHAT'S ACTUALLY GOING ON. GUESS WE'RE ALL *REALLY* IN THE DARK.
JUDGMENT DAY
_PAUL LEVITZ & SONNY LIEW STORYTELLERS
LEE LOUGHRIDGE_ COLORIST
_SAIDA TEMOFONTE LETTERER
BRENDAN McCARTHY_ COVER
_DAVID WOHL EDITOR
_MARIE JAVINS GROUP EDITOR
WHAT'S WITH THE SUN?
Lexington Av 58 Street
IT'S THE RISING-- JESUS SAVE *ME!*
IT'S LOUSY WEATHER, YOU NUT.

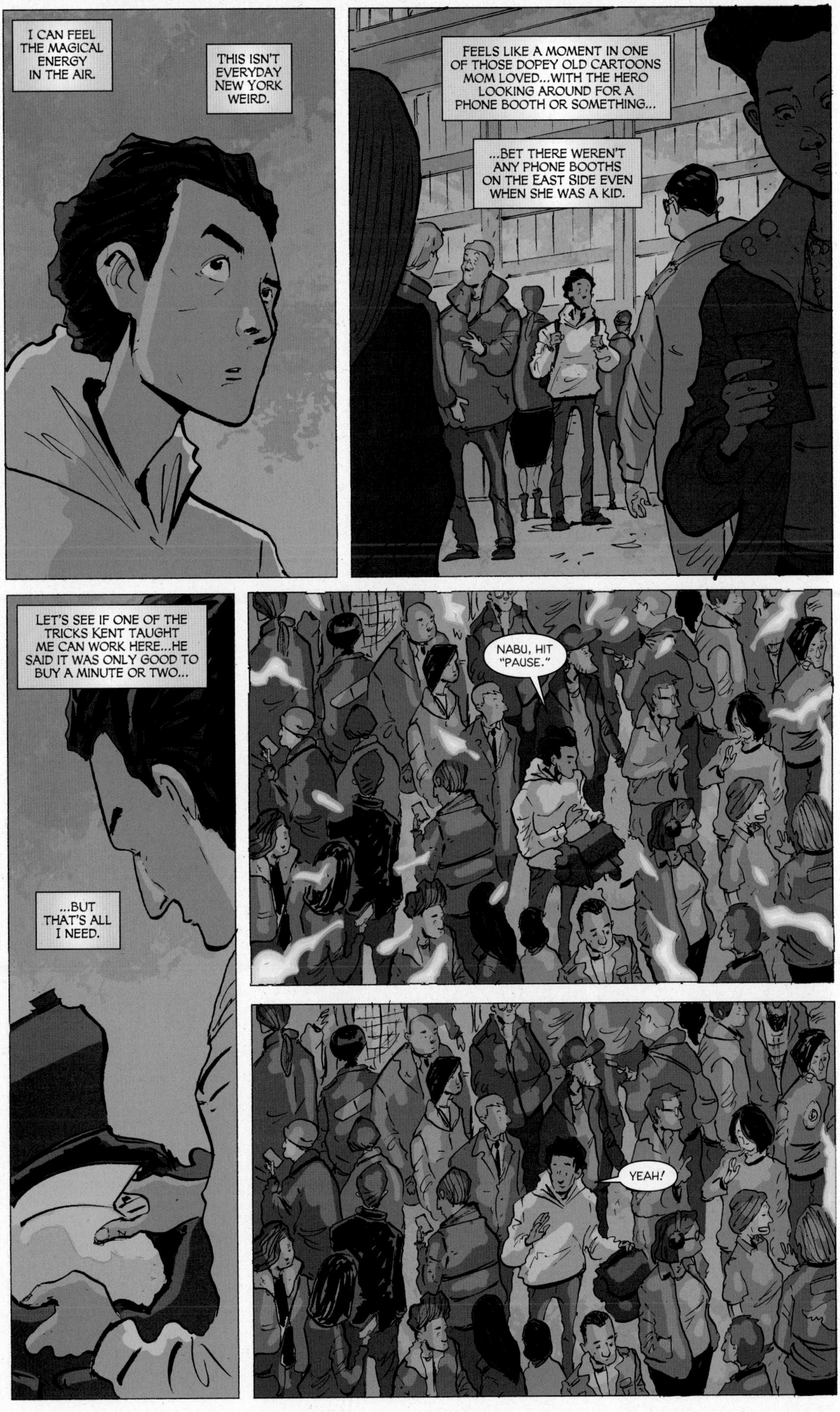
I CAN FEEL THE MAGICAL ENERGY IN THE AIR.
THIS ISN'T EVERYDAY NEW YORK WEIRD.
FEELS LIKE A MOMENT IN ONE OF THOSE DOPEY OLD CARTOONS MOM LOVED...WITH THE HERO LOOKING AROUND FOR A PHONE BOOTH OR SOMETHING...
...BET THERE WEREN'T ANY PHONE BOOTHS ON THE EAST SIDE EVEN WHEN SHE WAS A KID.
LET'S SEE IF ONE OF THE TRICKS KENT TAUGHT ME CAN WORK HERE...HE SAID IT WAS ONLY GOOD TO BUY A MINUTE OR TWO...
...BUT THAT'S ALL I NEED.
NABU, HIT "PAUSE."
YEAH!

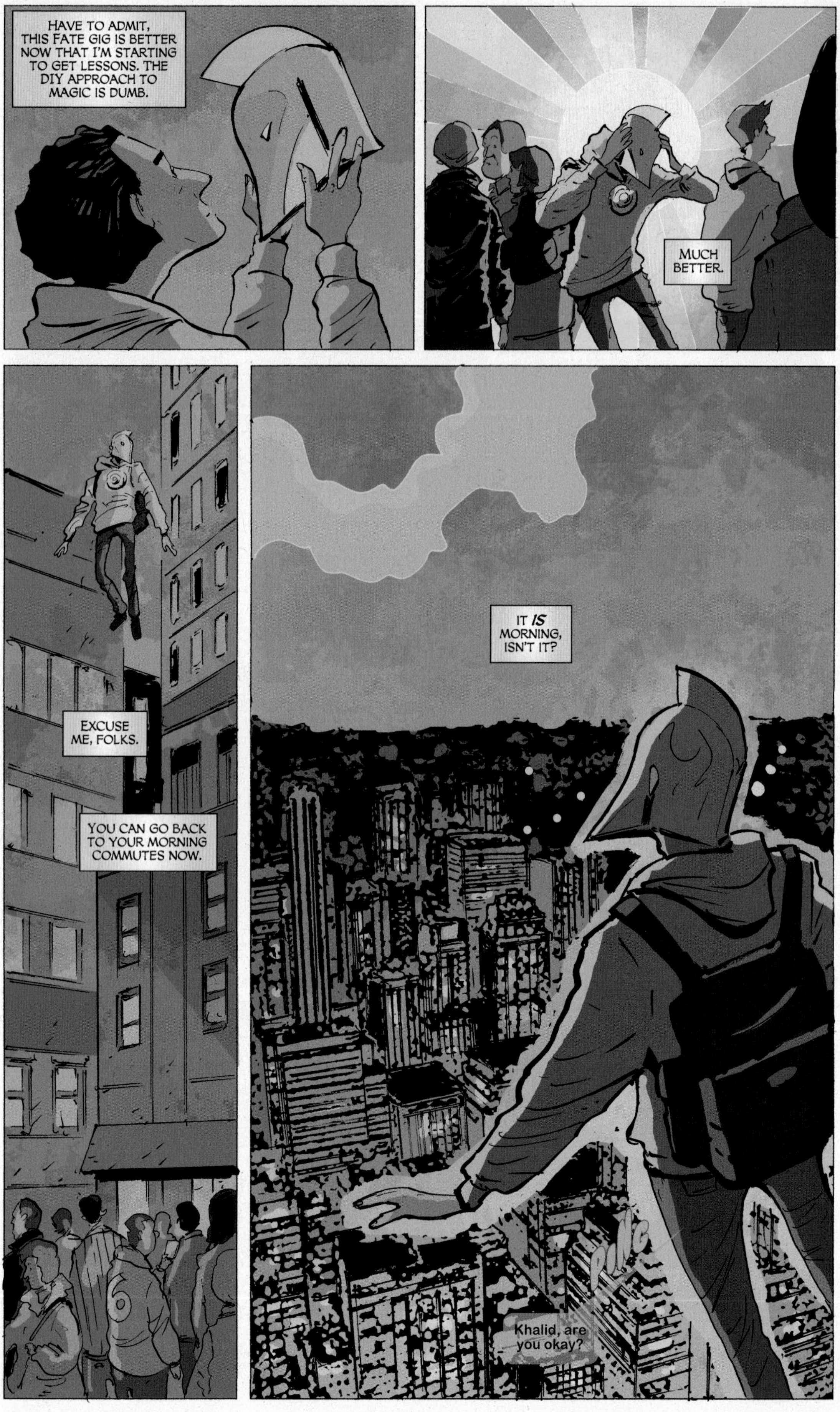
HAVE TO ADMIT, THIS FATE GIG IS BETTER NOW THAT I'M STARTING TO GET LESSONS. THE DIY APPROACH TO MAGIC IS DUMB.
MUCH BETTER.
EXCUSE ME, FOLKS.
YOU CAN GO BACK TO YOUR MORNING COMMUTES NOW.
IT *IS* MORNING, ISN'T IT?
PING
Khalid, are you okay?

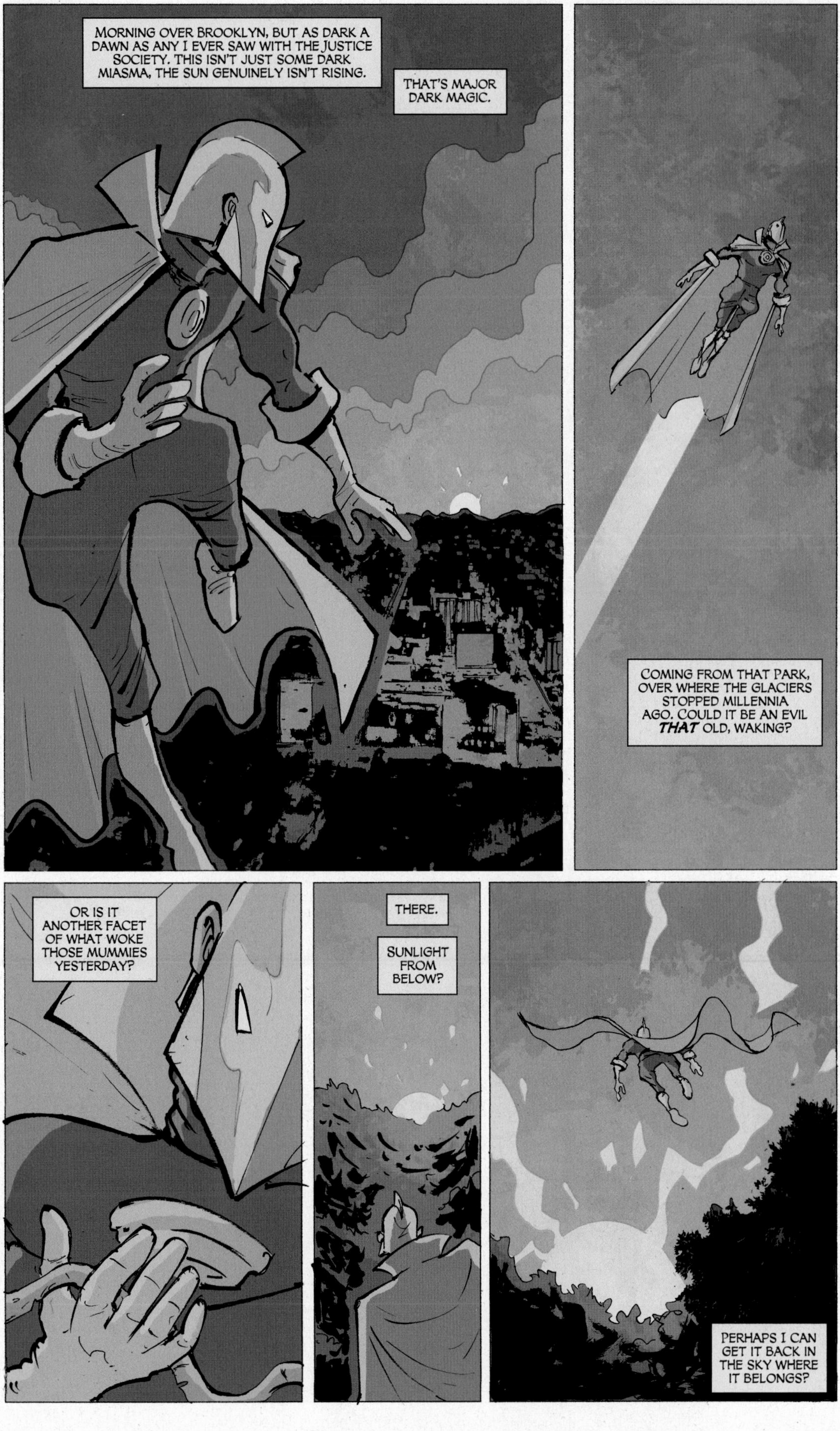
MORNING OVER BROOKLYN, BUT AS DARK A DAWN AS ANY I EVER SAW WITH THE JUSTICE SOCIETY. THIS ISN'T JUST SOME DARK MIASMA, THE SUN GENUINELY ISN'T RISING.
THAT'S MAJOR DARK MAGIC.
COMING FROM THAT PARK, OVER WHERE THE GLACIERS STOPPED MILLENNIA AGO. COULD IT BE AN EVIL *THAT* OLD, WAKING?
OR IS IT ANOTHER FACET OF WHAT WOKE THOSE MUMMIES YESTERDAY?
THERE.
SUNLIGHT FROM BELOW?
PERHAPS I CAN GET IT BACK IN THE SKY WHERE IT BELONGS?

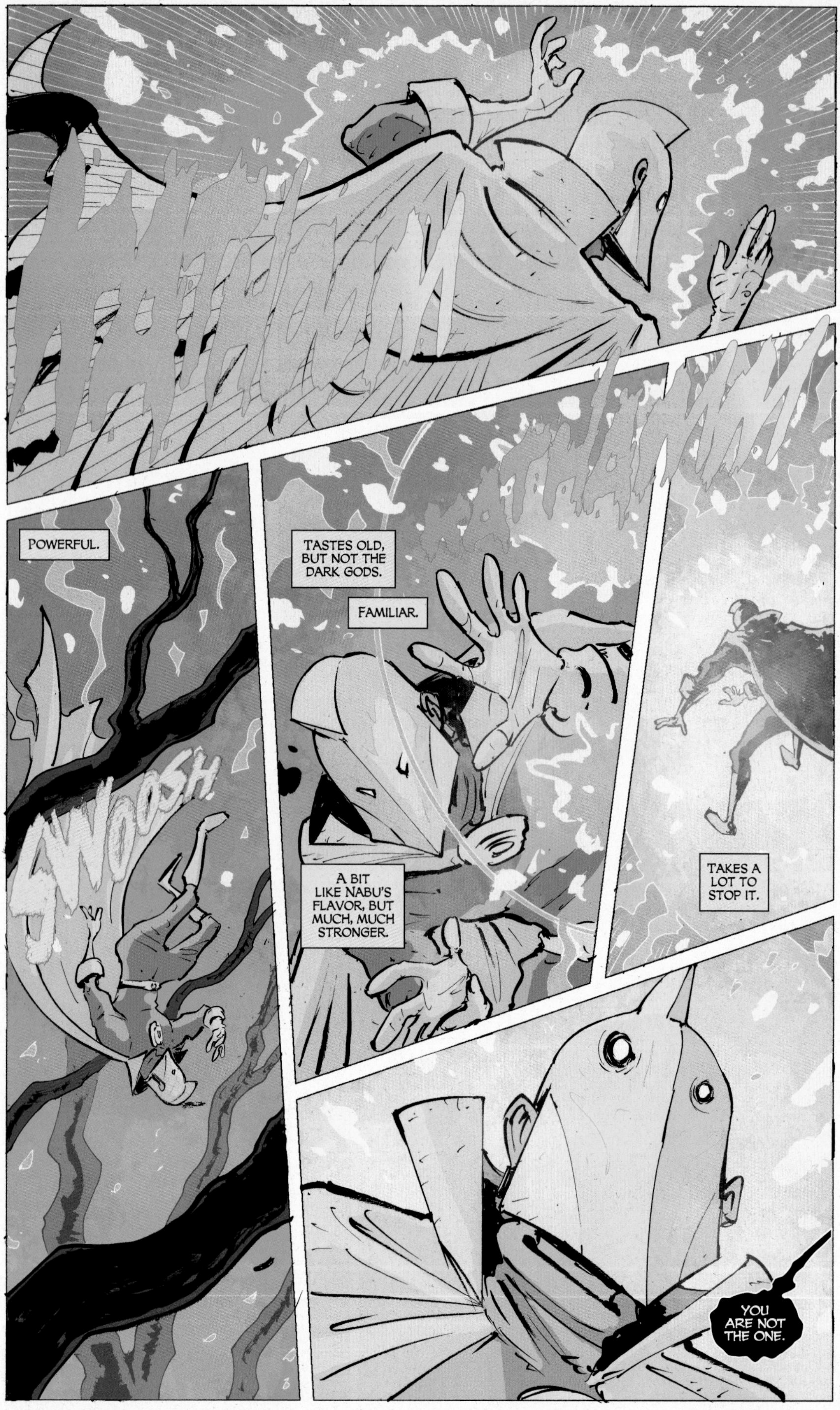
POWERFUL.
WOOSH.
TASTES OLD, BUT NOT THE DARK GODS.
FAMILIAR.
A BIT LIKE NABU'S FLAVOR, BUT MUCH, MUCH STRONGER.
TAKES A LOT TO STOP IT.
YOU ARE NOT THE ONE.

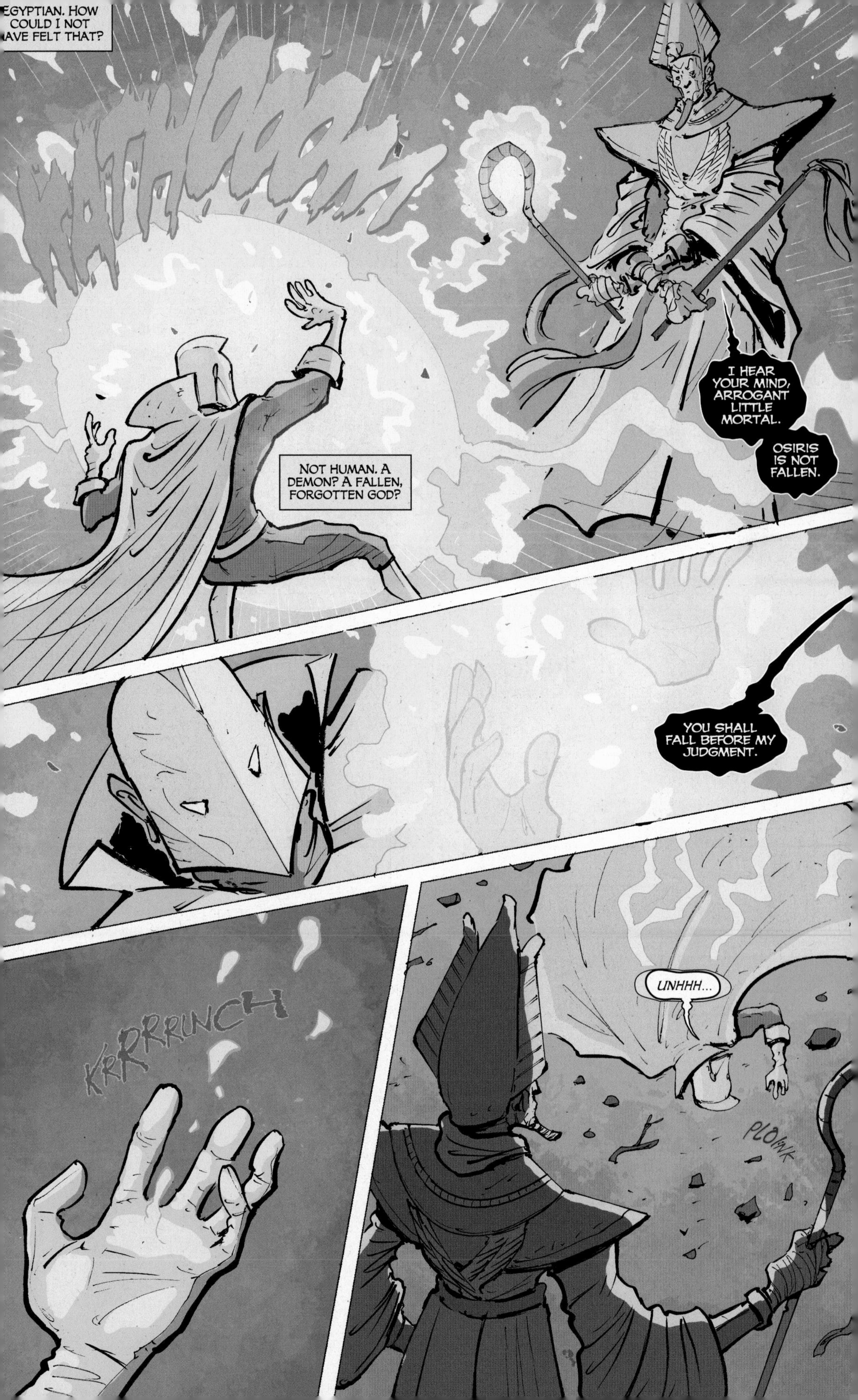
EGYPTIAN. HOW COULD I NOT HAVE FELT THAT?
WHHOOOM
NOT HUMAN. A DEMON? A FALLEN, FORGOTTEN GOD?
I HEAR YOUR MIND, ARROGANT LITTLE MORTAL.
OSIRIS IS NOT FALLEN.
YOU SHALL FALL BEFORE MY JUDGMENT.
KRRRRUNCH
UNHHH...
PLOINK

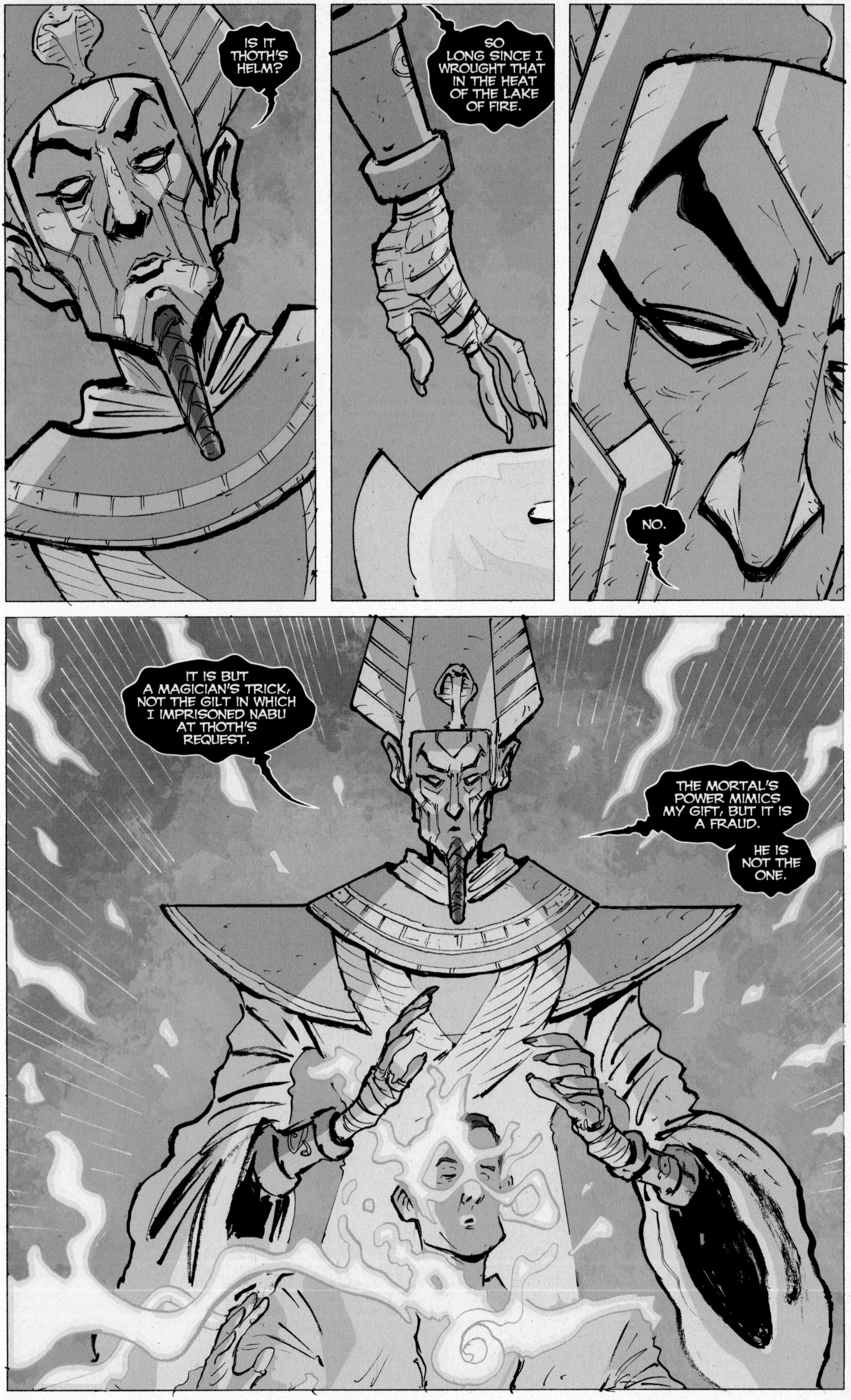
IS IT THOTH'S HELM?
SO LONG SINCE I WROUGHT THAT IN THE HEAT OF THE LAKE OF FIRE.
NO.
IT IS BUT A MAGICIAN'S TRICK, NOT THE GILT IN WHICH I IMPRISONED NABU AT THOTH'S REQUEST.
THE MORTAL'S POWER MIMICS MY GIFT, BUT IT IS A FRAUD.
HE IS NOT THE ONE.

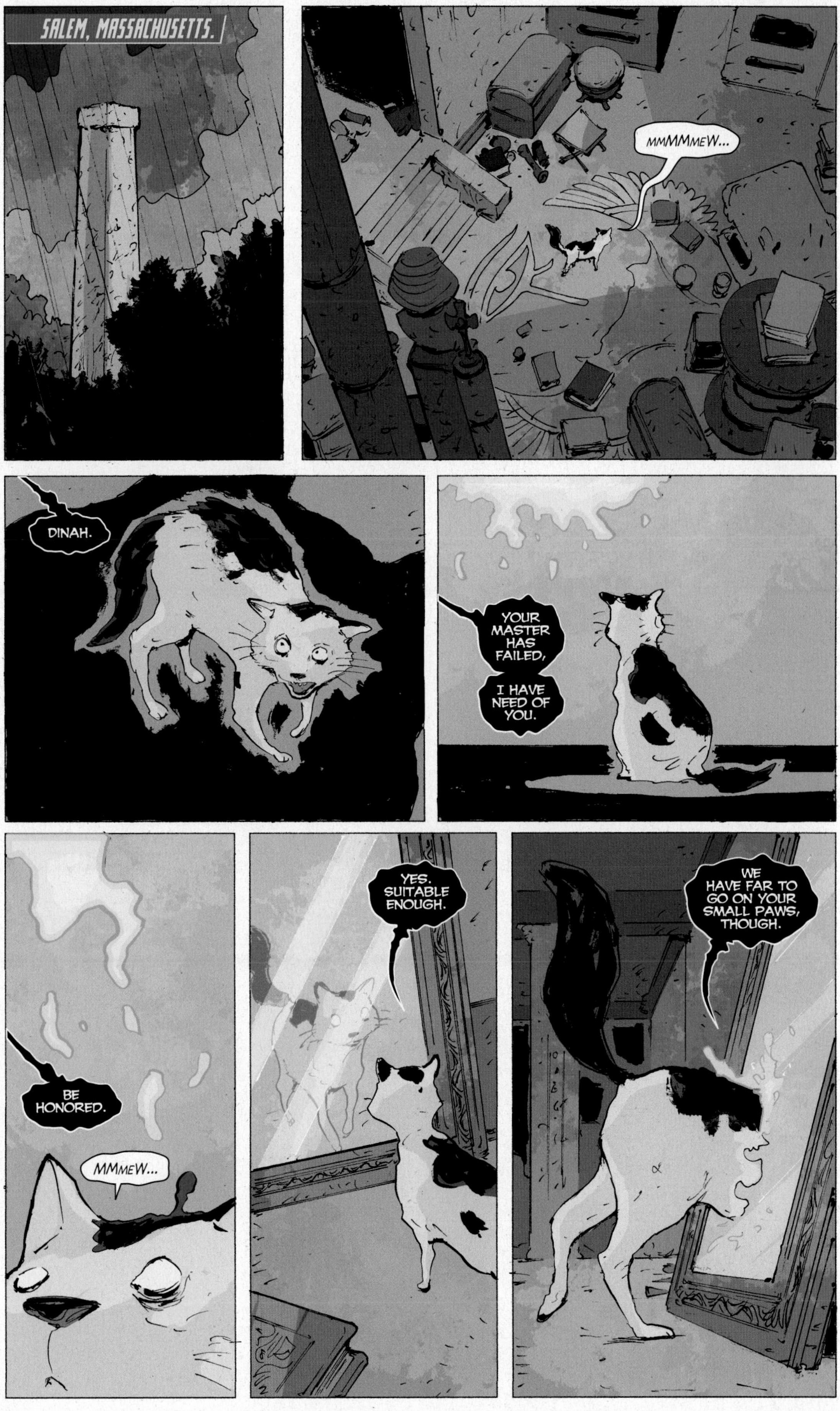
SALEM, MASSACHUSETTS.
MMMMMEW...
DINAH.
YOUR MASTER HAS FAILED,
I HAVE NEED OF YOU.
BE HONORED.
MMMEW...
YES. SUITABLE ENOUGH.
WE HAVE FAR TO GO ON YOUR SMALL PAWS, THOUGH.

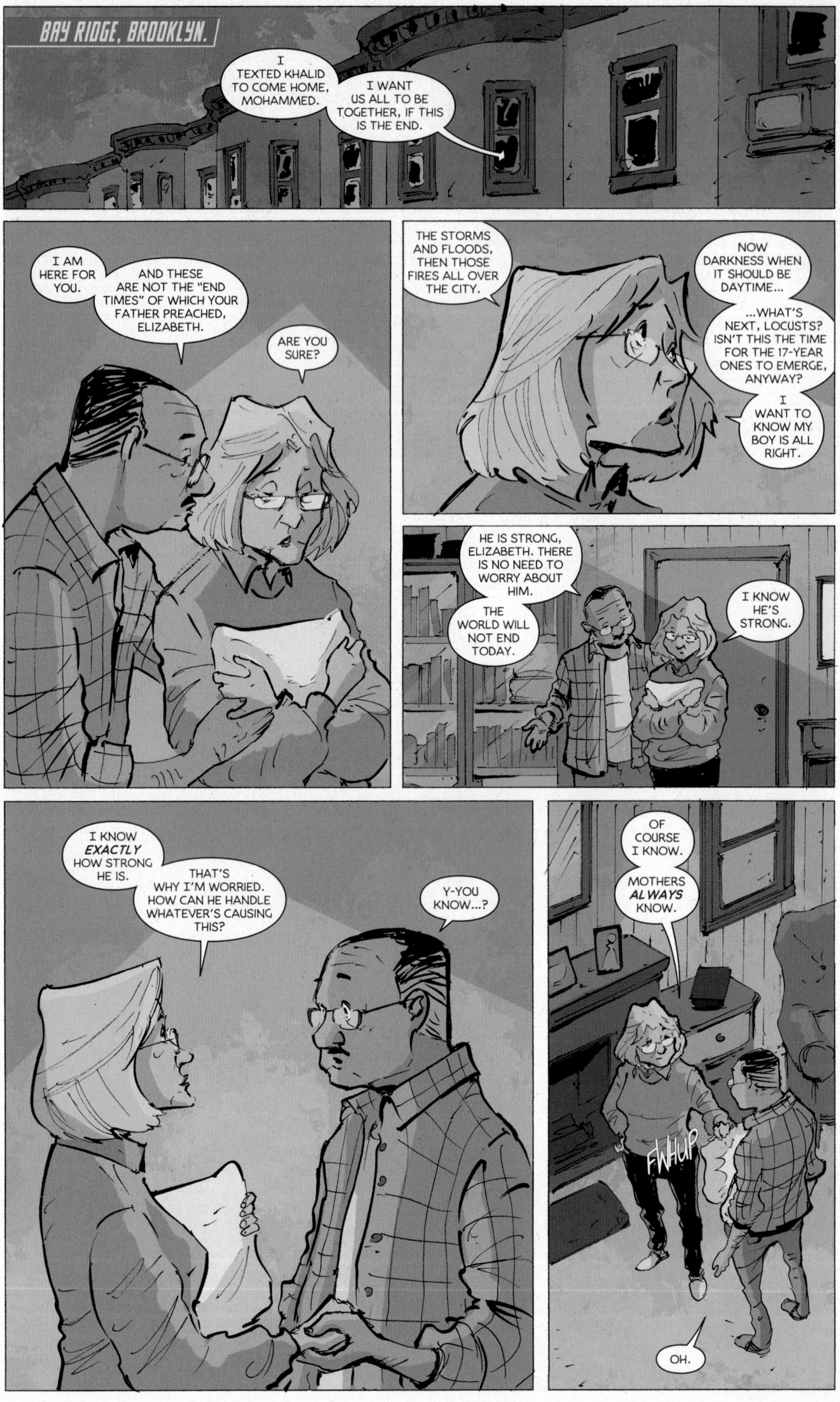
BAY RIDGE, BROOKLYN.
I TEXTED KHALID TO COME HOME, MOHAMMED.
I WANT US ALL TO BE TOGETHER, IF THIS IS THE END.
I AM HERE FOR YOU.
AND THESE ARE NOT THE "END TIMES" OF WHICH YOUR FATHER PREACHED, ELIZABETH.
ARE YOU SURE?
THE STORMS AND FLOODS, THEN THOSE FIRES ALL OVER THE CITY.
NOW DARKNESS WHEN IT SHOULD BE DAYTIME...
...WHAT'S NEXT, LOCUSTS? ISN'T THIS THE TIME FOR THE 17-YEAR ONES TO EMERGE, ANYWAY?
I WANT TO KNOW MY BOY IS ALL RIGHT.
HE IS STRONG, ELIZABETH. THERE IS NO NEED TO WORRY ABOUT HIM.
THE WORLD WILL NOT END TODAY.
I KNOW HE'S STRONG.
I KNOW *EXACTLY* HOW STRONG HE IS.
THAT'S WHY I'M WORRIED. HOW CAN HE HANDLE WHATEVER'S CAUSING THIS?
Y-YOU KNOW...?
OF COURSE I KNOW.
MOTHERS *ALWAYS* KNOW.
FWHUP
OH.

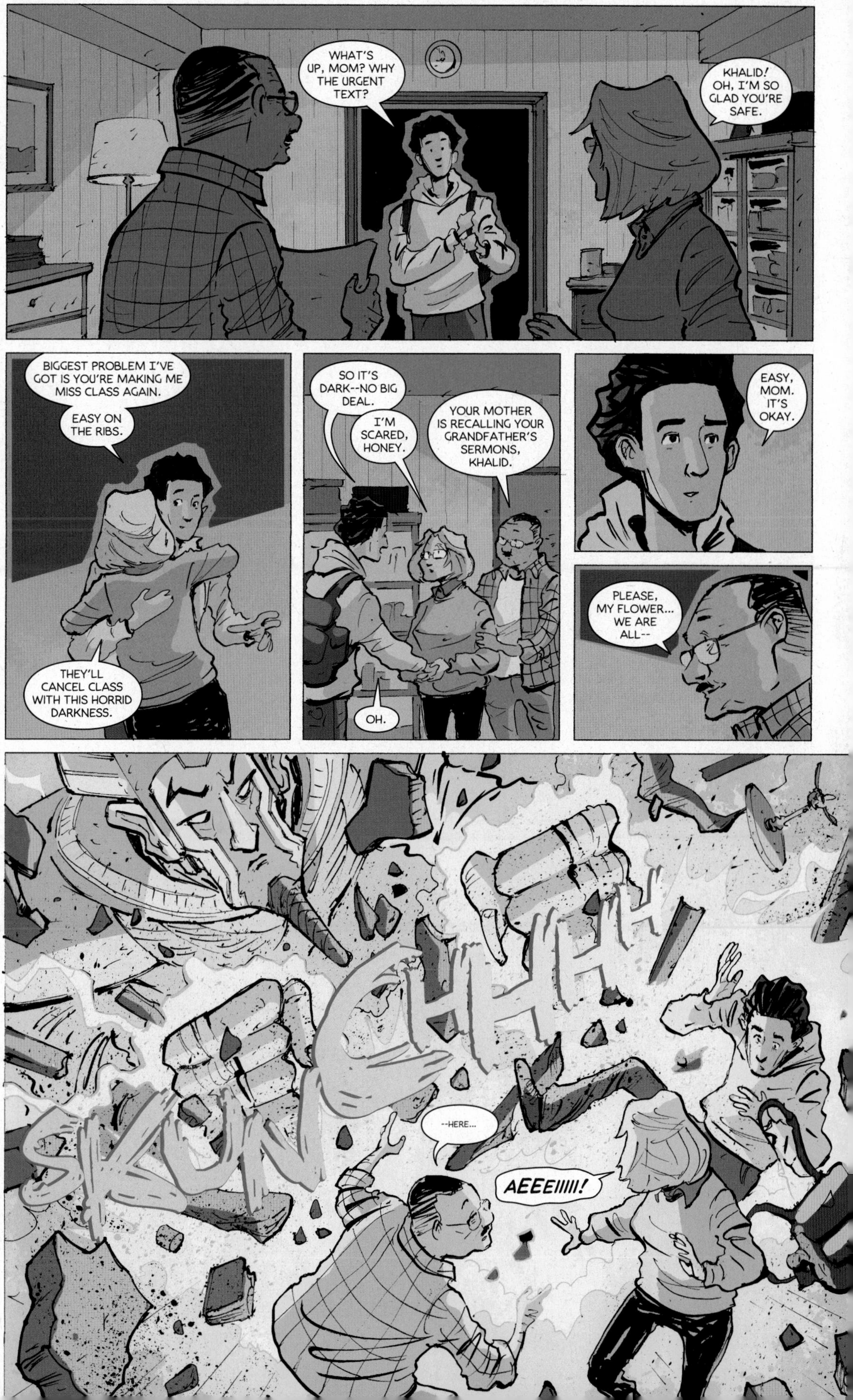
WHAT'S UP, MOM? WHY THE URGENT TEXT?
KHALID! OH, I'M SO GLAD YOU'RE SAFE.
BIGGEST PROBLEM I'VE GOT IS YOU'RE MAKING ME MISS CLASS AGAIN.
EASY ON THE RIBS.
THEY'LL CANCEL CLASS WITH THIS HORRID DARKNESS.
SO IT'S DARK--NO BIG DEAL.
I'M SCARED, HONEY.
YOUR MOTHER IS RECALLING YOUR GRANDFATHER'S SERMONS, KHALID.
OH.
EASY, MOM. IT'S OKAY.
PLEASE, MY FLOWER... WE ARE ALL--
SKUNCHHH
--HERE...
AEEEIIIII!

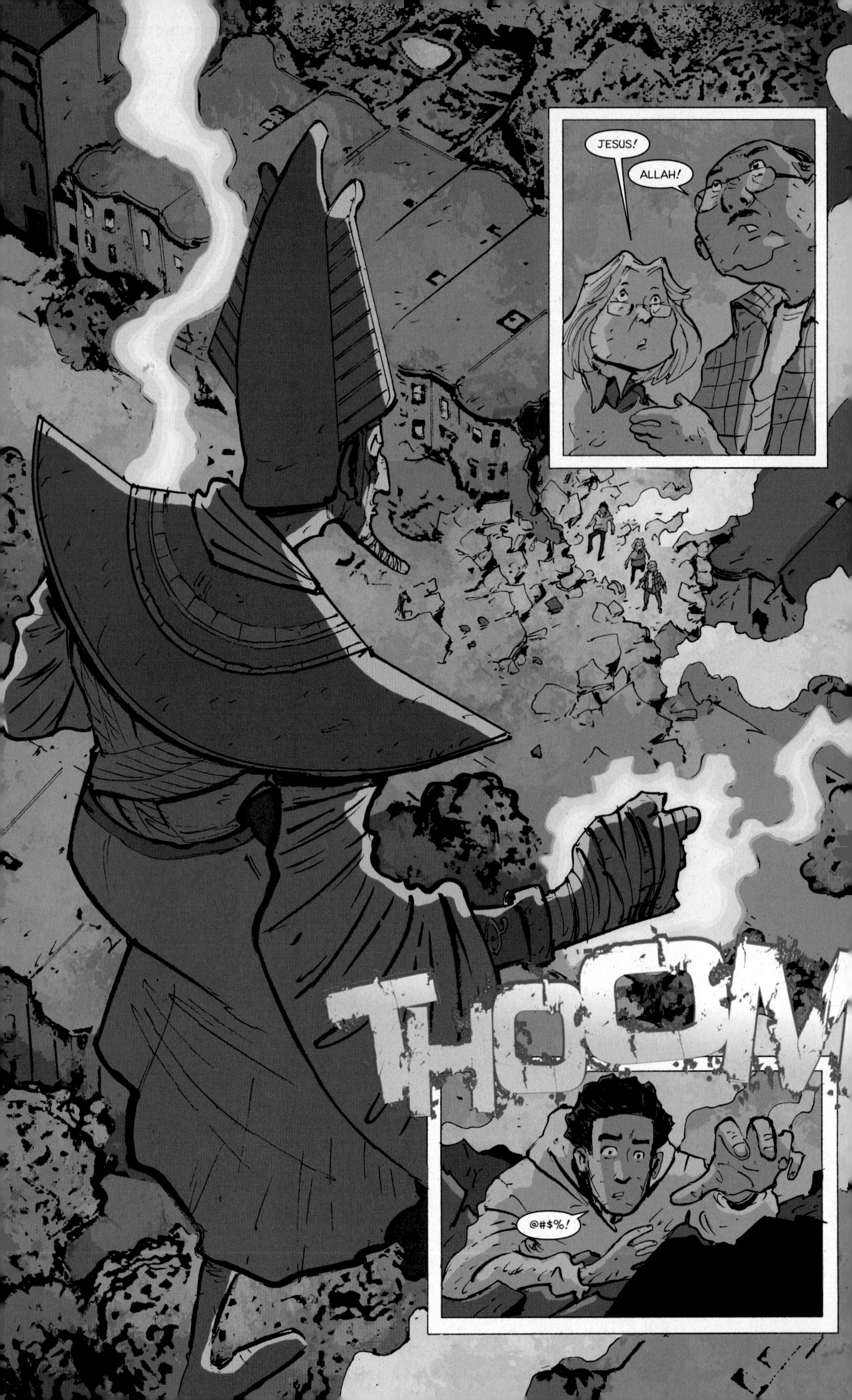
JESUS!
ALLAH!
THOOM
@#$%!

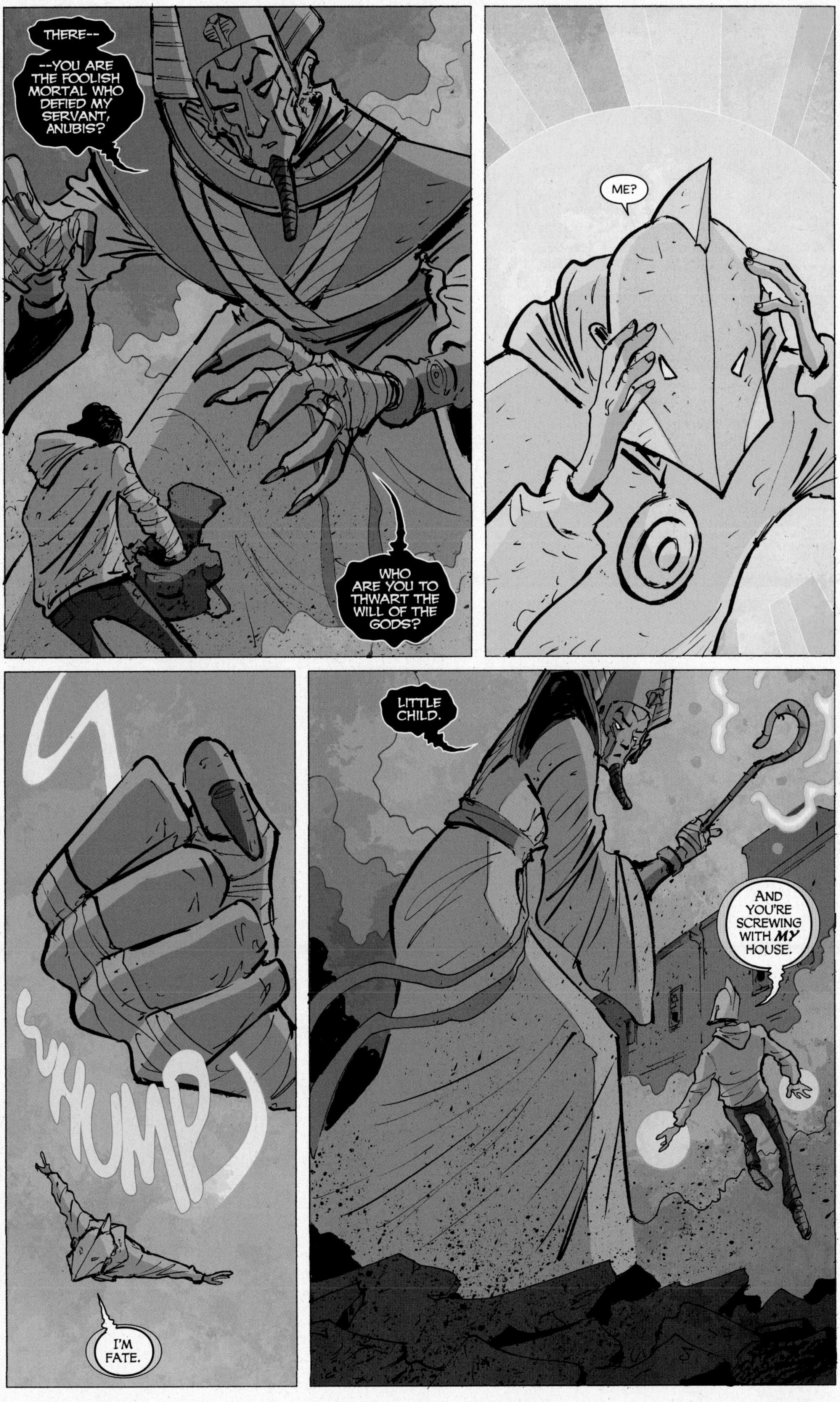
THERE--
--YOU ARE THE FOOLISH MORTAL WHO DEFIED MY SERVANT, ANUBIS?
WHO ARE YOU TO THWART THE WILL OF THE GODS?
ME?
WHUMP
I'M FATE.
LITTLE CHILD.
AND YOU'RE SCREWING WITH MY HOUSE.

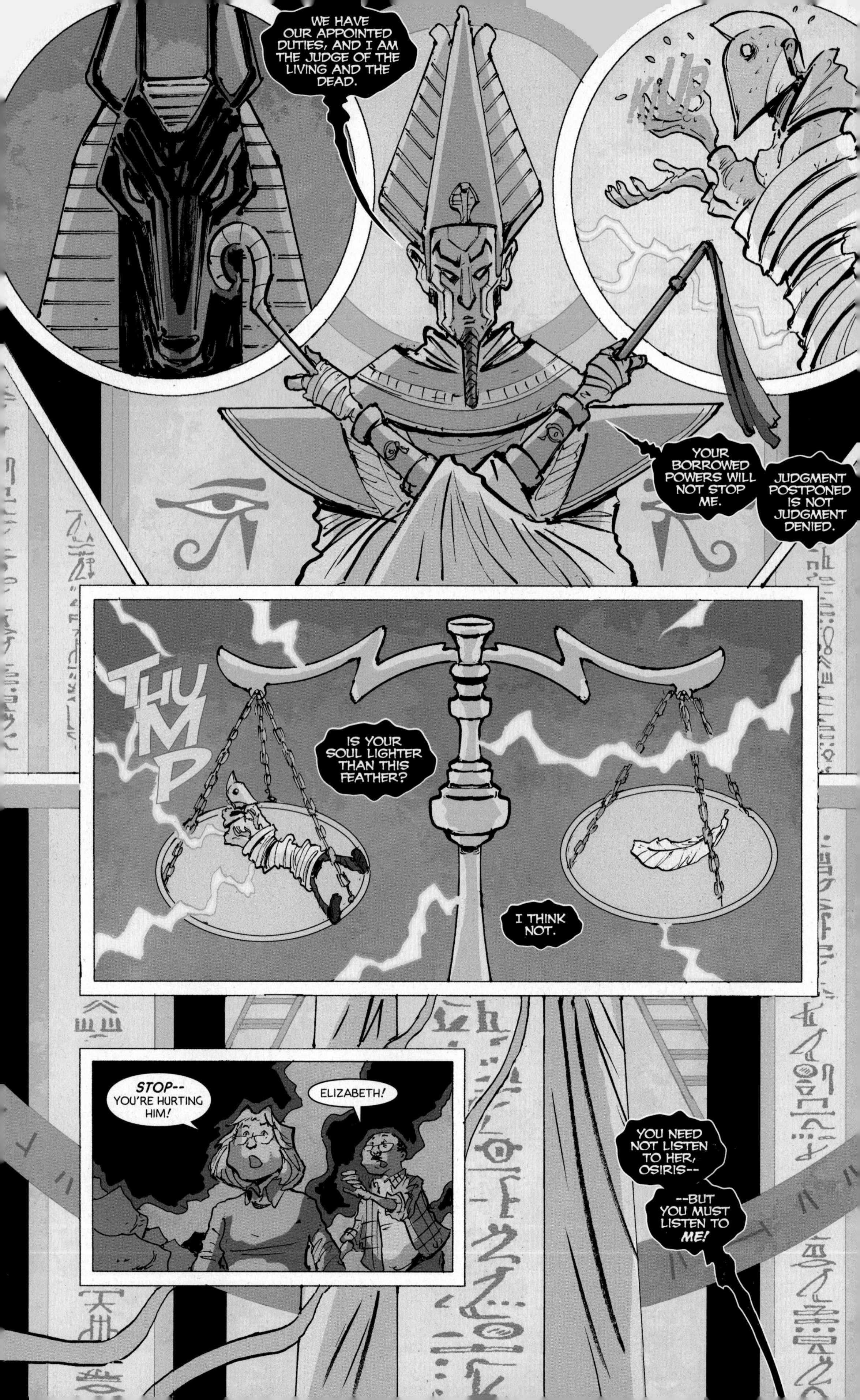
WE HAVE OUR APPOINTED DUTIES, AND I AM THE JUDGE OF THE LIVING AND THE DEAD.
KLUP
YOUR BORROWED POWERS WILL NOT STOP ME.
JUDGMENT POSTPONED IS NOT JUDGMENT DENIED.
THUMP
IS YOUR SOUL LIGHTER THAN THIS FEATHER?
I THINK NOT.
STOP-- YOU'RE HURTING HIM!
ELIZABETH!
YOU NEED NOT LISTEN TO HER, OSIRIS--
--BUT YOU MUST LISTEN TO ME!

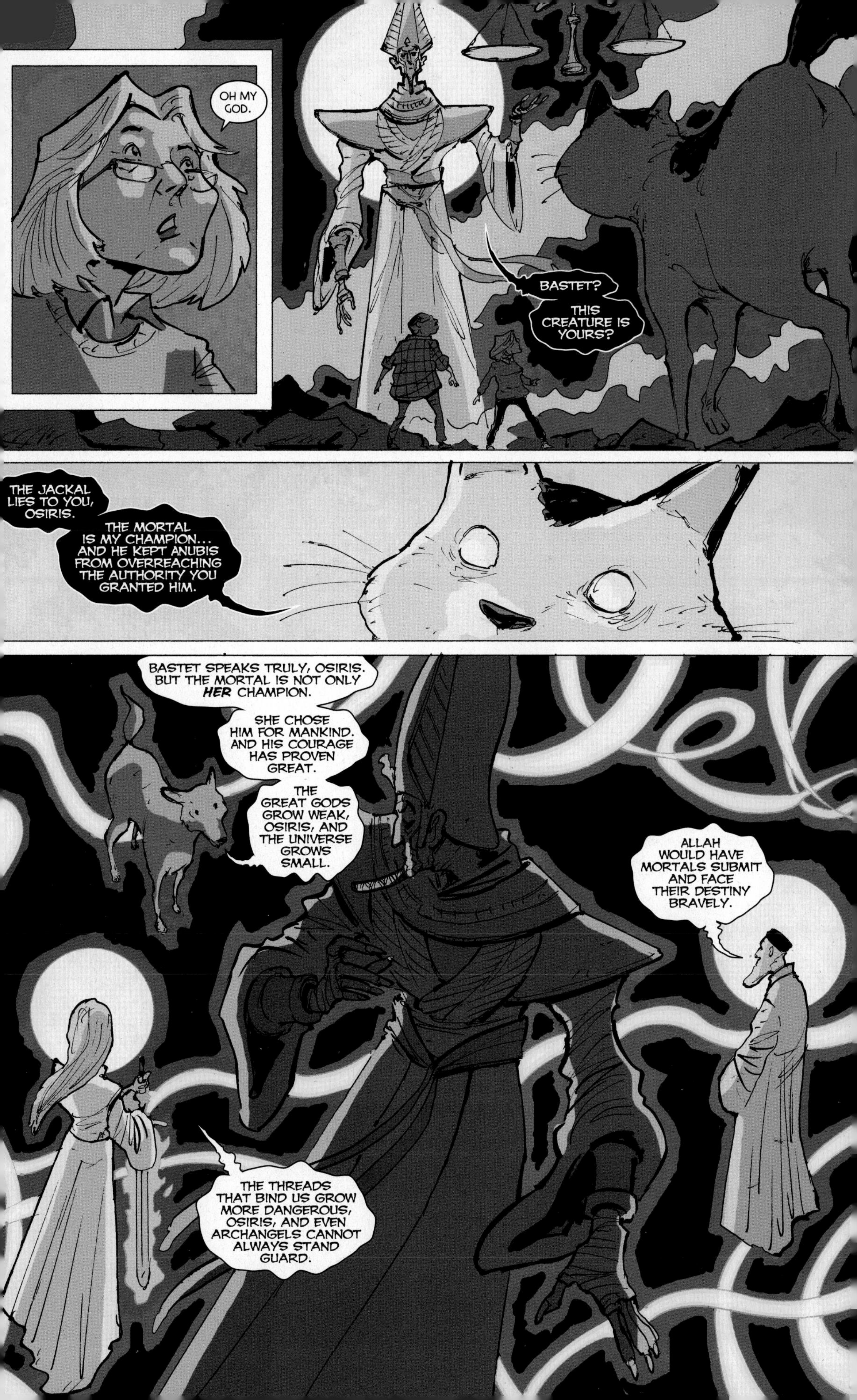
OH MY GOD.
BASTET? THIS CREATURE IS YOURS?
THE JACKAL LIES TO YOU, OSIRIS.
THE MORTAL IS MY CHAMPION... AND HE KEPT ANUBIS FROM OVERREACHING THE AUTHORITY YOU GRANTED HIM.
BASTET SPEAKS TRULY, OSIRIS. BUT THE MORTAL IS NOT ONLY *HER* CHAMPION.
SHE CHOSE HIM FOR MANKIND. AND HIS COURAGE HAS PROVEN GREAT.
THE GREAT GODS GROW WEAK, OSIRIS, AND THE UNIVERSE GROWS SMALL.
ALLAH WOULD HAVE MORTALS SUBMIT AND FACE THEIR DESTINY BRAVELY.
THE THREADS THAT BIND US GROW MORE DANGEROUS, OSIRIS, AND EVEN ARCHANGELS CANNOT ALWAYS STAND GUARD.

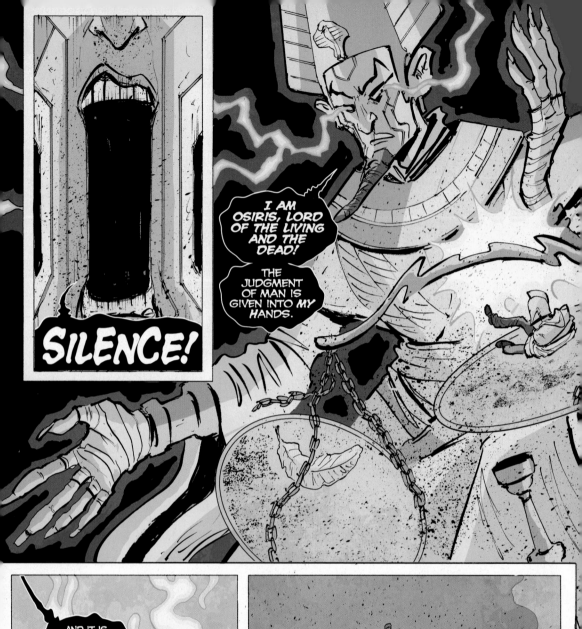

SILENCE!

I AM OSIRIS, LORD OF THE LIVING AND THE DEAD!

THE JUDGMENT OF MAN IS GIVEN INTO *MY* HANDS.

AND IT IS *MY* JUDGMENT THAT WILL BE PASSED ON THIS MORTAL.

AND IT IS *MY* JUDGMENT THAT HE MAY *LIVE.*

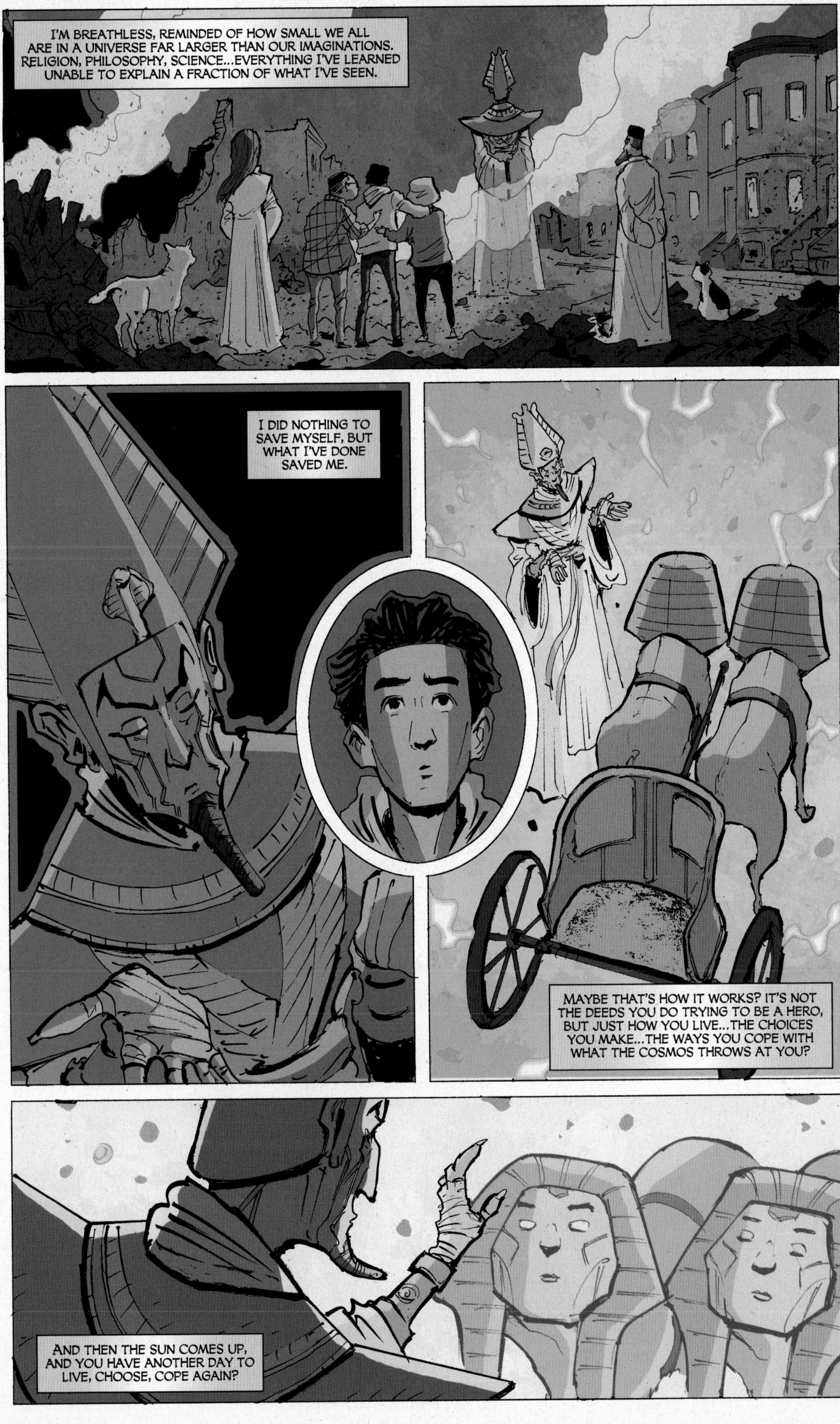
I'M BREATHLESS, REMINDED OF HOW SMALL WE ALL ARE IN A UNIVERSE FAR LARGER THAN OUR IMAGINATIONS. RELIGION, PHILOSOPHY, SCIENCE...EVERYTHING I'VE LEARNED UNABLE TO EXPLAIN A FRACTION OF WHAT I'VE SEEN.
I DID NOTHING TO SAVE MYSELF, BUT WHAT I'VE DONE SAVED ME.
MAYBE THAT'S HOW IT WORKS? IT'S NOT THE DEEDS YOU DO TRYING TO BE A HERO, BUT JUST HOW YOU LIVE...THE CHOICES YOU MAKE...THE WAYS YOU COPE WITH WHAT THE COSMOS THROWS AT YOU?
AND THEN THE SUN COMES UP, AND YOU HAVE ANOTHER DAY TO LIVE, CHOOSE, COPE AGAIN?

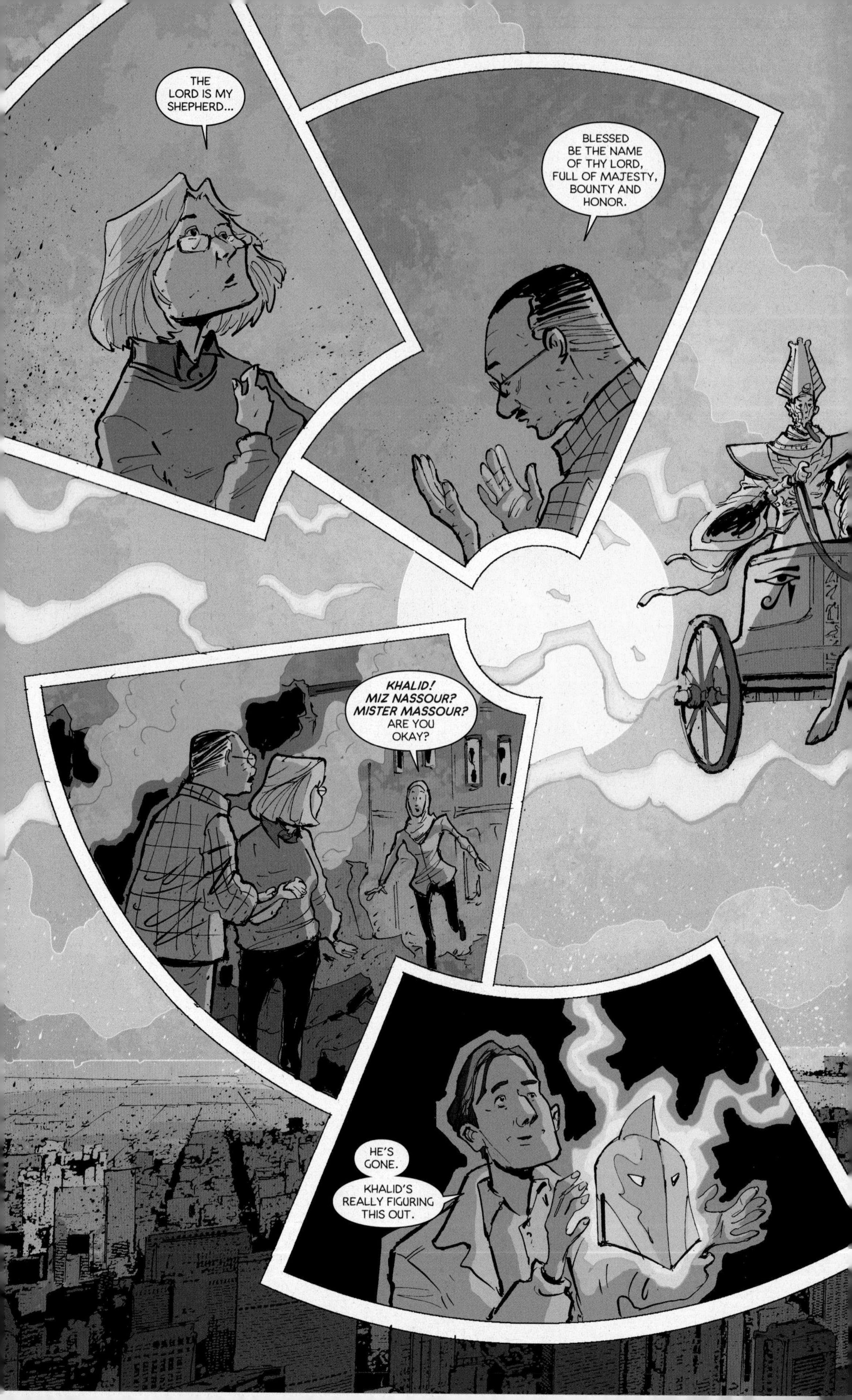
THE LORD IS MY SHEPHERD...
BLESSED BE THE NAME OF THY LORD, FULL OF MAJESTY, BOUNTY AND HONOR.
KHALID! MIZ NASSOUR? MISTER MASSOUR? ARE YOU OKAY?
HE'S GONE.
KHALID'S REALLY FIGURING THIS OUT.

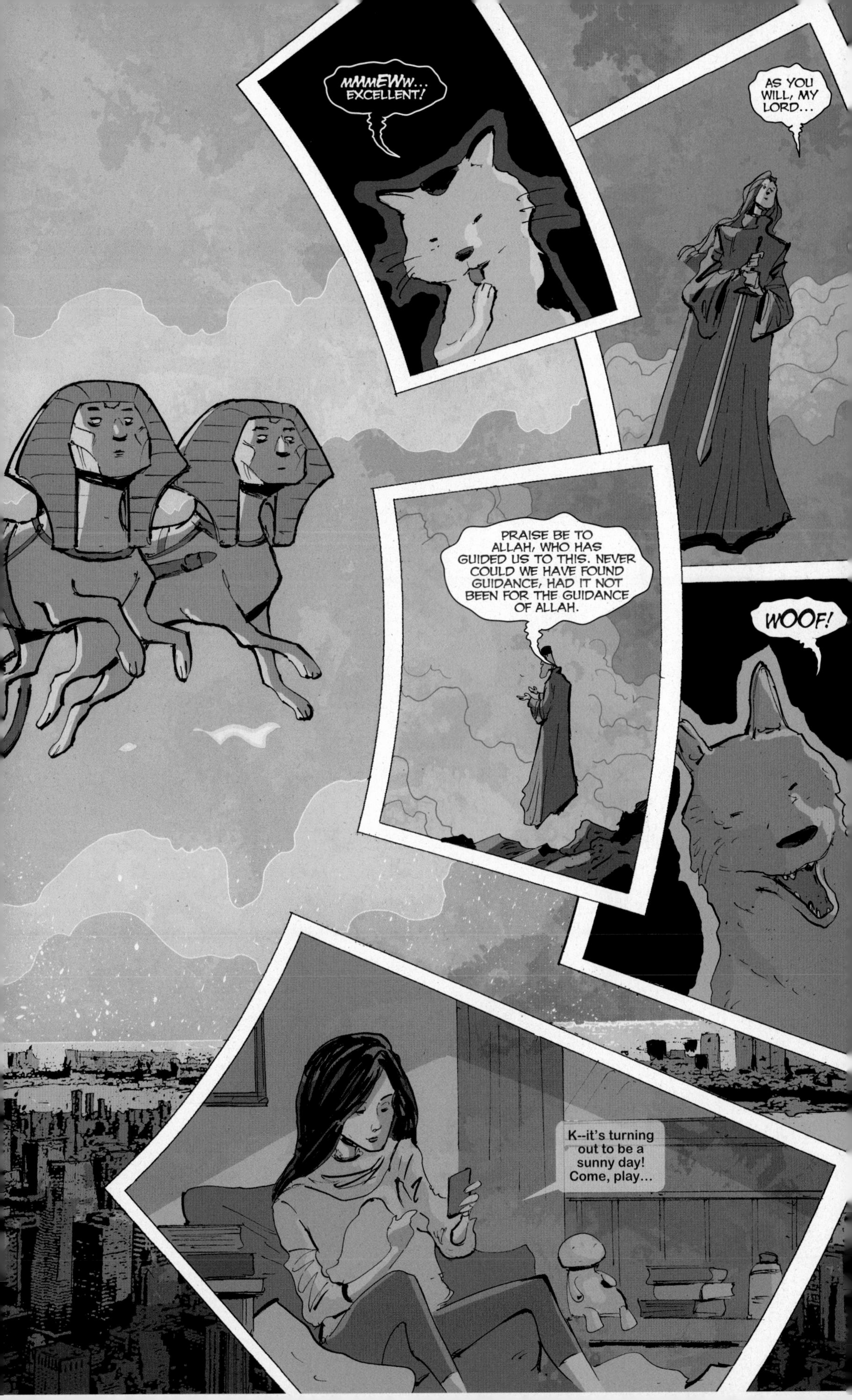
MMMEWW... EXCELLENT!
AS YOU WILL, MY LORD...
PRAISE BE TO ALLAH, WHO HAS GUIDED US TO THIS. NEVER COULD WE HAVE FOUND GUIDANCE, HAD IT NOT BEEN FOR THE GUIDANCE OF ALLAH.
WOOF!
K--it's turning out to be a sunny day! Come, play...

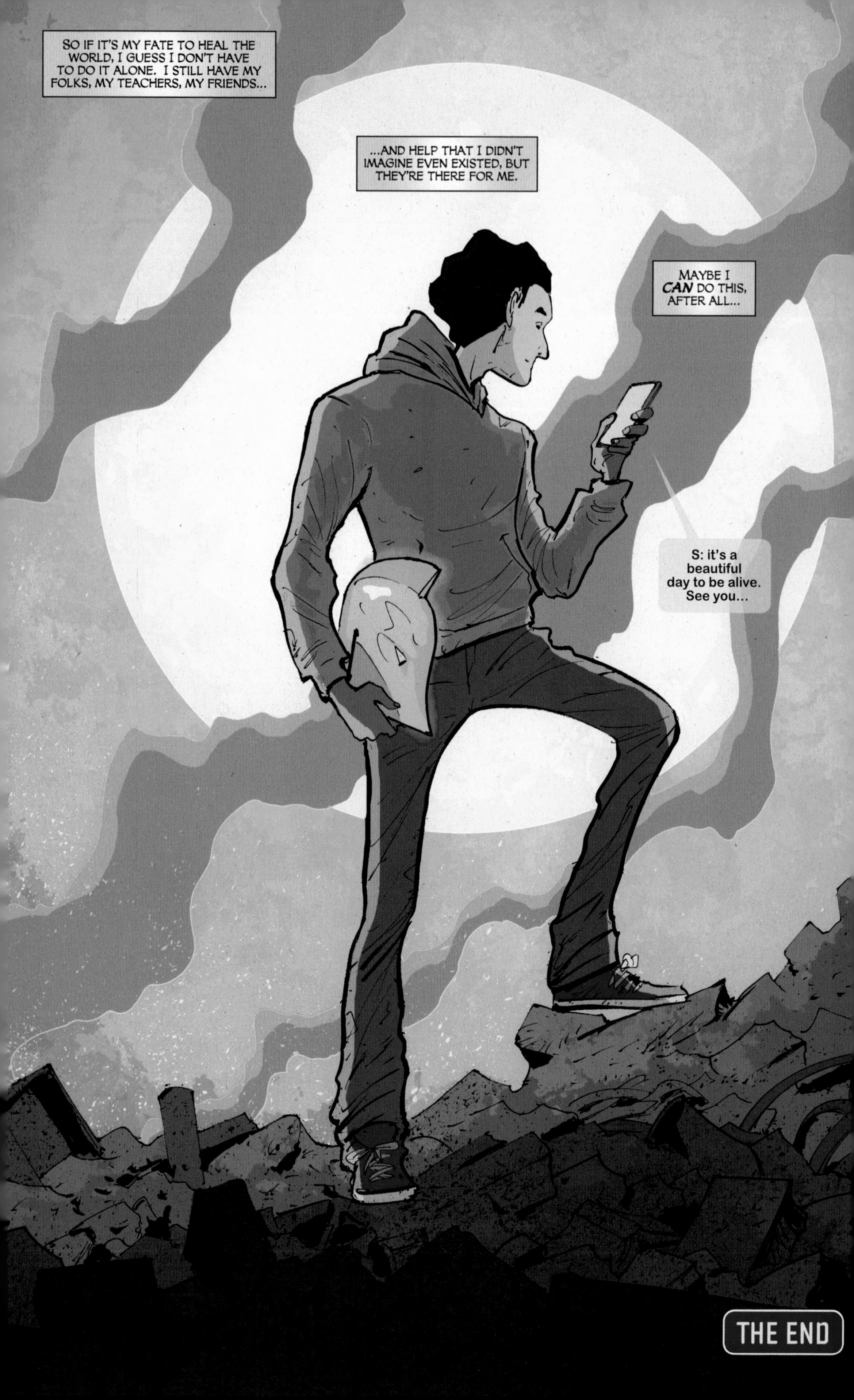
SO IF IT'S MY FATE TO HEAL THE WORLD, I GUESS I DON'T HAVE TO DO IT ALONE. I STILL HAVE MY FOLKS, MY TEACHERS, MY FRIENDS...
...AND HELP THAT I DIDN'T IMAGINE EVEN EXISTED, BUT THEY'RE THERE FOR ME.
MAYBE I *CAN* DO THIS, AFTER ALL...
S: it's a beautiful day to be alive. See you...
THE END

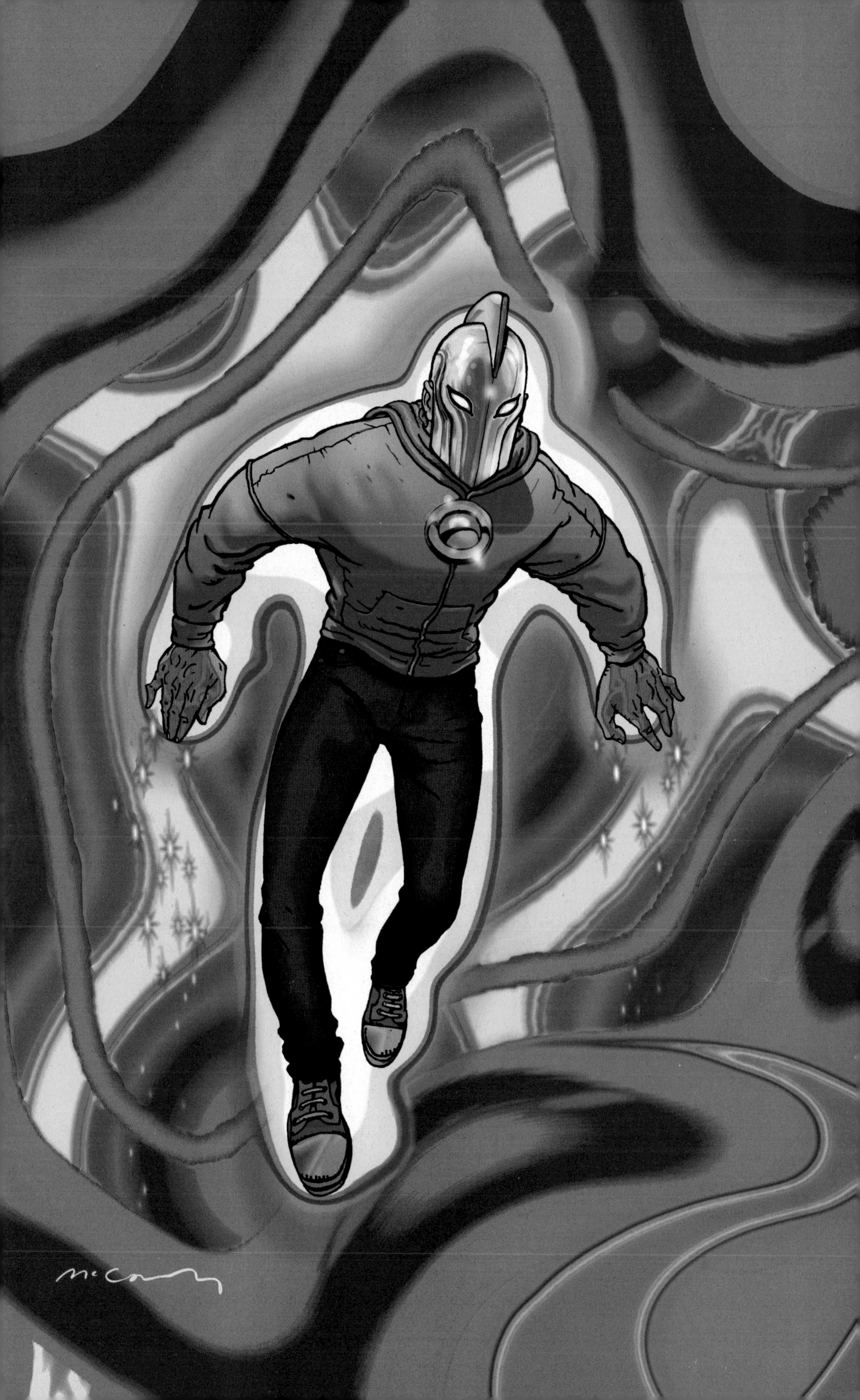

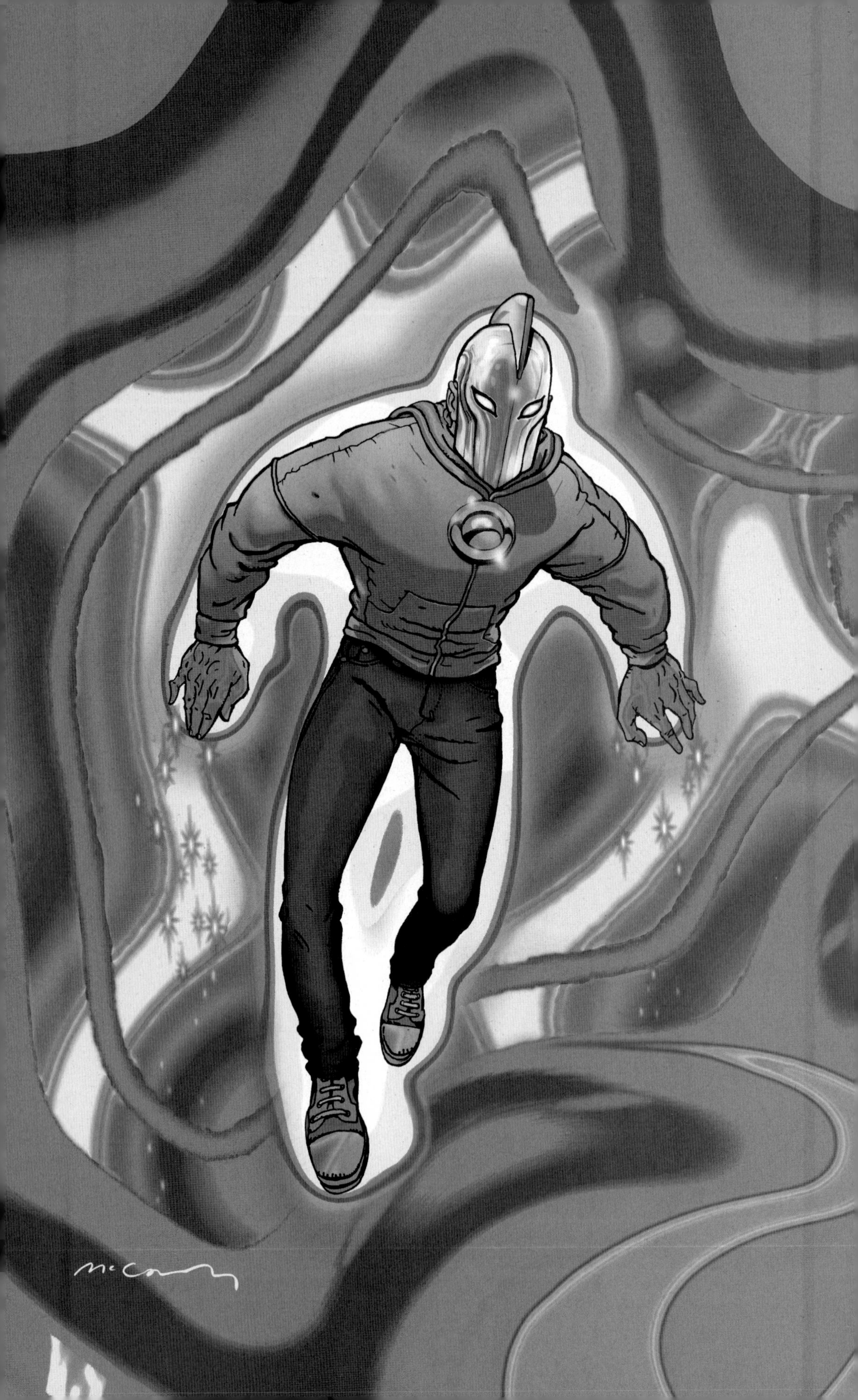

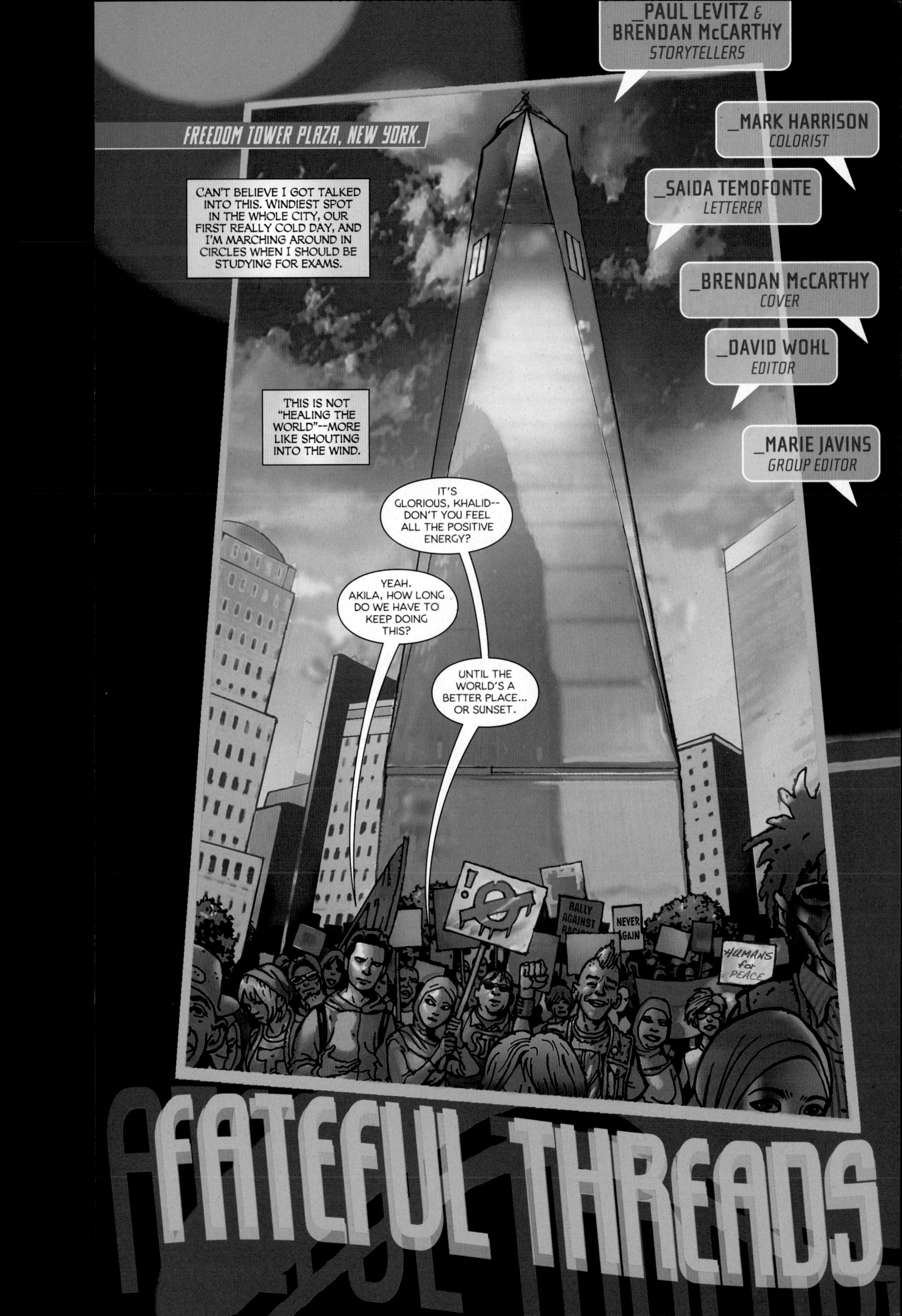
_PAUL LEVITZ & BRENDAN McCARTHY STORYTELLERS
_MARK HARRISON COLORIST
_SAIDA TEMOFONTE LETTERER
_BRENDAN McCARTHY COVER
_DAVID WOHL EDITOR
_MARIE JAVINS GROUP EDITOR
FREEDOM TOWER PLAZA, NEW YORK.
CAN'T BELIEVE I GOT TALKED INTO THIS. WINDIEST SPOT IN THE WHOLE CITY, OUR FIRST REALLY COLD DAY, AND I'M MARCHING AROUND IN CIRCLES WHEN I SHOULD BE STUDYING FOR EXAMS.
THIS IS NOT "HEALING THE WORLD"--MORE LIKE SHOUTING INTO THE WIND.
IT'S GLORIOUS, KHALID--DON'T YOU FEEL ALL THE POSITIVE ENERGY?
YEAH. AKILA, HOW LONG DO WE HAVE TO KEEP DOING THIS?
UNTIL THE WORLD'S A BETTER PLACE... OR SUNSET.
RALLY AGAINST RACISM
NEVER AGAIN
HUMANS for PEACE
A FATEFUL THREADS

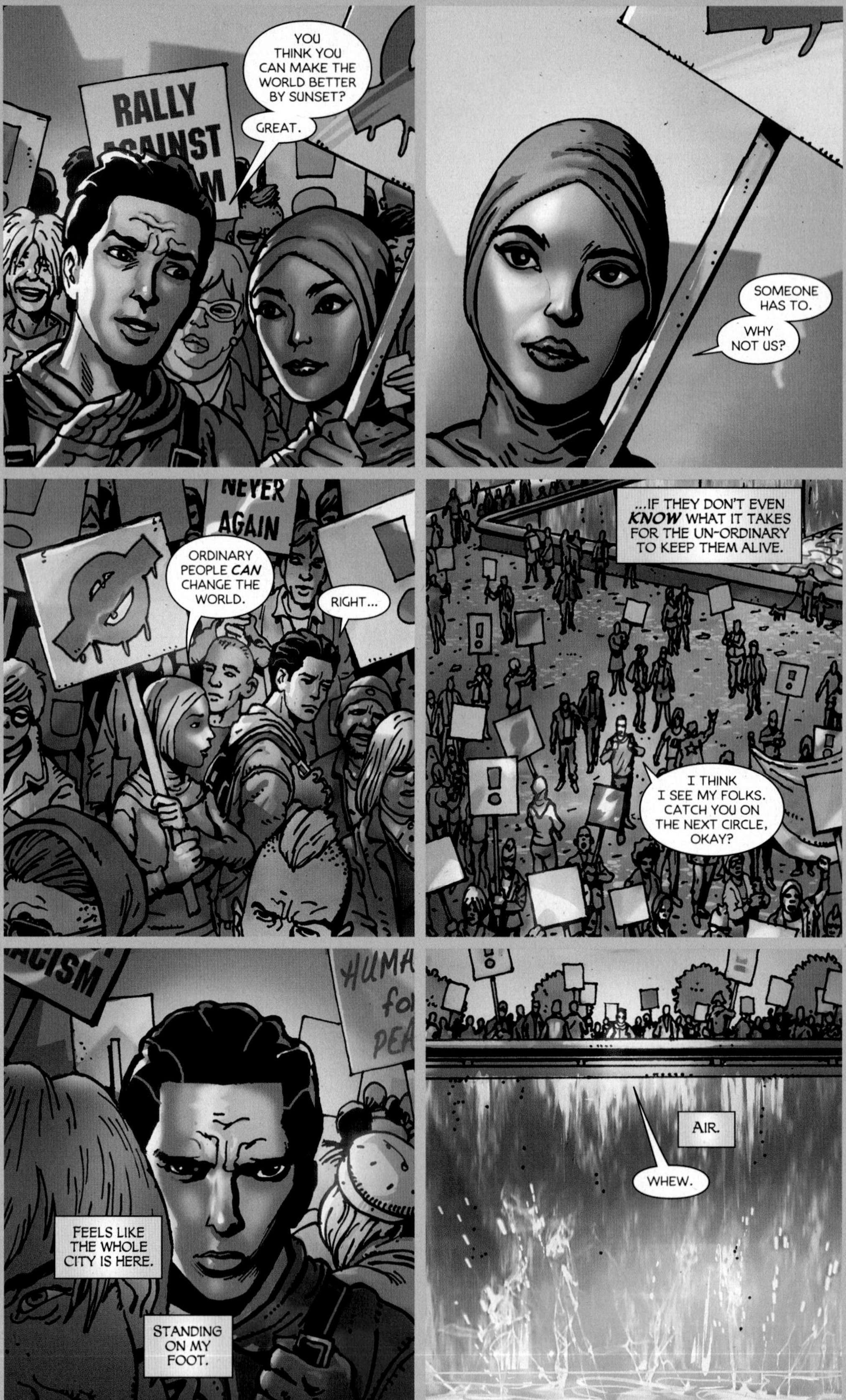
RALLY AGAINST
YOU THINK YOU CAN MAKE THE WORLD BETTER BY SUNSET?
GREAT.
SOMEONE HAS TO.
WHY NOT US?
NEVER AGAIN
ORDINARY PEOPLE CAN CHANGE THE WORLD.
RIGHT...
...IF THEY DON'T EVEN KNOW WHAT IT TAKES FOR THE UN-ORDINARY TO KEEP THEM ALIVE.
I THINK I SEE MY FOLKS. CATCH YOU ON THE NEXT CIRCLE, OKAY?
ACISM
HUMA fo PEA
FEELS LIKE THE WHOLE CITY IS HERE.
STANDING ON MY FOOT.
AIR.
WHEW.

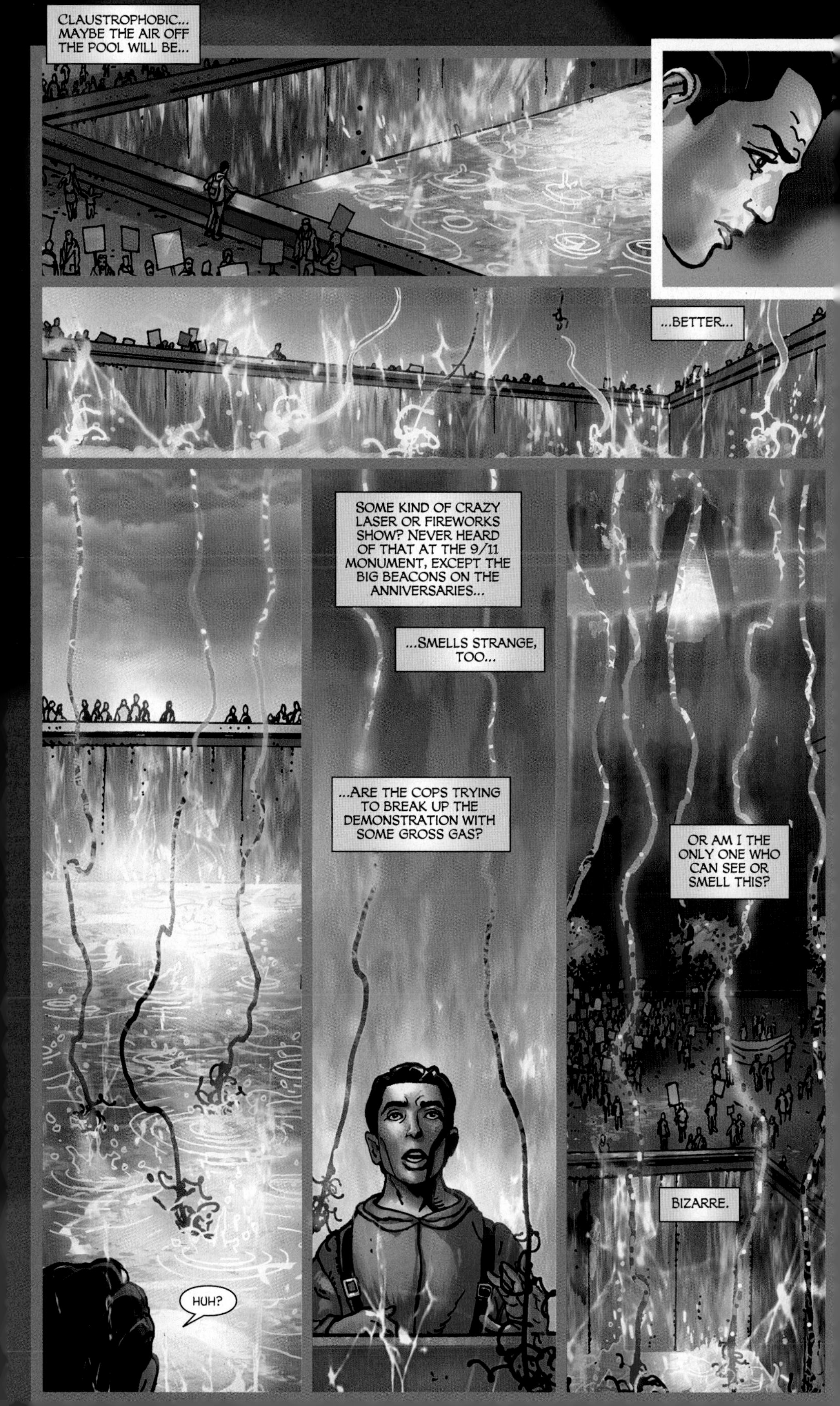
CLAUSTROPHOBIC... MAYBE THE AIR OFF THE POOL WILL BE...
...BETTER...
SOME KIND OF CRAZY LASER OR FIREWORKS SHOW? NEVER HEARD OF THAT AT THE 9/11 MONUMENT, EXCEPT THE BIG BEACONS ON THE ANNIVERSARIES...
...SMELLS STRANGE, TOO...
...ARE THE COPS TRYING TO BREAK UP THE DEMONSTRATION WITH SOME GROSS GAS?
HUH?
OR AM I THE ONLY ONE WHO CAN SEE OR SMELL THIS?
BIZARRE.

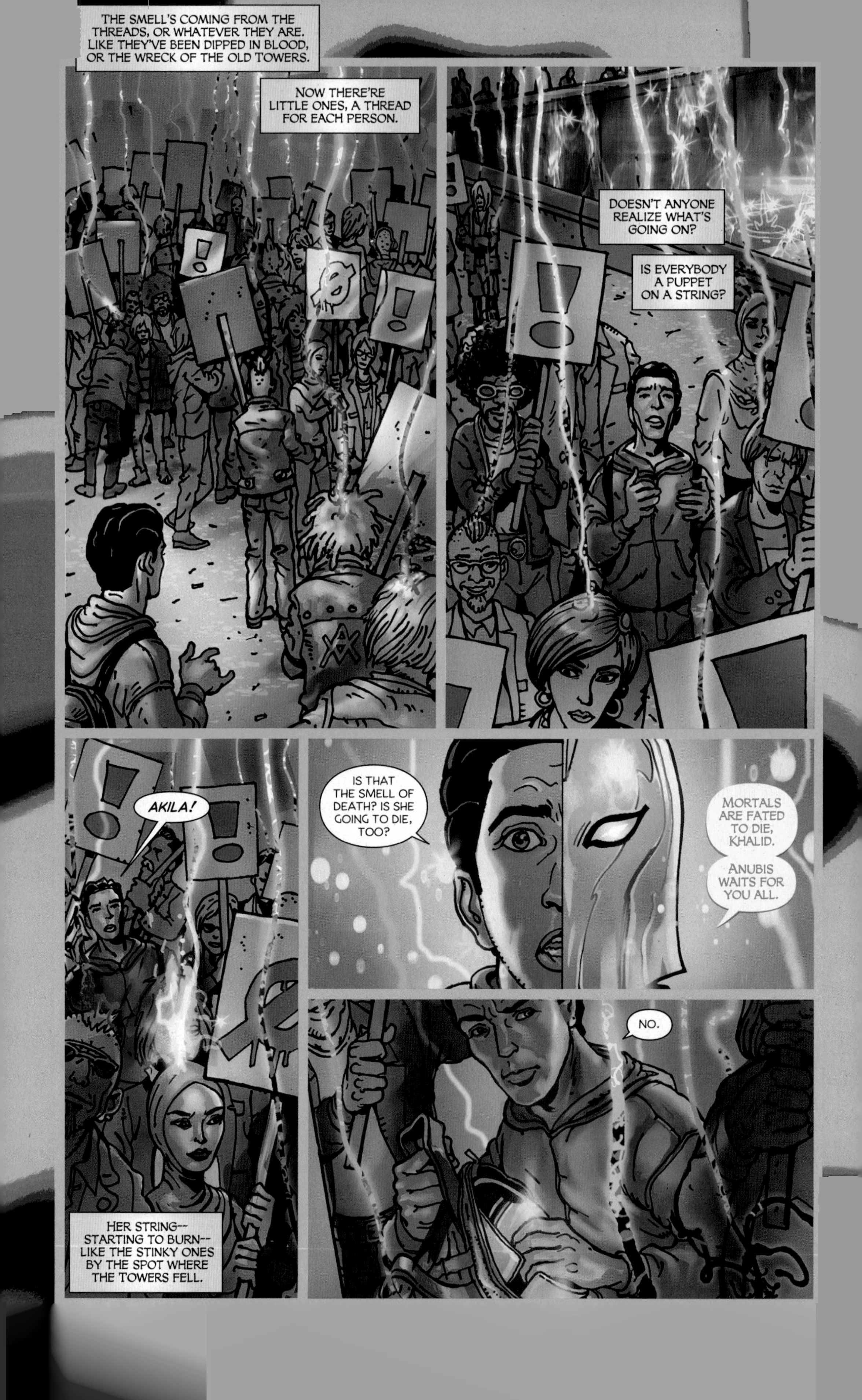
THE SMELL'S COMING FROM THE THREADS, OR WHATEVER THEY ARE. LIKE THEY'VE BEEN DIPPED IN BLOOD, OR THE WRECK OF THE OLD TOWERS.
NOW THERE'RE LITTLE ONES, A THREAD FOR EACH PERSON.
DOESN'T ANYONE REALIZE WHAT'S GOING ON?
IS EVERYBODY A PUPPET ON A STRING?
AKILA!
HER STRING-- STARTING TO BURN-- LIKE THE STINKY ONES BY THE SPOT WHERE THE TOWERS FELL.
IS THAT THE SMELL OF DEATH? IS SHE GOING TO DIE, TOO?
MORTALS ARE FATED TO DIE, KHALID.
ANUBIS WAITS FOR YOU ALL.
NO.

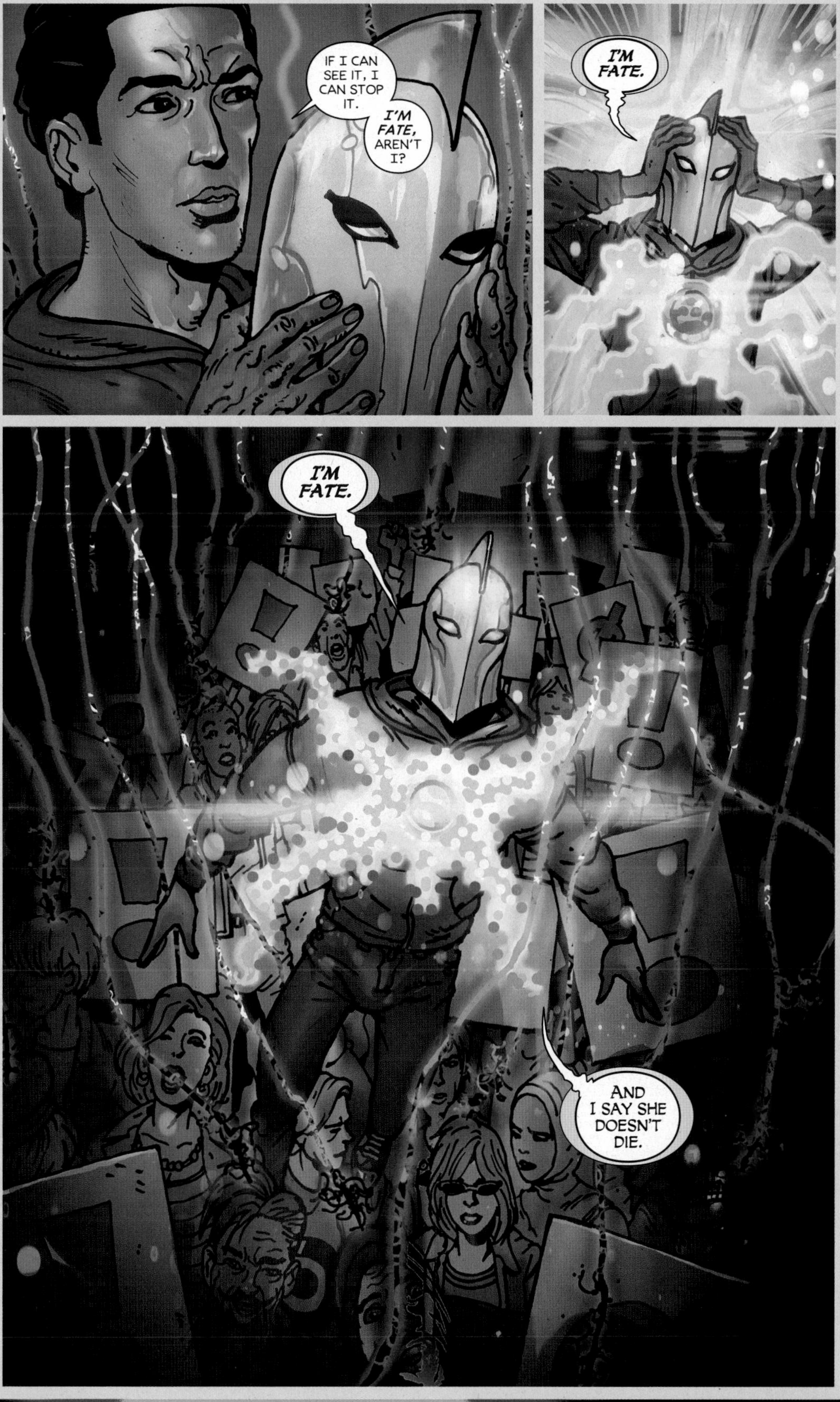
IF I CAN SEE IT, I CAN STOP IT.
I'M FATE, AREN'T I?
I'M FATE.
I'M FATE.
AND I SAY SHE DOESN'T DIE.

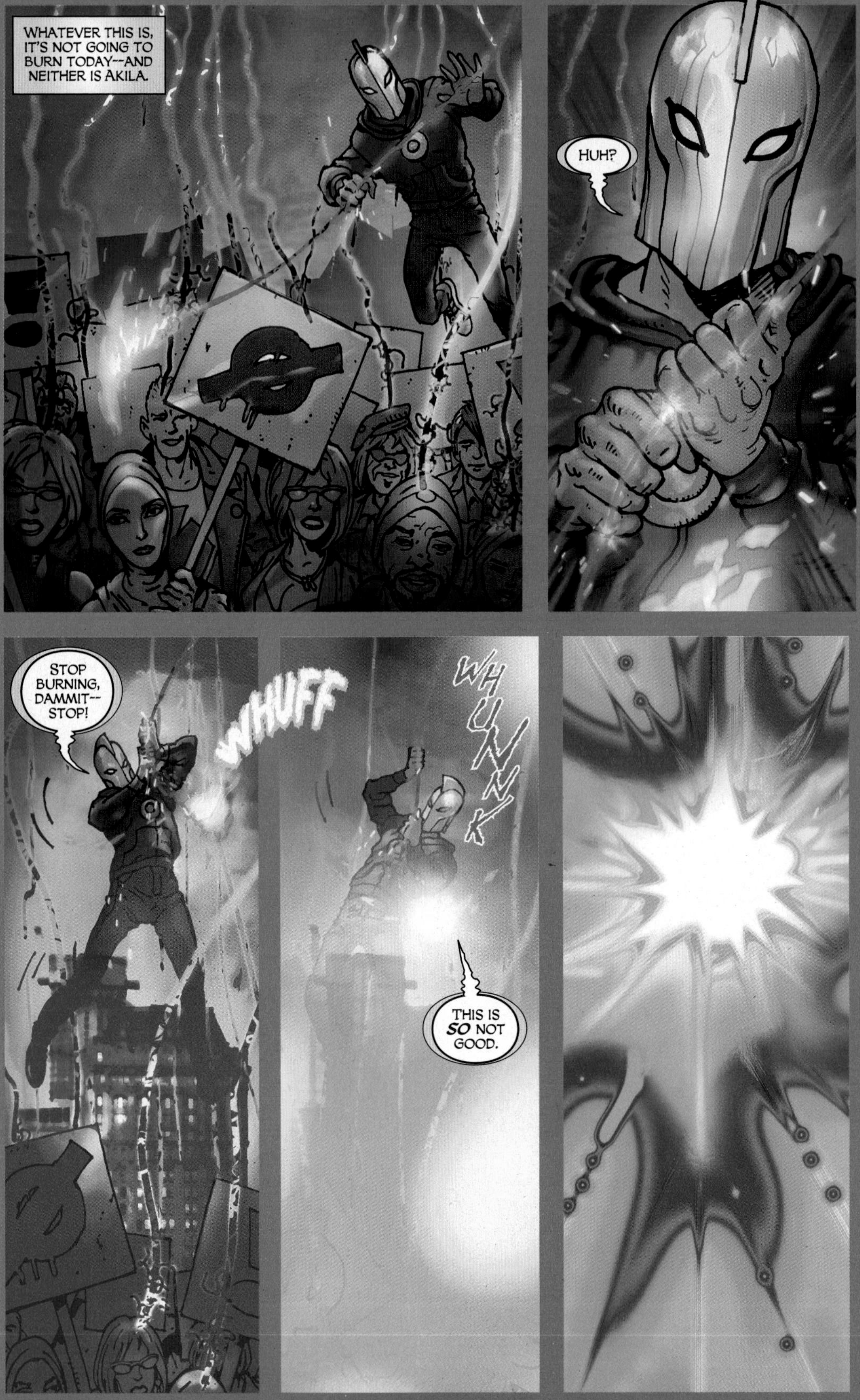
WHATEVER THIS IS, IT'S NOT GOING TO BURN TODAY--AND NEITHER IS AKILA.
HUH?
STOP BURNING, DAMMIT-- STOP!
WHUFF
WHUNNK
THIS IS SO NOT GOOD.

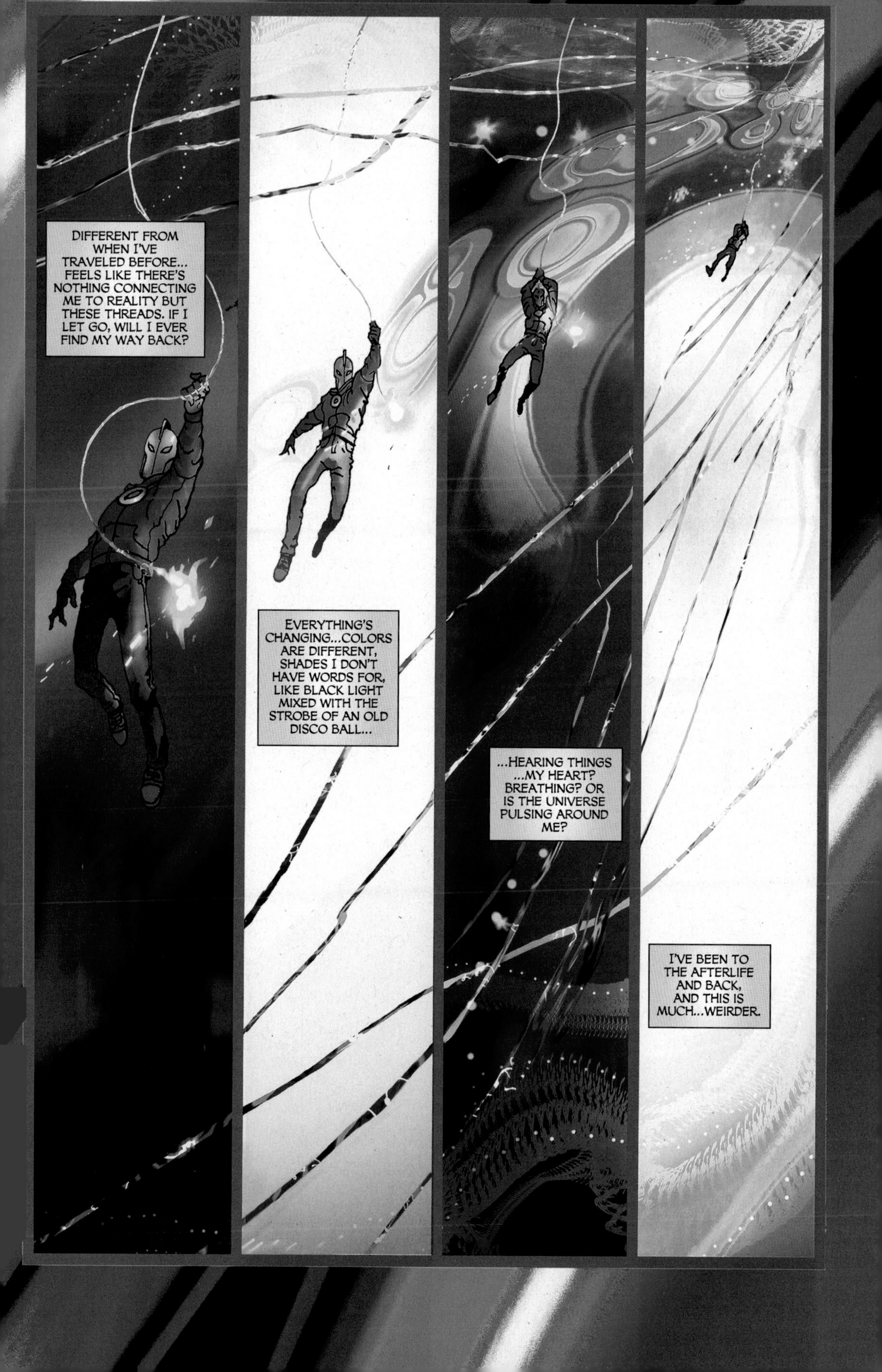
DIFFERENT FROM WHEN I'VE TRAVELED BEFORE... FEELS LIKE THERE'S NOTHING CONNECTING ME TO REALITY BUT THESE THREADS. IF I LET GO, WILL I EVER FIND MY WAY BACK?
EVERYTHING'S CHANGING...COLORS ARE DIFFERENT, SHADES I DON'T HAVE WORDS FOR, LIKE BLACK LIGHT MIXED WITH THE STROBE OF AN OLD DISCO BALL...
...HEARING THINGS ...MY HEART? BREATHING? OR IS THE UNIVERSE PULSING AROUND ME?
I'VE BEEN TO THE AFTERLIFE AND BACK, AND THIS IS MUCH...WEIRDER.

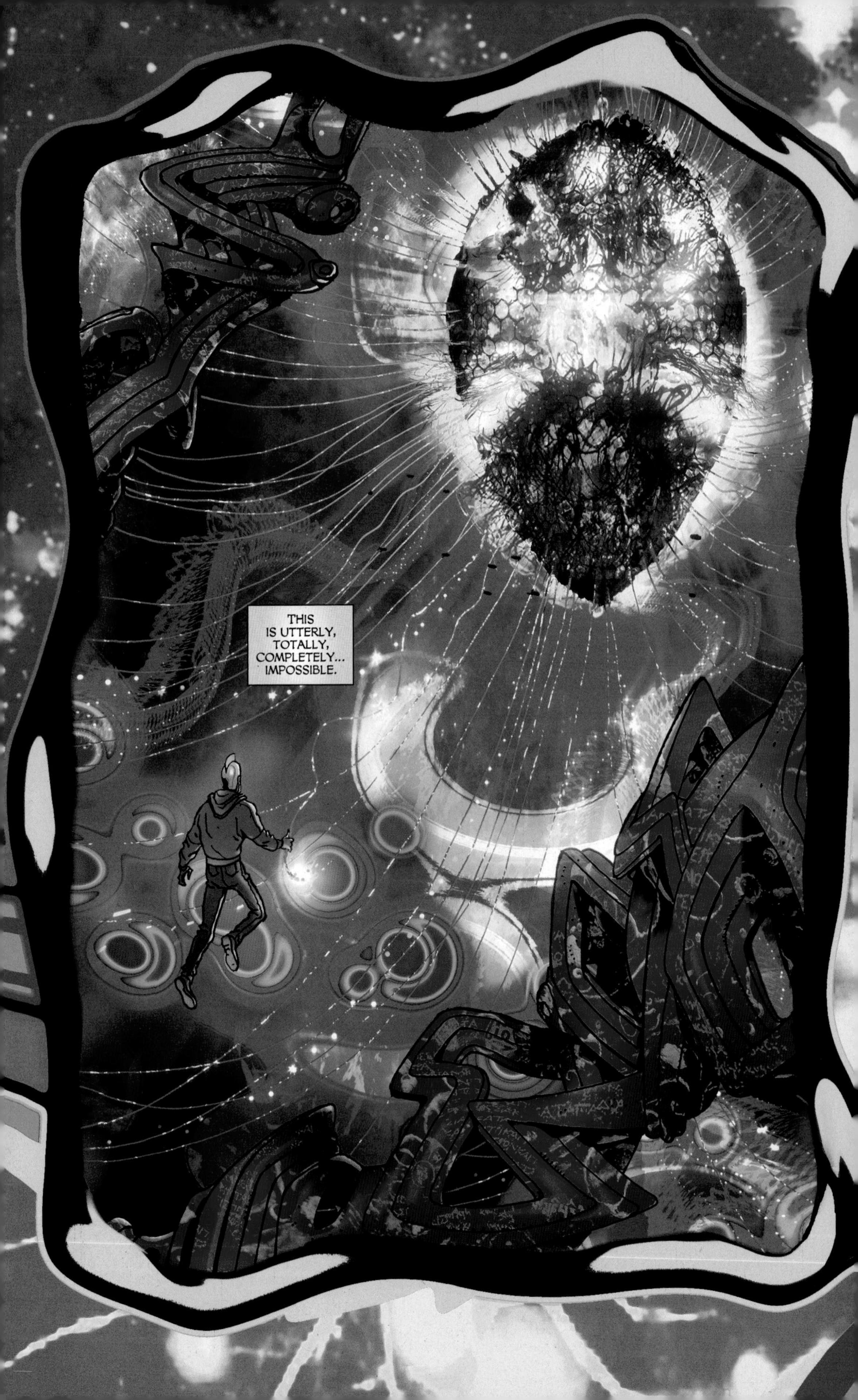
THIS IS UTTERLY, TOTALLY, COMPLETELY... IMPOSSIBLE.

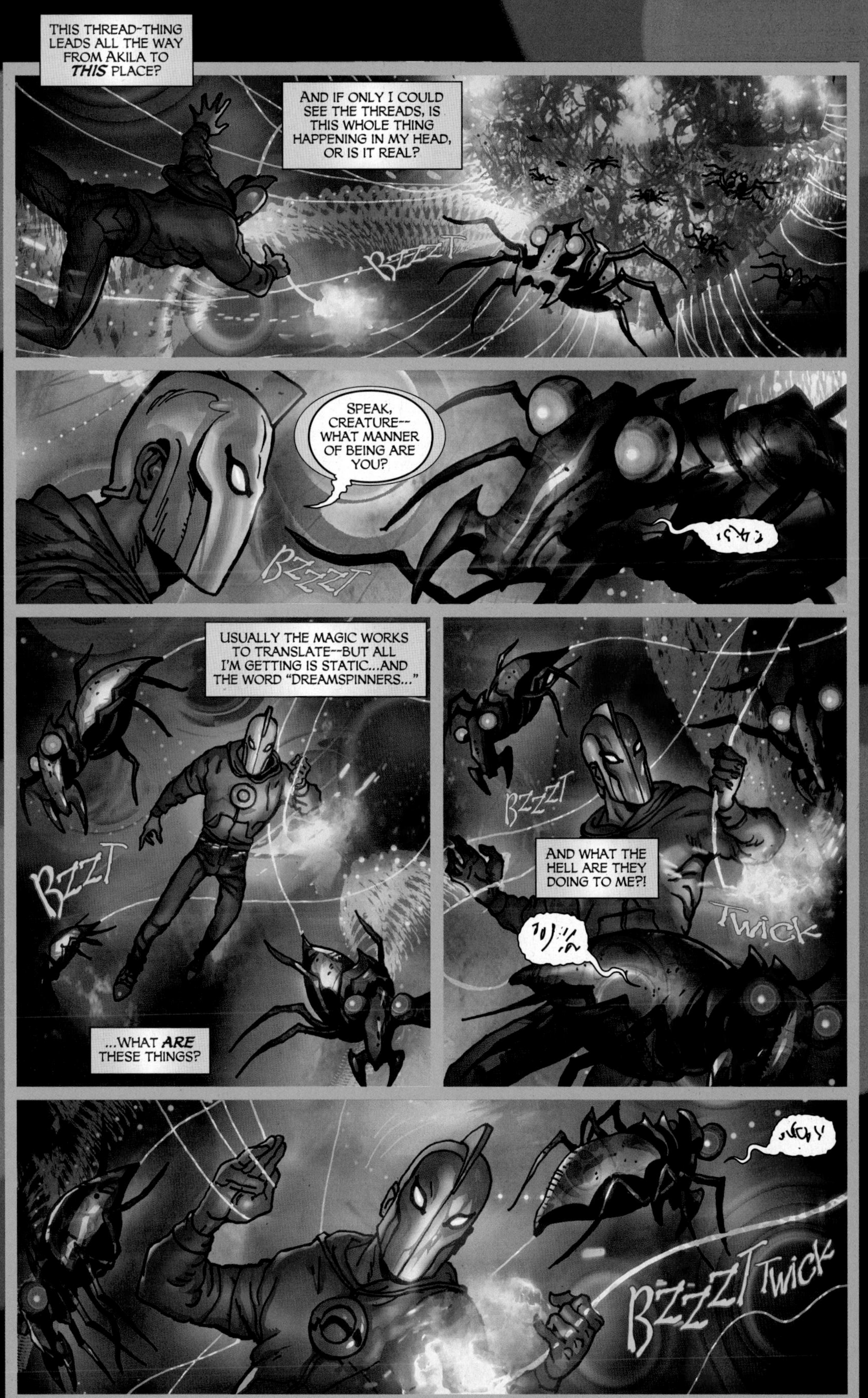
THIS THREAD-THING LEADS ALL THE WAY FROM AKILA TO *THIS* PLACE?
AND IF ONLY I COULD SEE THE THREADS, IS THIS WHOLE THING HAPPENING IN MY HEAD, OR IS IT REAL?
BZZZT
SPEAK, CREATURE-- WHAT MANNER OF BEING ARE YOU?
BZZZT
USUALLY THE MAGIC WORKS TO TRANSLATE--BUT ALL I'M GETTING IS STATIC...AND THE WORD "DREAMSPINNERS..."
BZZT
...WHAT *ARE* THESE THINGS?
BZZZT
AND WHAT THE HELL ARE THEY DOING TO ME?!
TWICK
BZZZT TWICK

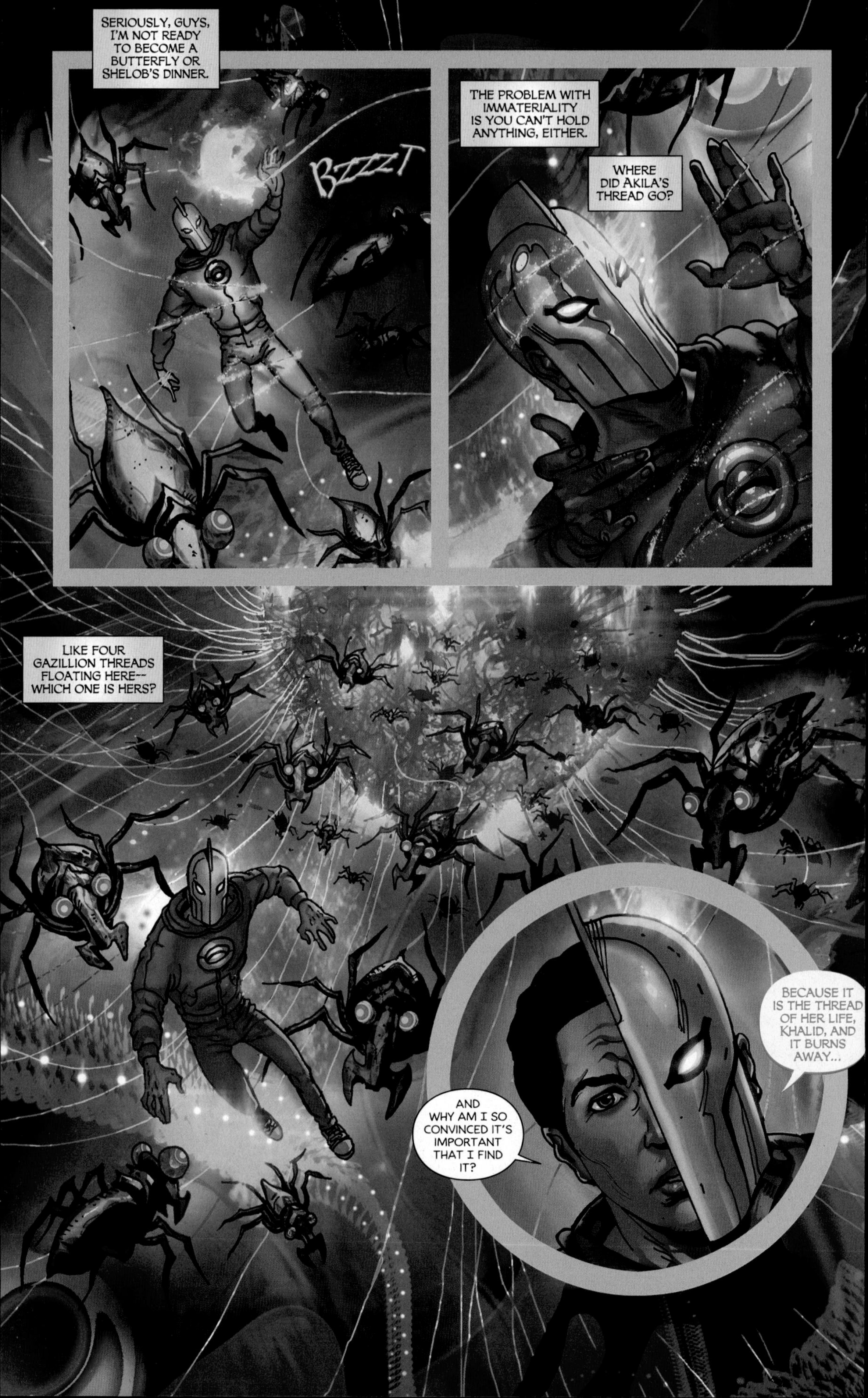
SERIOUSLY, GUYS, I'M NOT READY TO BECOME A BUTTERFLY OR SHELOB'S DINNER.
BZZZT
THE PROBLEM WITH IMMATERIALITY IS YOU CAN'T HOLD ANYTHING, EITHER.
WHERE DID AKILA'S THREAD GO?
LIKE FOUR GAZILLION THREADS FLOATING HERE-- WHICH ONE IS HERS?
AND WHY AM I SO CONVINCED IT'S IMPORTANT THAT I FIND IT?
BECAUSE IT IS THE THREAD OF HER LIFE, KHALID, AND IT BURNS AWAY...

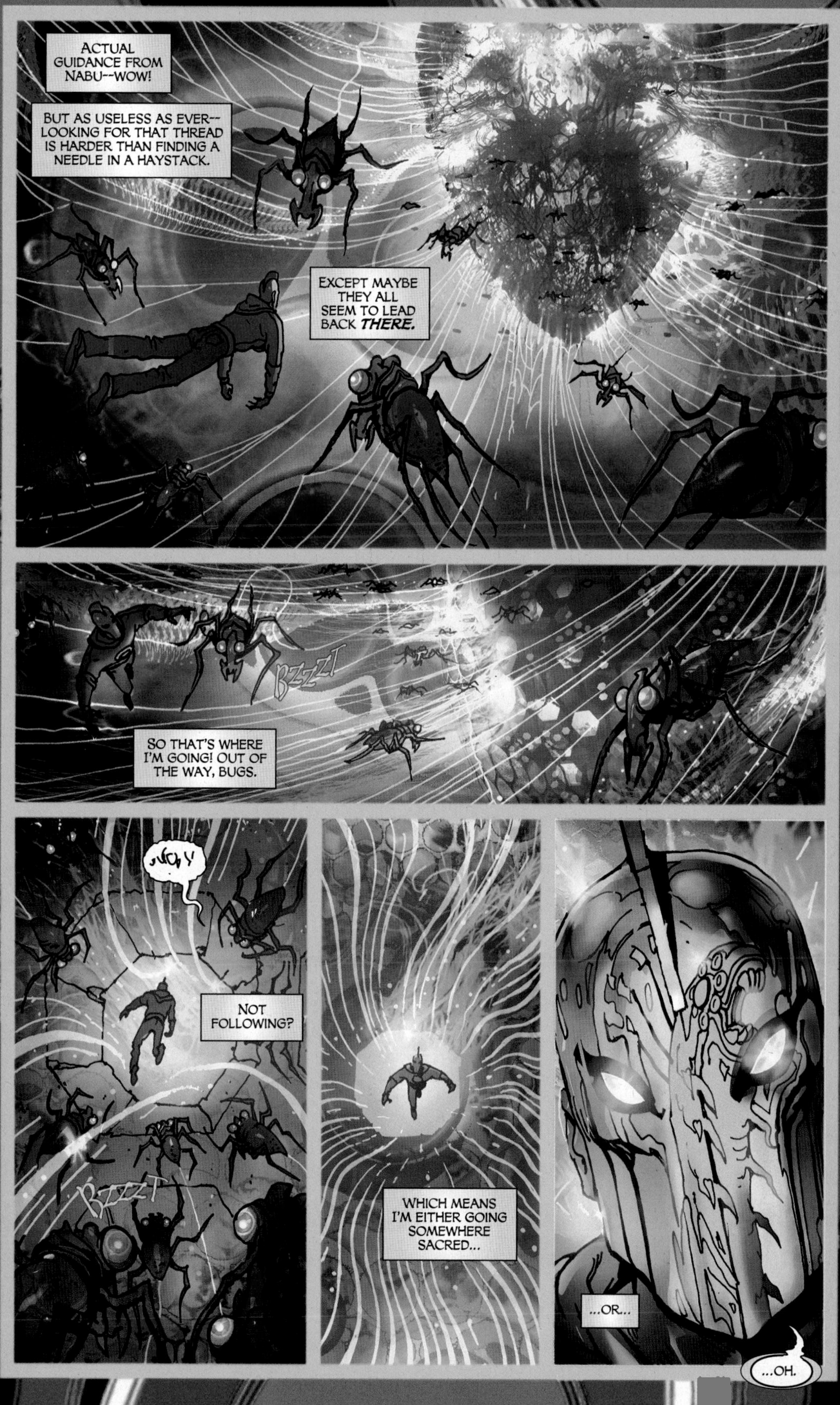
ACTUAL GUIDANCE FROM NABU--WOW!
BUT AS USELESS AS EVER--LOOKING FOR THAT THREAD IS HARDER THAN FINDING A NEEDLE IN A HAYSTACK.
EXCEPT MAYBE THEY ALL SEEM TO LEAD BACK *THERE.*
BZZZT
SO THAT'S WHERE I'M GOING! OUT OF THE WAY, BUGS.
NOT FOLLOWING?
BZZZT
WHICH MEANS I'M EITHER GOING SOMEWHERE SACRED...
...OR...
...OH.

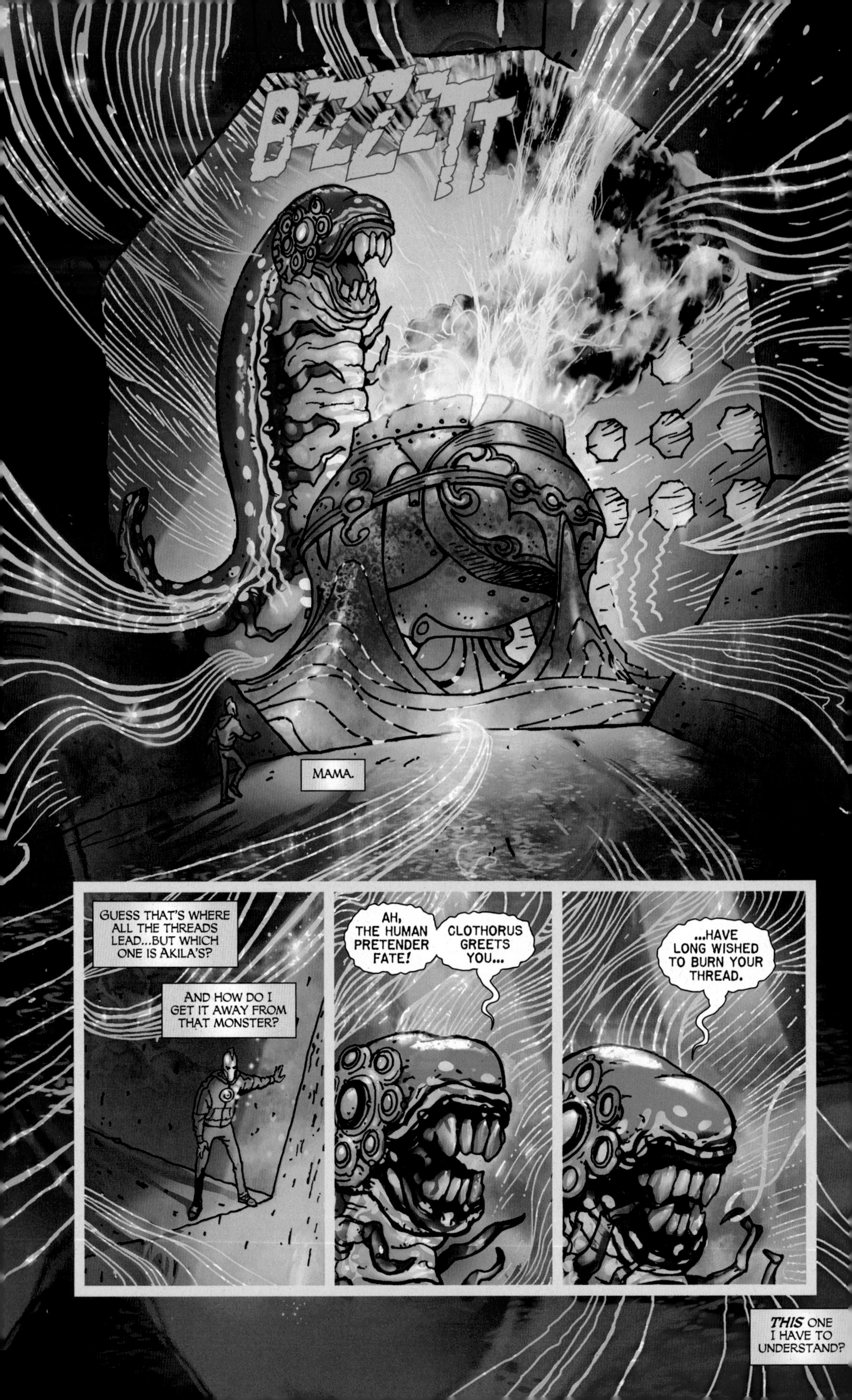
BZZZTT
MAMA.
GUESS THAT'S WHERE ALL THE THREADS LEAD...BUT WHICH ONE IS AKILA'S?
AND HOW DO I GET IT AWAY FROM THAT MONSTER?
AH, THE HUMAN PRETENDER FATE!
CLOTHORUS GREETS YOU...
...HAVE LONG WISHED TO BURN YOUR THREAD.
THIS ONE I HAVE TO UNDERSTAND?

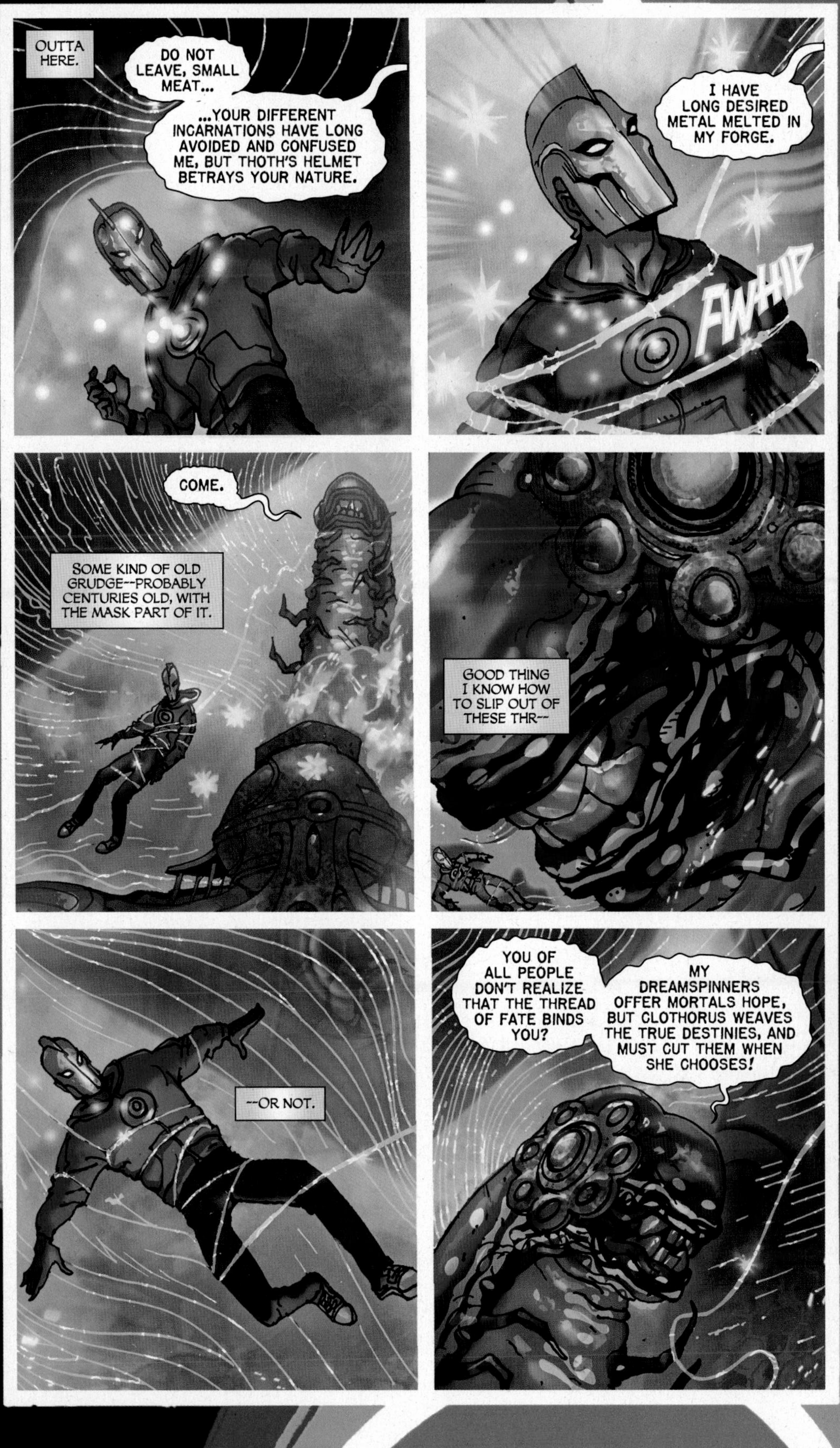
OUTTA HERE.
DO NOT LEAVE, SMALL MEAT...
...YOUR DIFFERENT INCARNATIONS HAVE LONG AVOIDED AND CONFUSED ME, BUT THOTH'S HELMET BETRAYS YOUR NATURE.
I HAVE LONG DESIRED METAL MELTED IN MY FORGE.
FWHIP
COME.
SOME KIND OF OLD GRUDGE--PROBABLY CENTURIES OLD, WITH THE MASK PART OF IT.
GOOD THING I KNOW HOW TO SLIP OUT OF THESE THR--
--OR NOT.
YOU OF ALL PEOPLE DON'T REALIZE THAT THE THREAD OF FATE BINDS YOU?
MY DREAMSPINNERS OFFER MORTALS HOPE, BUT CLOTHORUS WEAVES THE TRUE DESTINIES, AND MUST CUT THEM WHEN SHE CHOOSES!

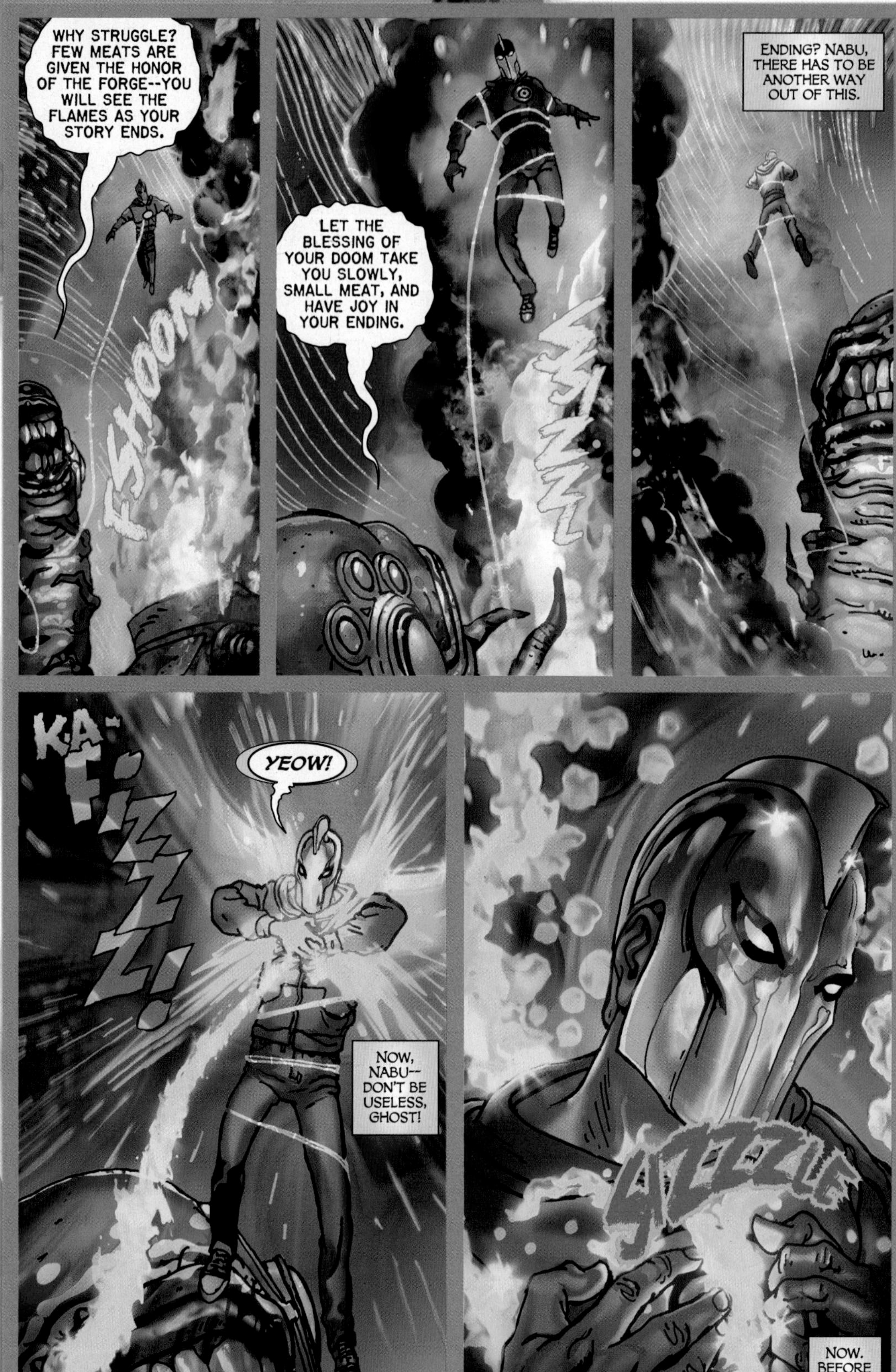

WHY STRUGGLE? FEW MEATS ARE GIVEN THE HONOR OF THE FORGE--YOU WILL SEE THE FLAMES AS YOUR STORY ENDS.
FSHOOM
LET THE BLESSING OF YOUR DOOM TAKE YOU SLOWLY, SMALL MEAT, AND HAVE JOY IN YOUR ENDING.
ENDING? NABU, THERE HAS TO BE ANOTHER WAY OUT OF THIS.
KA-FIZZZZ!
YEOW!
NOW, NABU--DON'T BE USELESS, GHOST!
NOW. BEFORE I'M TOAST.

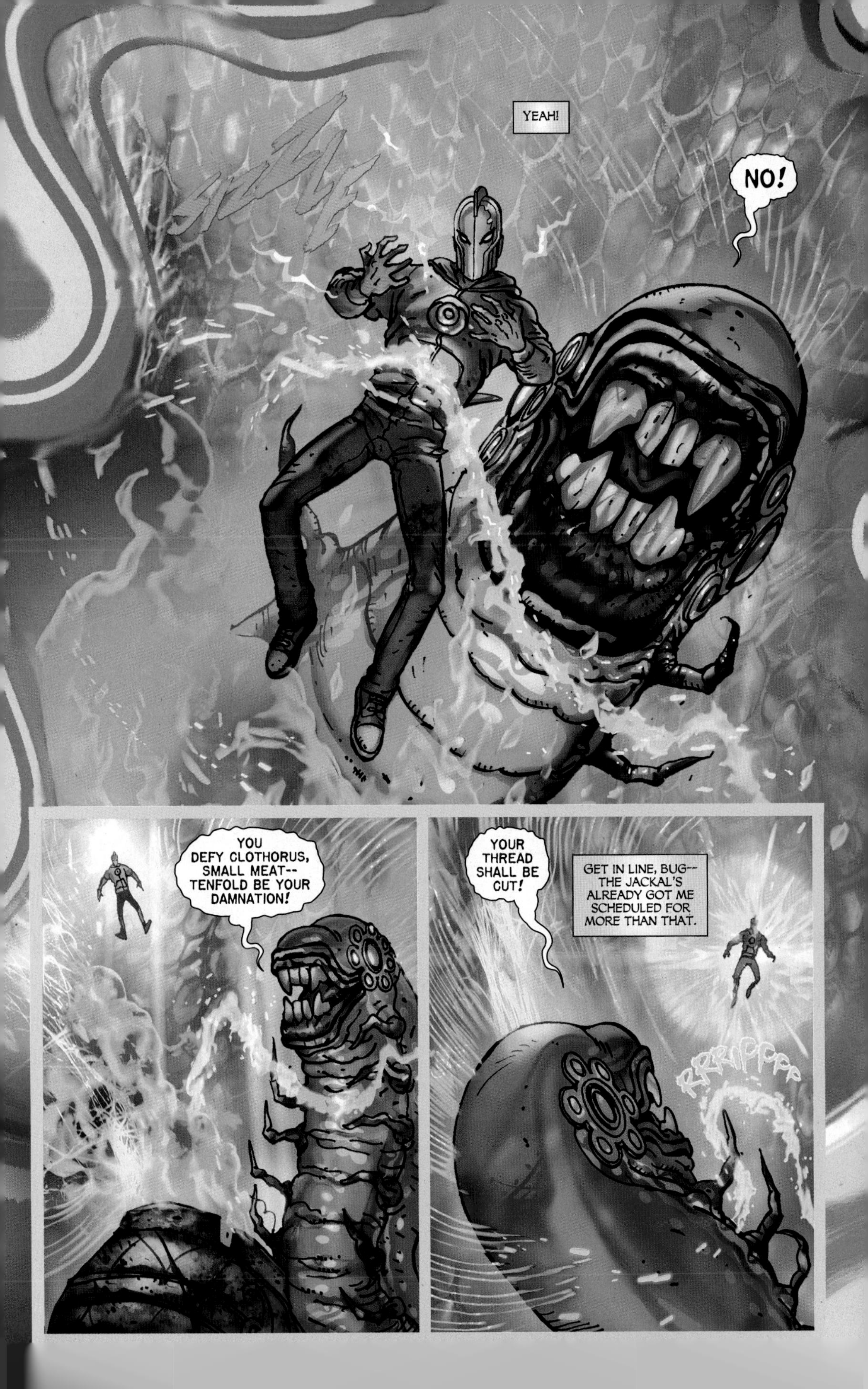
YEAH!
NO!
YOU DEFY CLOTHORUS, SMALL MEAT-- TENFOLD BE YOUR DAMNATION!
YOUR THREAD SHALL BE CUT!
GET IN LINE, BUG-- THE JACKAL'S ALREADY GOT ME SCHEDULED FOR MORE THAN THAT.

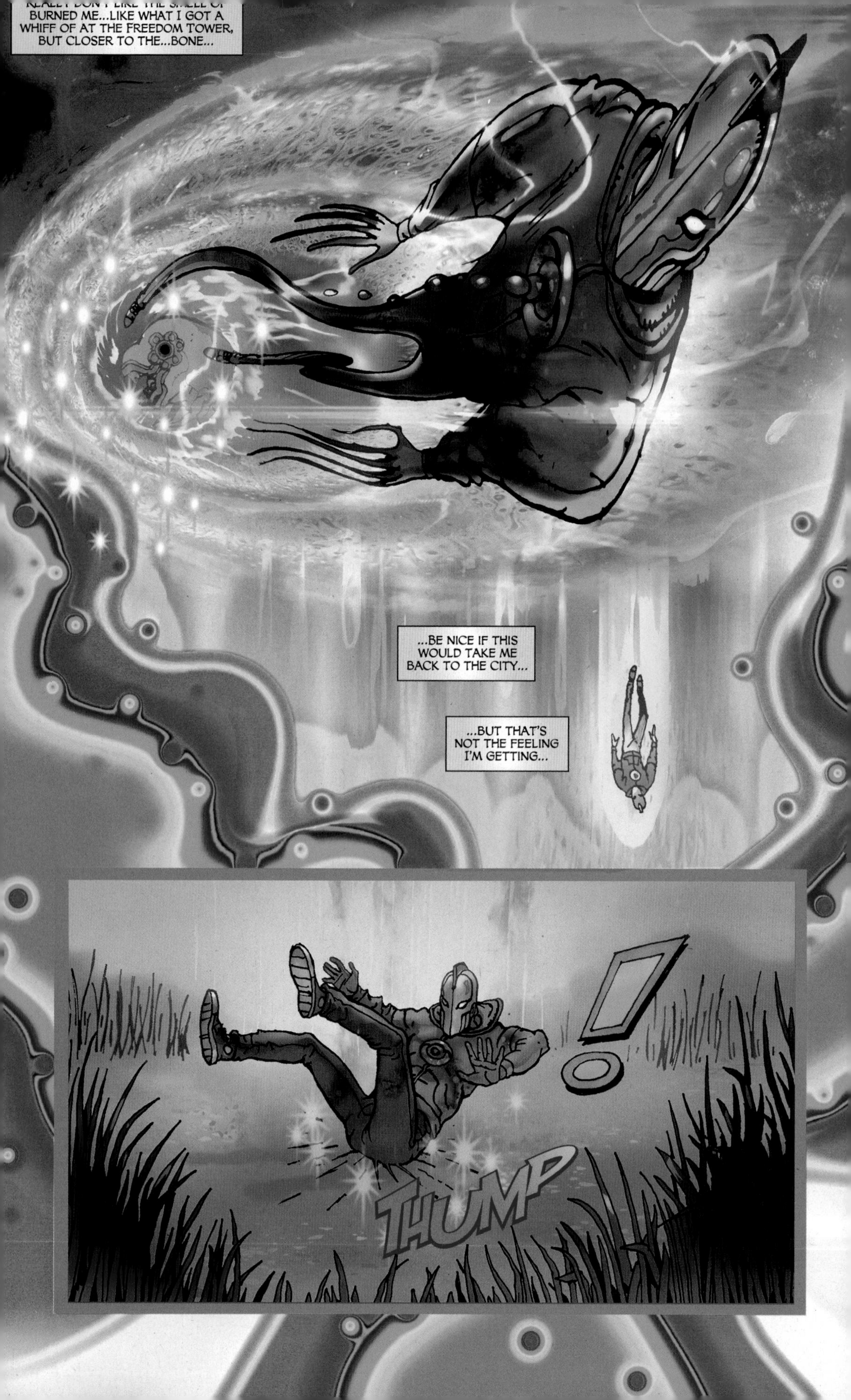
BURNED ME...LIKE WHAT I GOT A WHIFF OF AT THE FREEDOM TOWER, BUT CLOSER TO THE...BONE...
...BE NICE IF THIS WOULD TAKE ME BACK TO THE CITY...
...BUT THAT'S NOT THE FEELING I'M GETTING...
THUMP

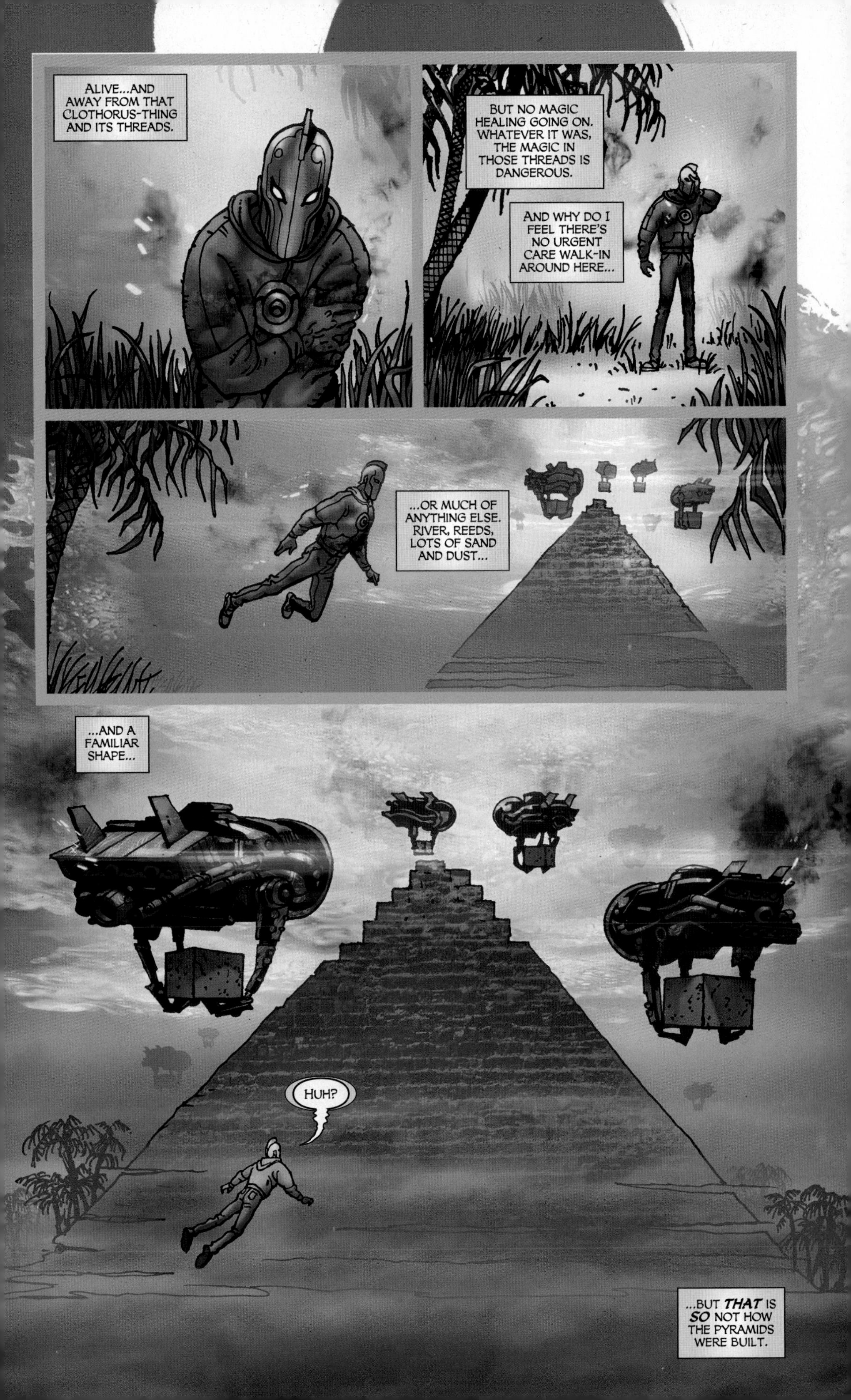
ALIVE...AND AWAY FROM THAT CLOTHORUS-THING AND ITS THREADS.
BUT NO MAGIC HEALING GOING ON. WHATEVER IT WAS, THE MAGIC IN THOSE THREADS IS DANGEROUS.
AND WHY DO I FEEL THERE'S NO URGENT CARE WALK-IN AROUND HERE...
...OR MUCH OF ANYTHING ELSE. RIVER, REEDS, LOTS OF SAND AND DUST...
...AND A FAMILIAR SHAPE...
HUH?
...BUT THAT IS SO NOT HOW THE PYRAMIDS WERE BUILT.

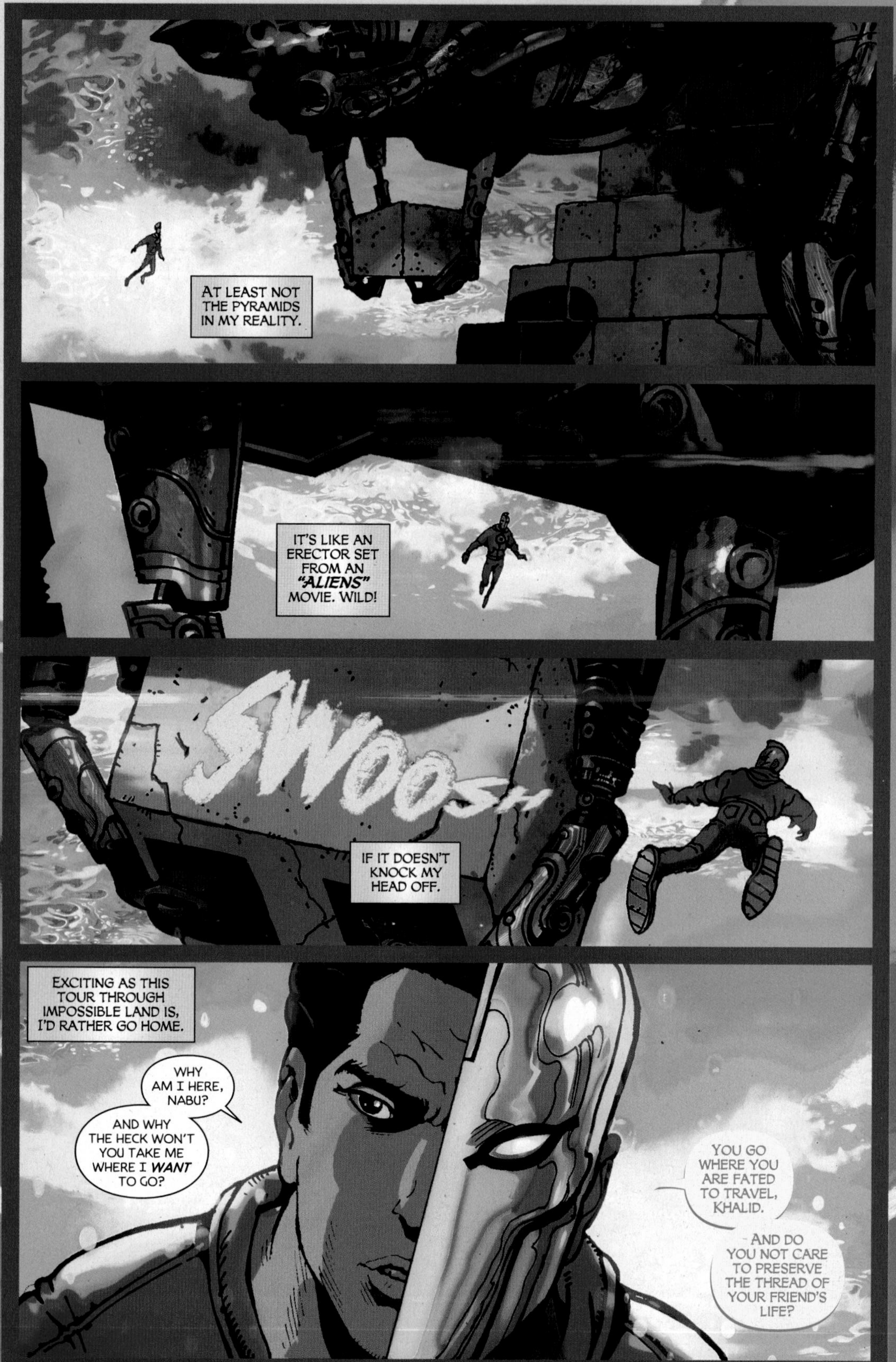
AT LEAST NOT THE PYRAMIDS IN MY REALITY.
IT'S LIKE AN ERECTOR SET FROM AN "ALIENS" MOVIE. WILD!
SWOOSH
IF IT DOESN'T KNOCK MY HEAD OFF.
EXCITING AS THIS TOUR THROUGH IMPOSSIBLE LAND IS, I'D RATHER GO HOME.
WHY AM I HERE, NABU?
AND WHY THE HECK WON'T YOU TAKE ME WHERE I WANT TO GO?
YOU GO WHERE YOU ARE FATED TO TRAVEL, KHALID.
AND DO YOU NOT CARE TO PRESERVE THE THREAD OF YOUR FRIEND'S LIFE?

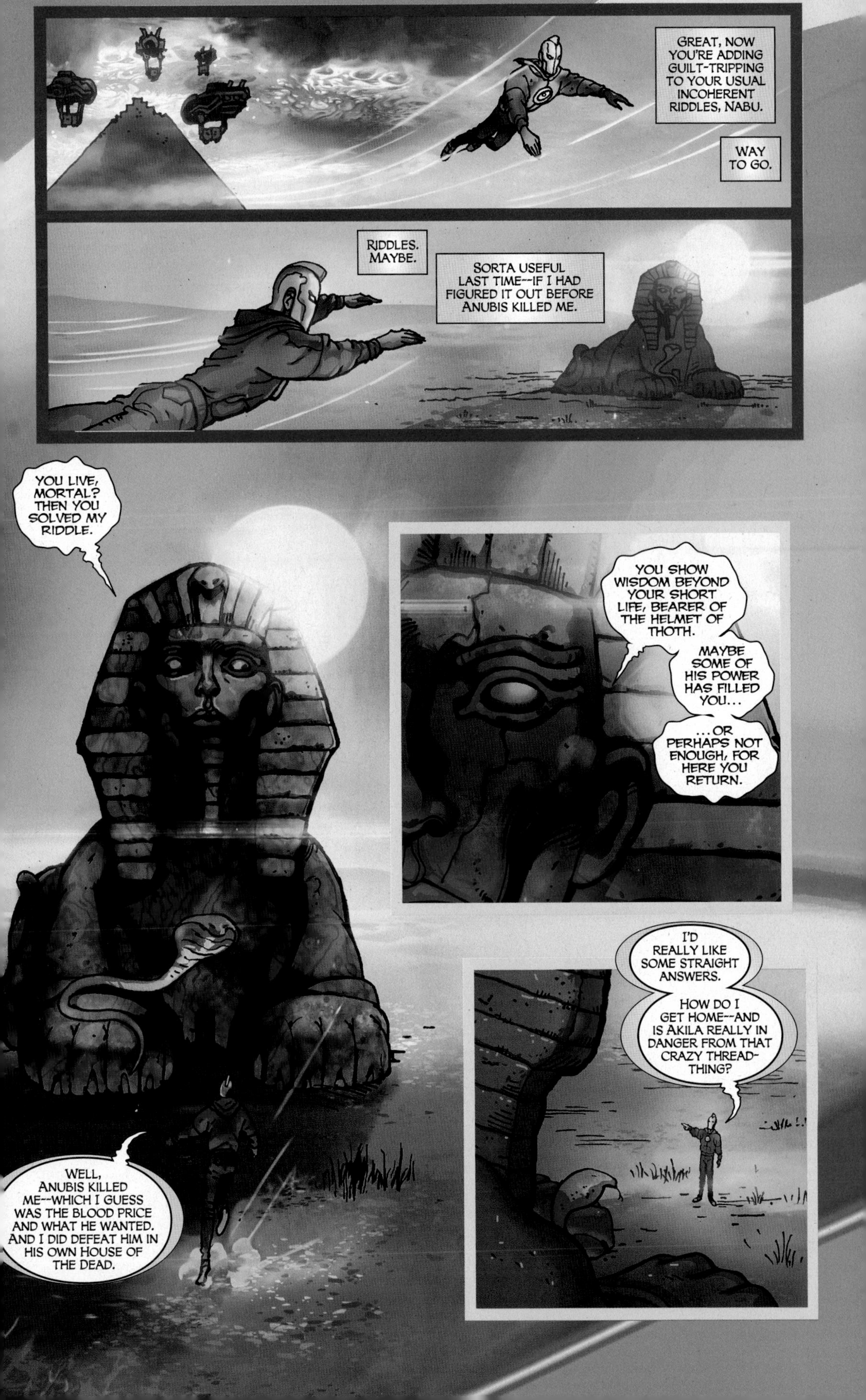
GREAT, NOW YOU'RE ADDING GUILT-TRIPPING TO YOUR USUAL INCOHERENT RIDDLES, NABU.
WAY TO GO.
RIDDLES. MAYBE.
SORTA USEFUL LAST TIME--IF I HAD FIGURED IT OUT BEFORE ANUBIS KILLED ME.
YOU LIVE, MORTAL? THEN YOU SOLVED MY RIDDLE.
WELL, ANUBIS KILLED ME--WHICH I GUESS WAS THE BLOOD PRICE AND WHAT HE WANTED. AND I DID DEFEAT HIM IN HIS OWN HOUSE OF THE DEAD.
YOU SHOW WISDOM BEYOND YOUR SHORT LIFE, BEARER OF THE HELMET OF THOTH.
MAYBE SOME OF HIS POWER HAS FILLED YOU...
...OR PERHAPS NOT ENOUGH, FOR HERE YOU RETURN.
I'D REALLY LIKE SOME STRAIGHT ANSWERS.
HOW DO I GET HOME--AND IS AKILA REALLY IN DANGER FROM THAT CRAZY THREAD-THING?

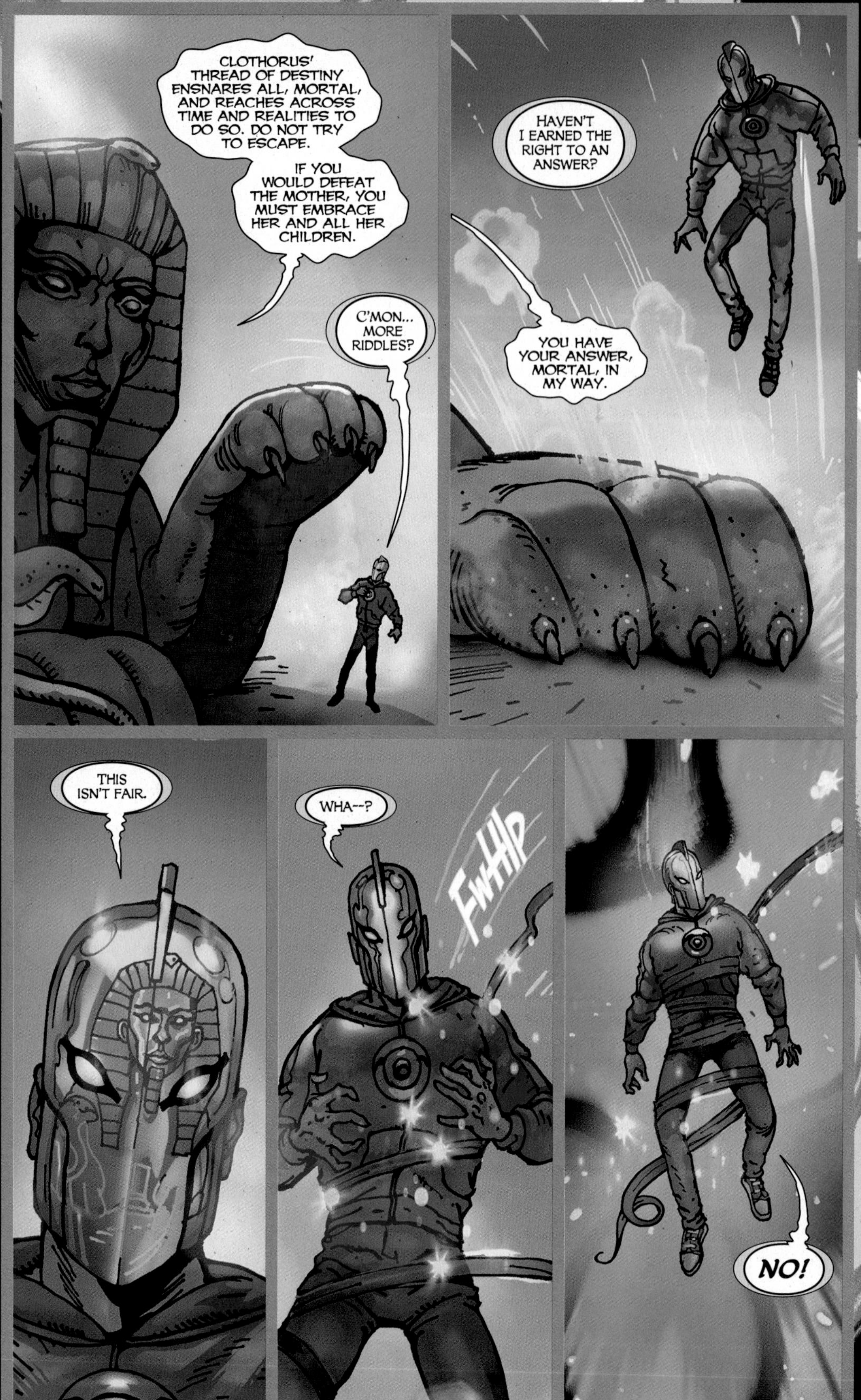
CLOTHORUS' THREAD OF DESTINY ENSNARES ALL, MORTAL, AND REACHES ACROSS TIME AND REALITIES TO DO SO. DO NOT TRY TO ESCAPE.
IF YOU WOULD DEFEAT THE MOTHER, YOU MUST EMBRACE HER AND ALL HER CHILDREN.
C'MON... MORE RIDDLES?
HAVEN'T I EARNED THE RIGHT TO AN ANSWER?
YOU HAVE YOUR ANSWER, MORTAL, IN MY WAY.
THIS ISN'T FAIR.
WHA--?
FWHIP
NO!

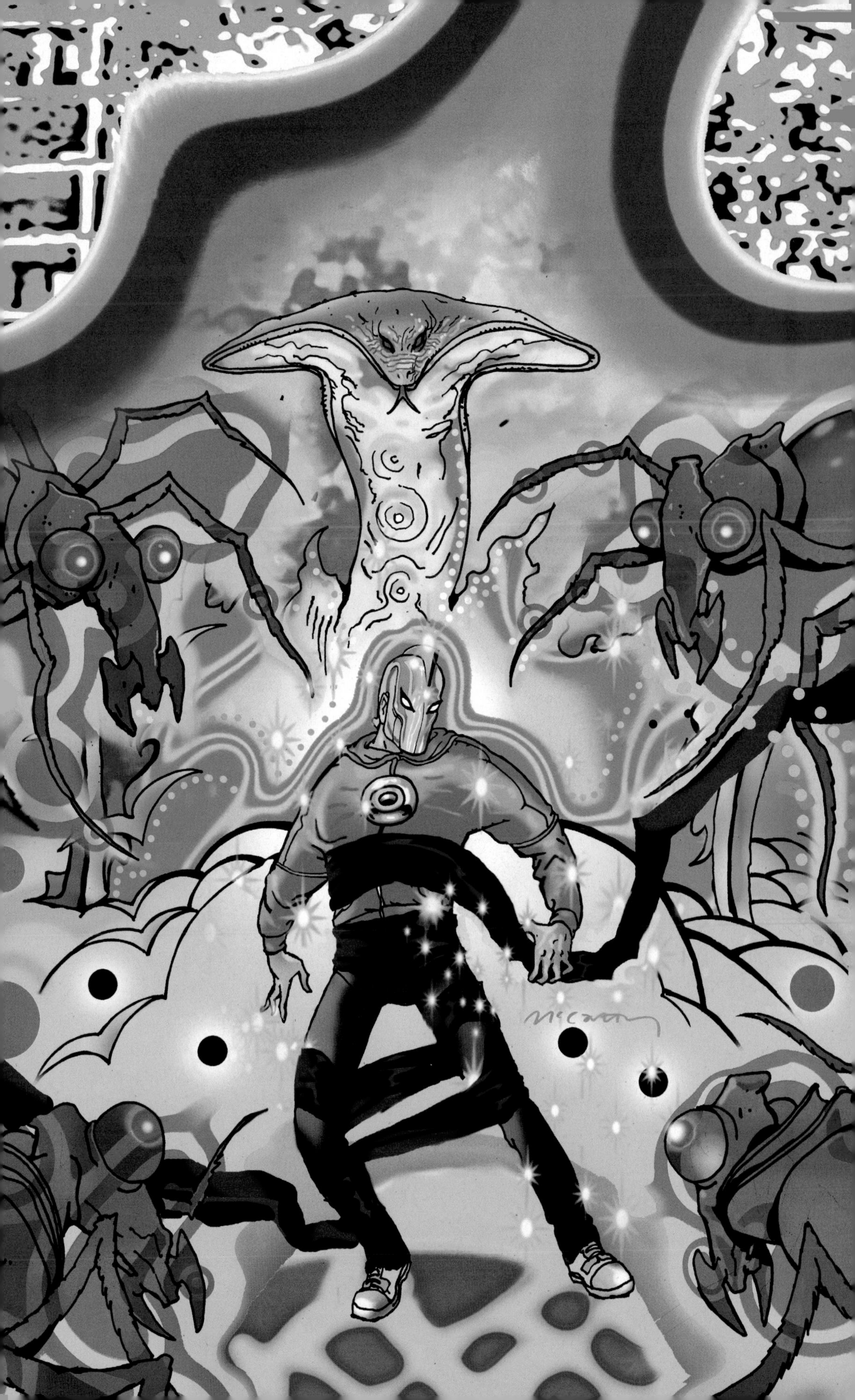

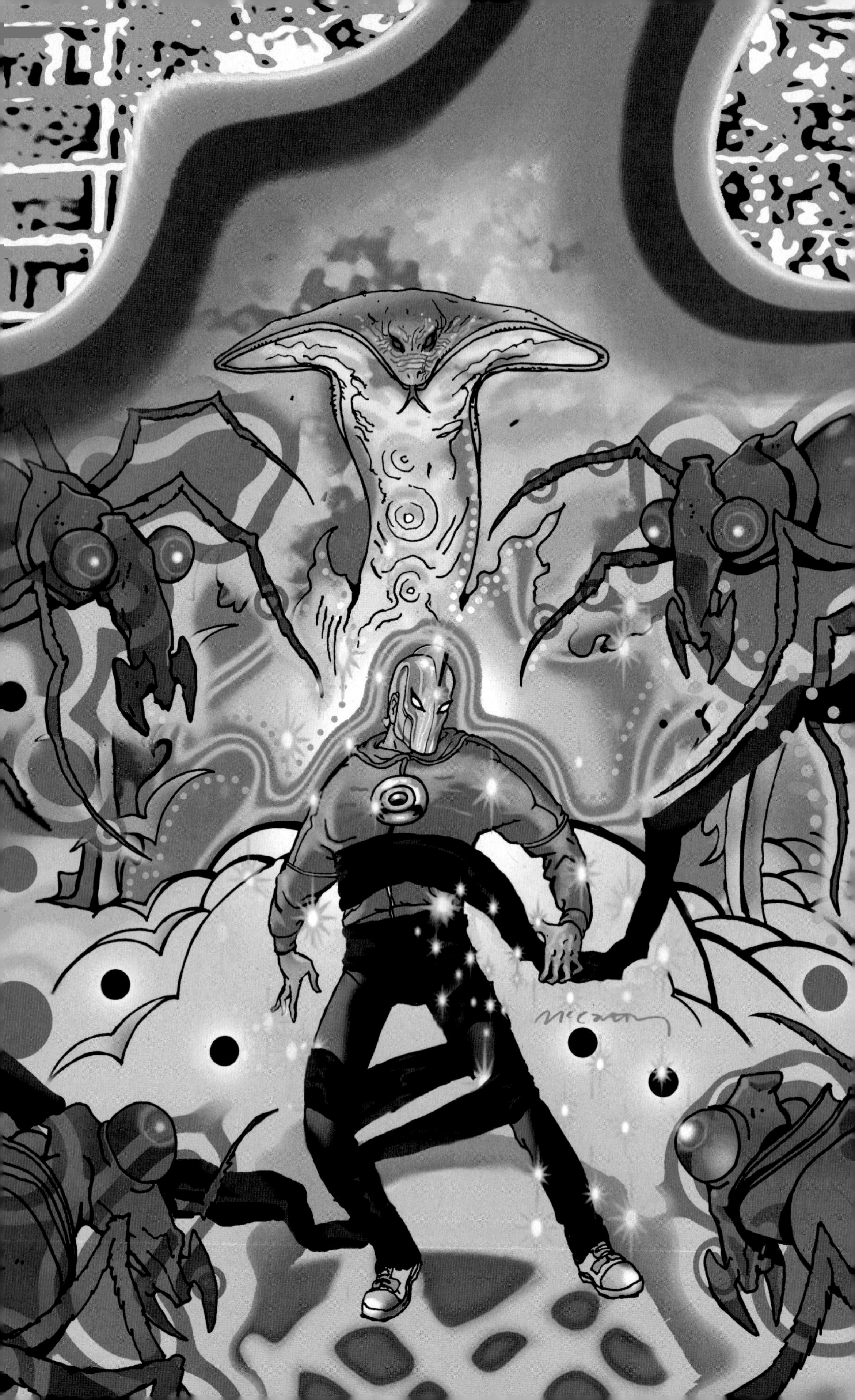

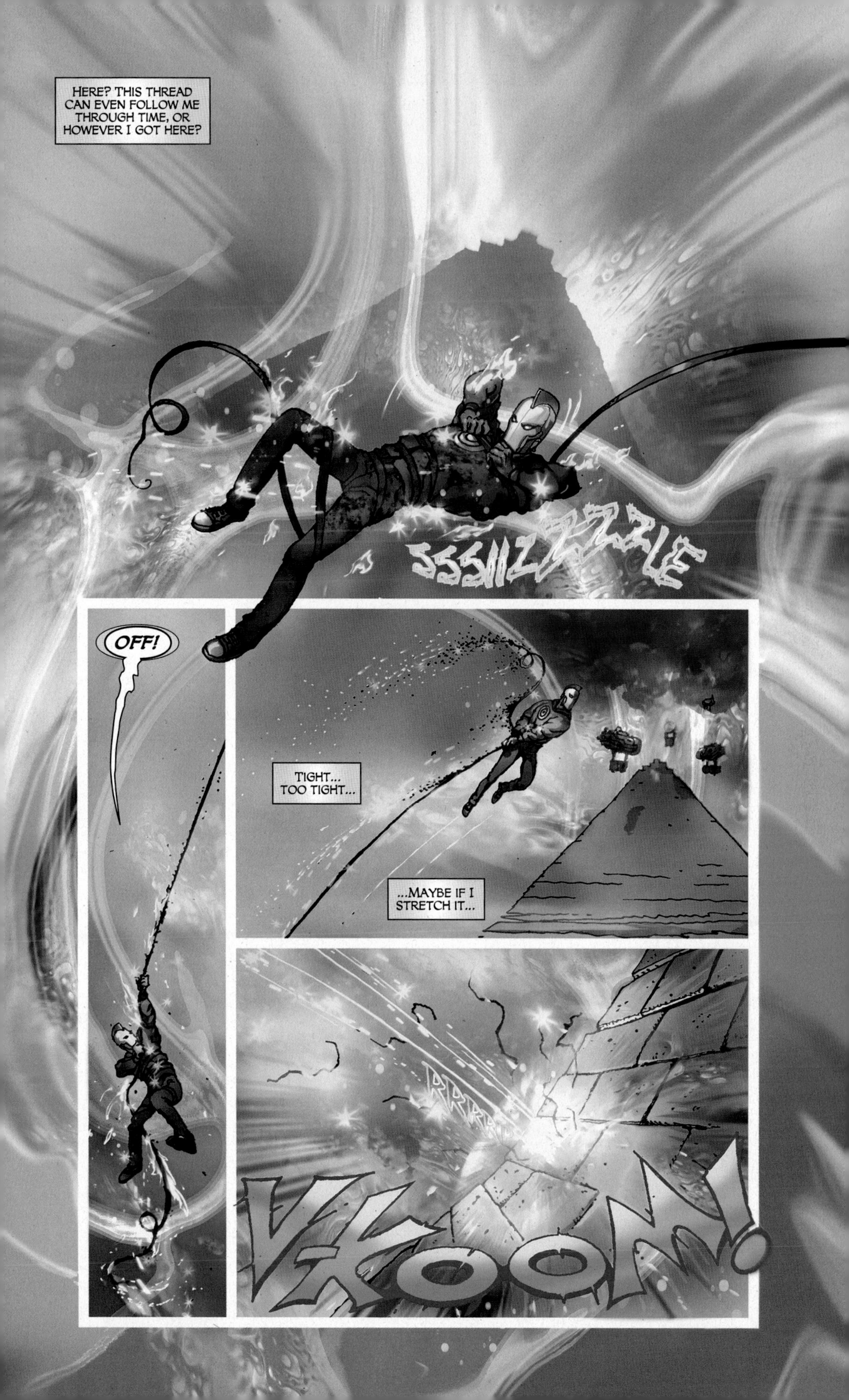
HERE? THIS THREAD
CAN EVEN FOLLOW ME
THROUGH TIME, OR
HOWEVER I GOT HERE?
SSSHIZZZZLE
OFF!
TIGHT...
TOO TIGHT...
...MAYBE IF I
STRETCH IT...
V-KOOM!

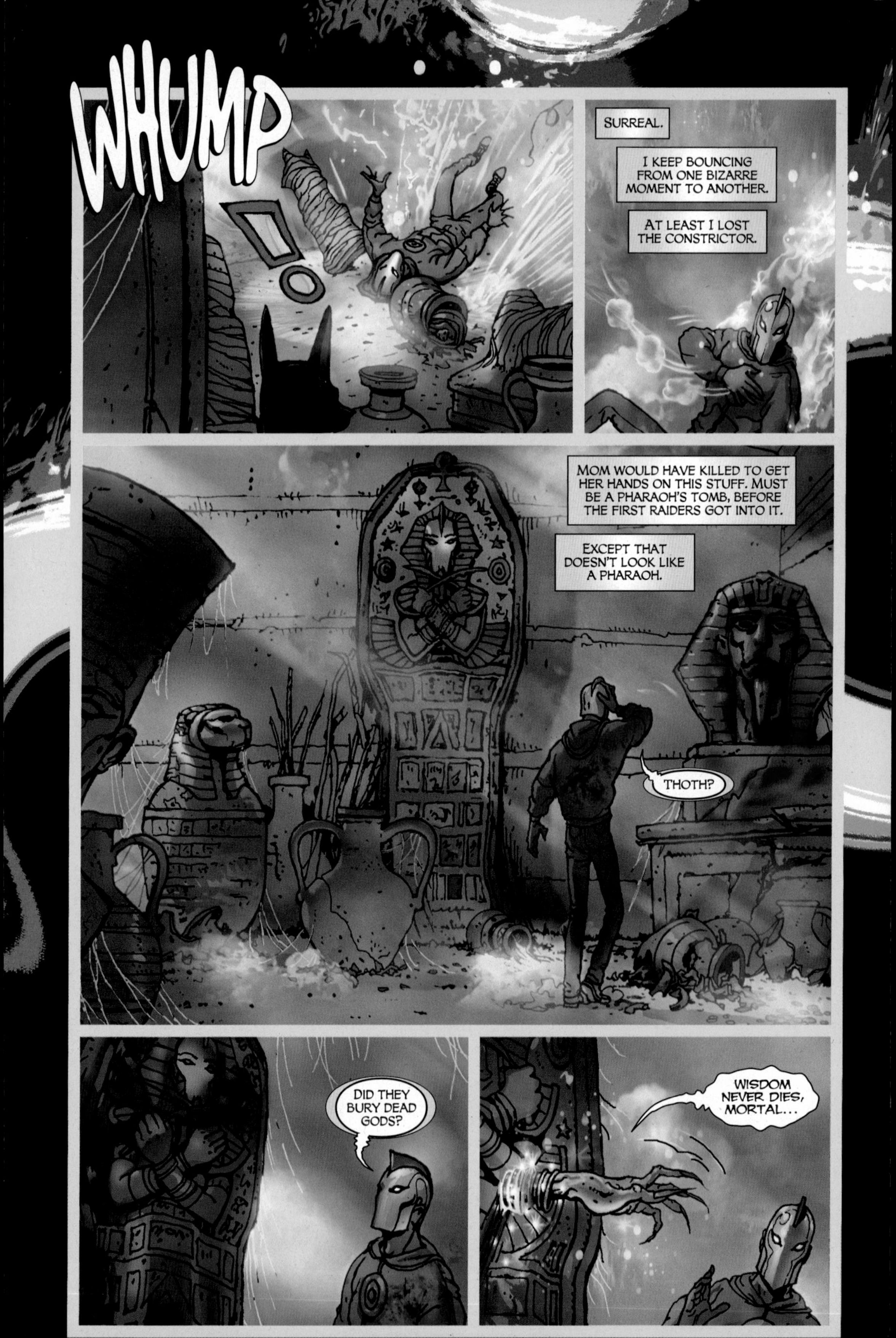
WHUMP
SURREAL.
I KEEP BOUNCING FROM ONE BIZARRE MOMENT TO ANOTHER.
AT LEAST I LOST THE CONSTRICTOR.
MOM WOULD HAVE KILLED TO GET HER HANDS ON THIS STUFF. MUST BE A PHARAOH'S TOMB, BEFORE THE FIRST RAIDERS GOT INTO IT.
EXCEPT THAT DOESN'T LOOK LIKE A PHARAOH.
THOTH?
DID THEY BURY DEAD GODS?
WISDOM NEVER DIES, MORTAL...

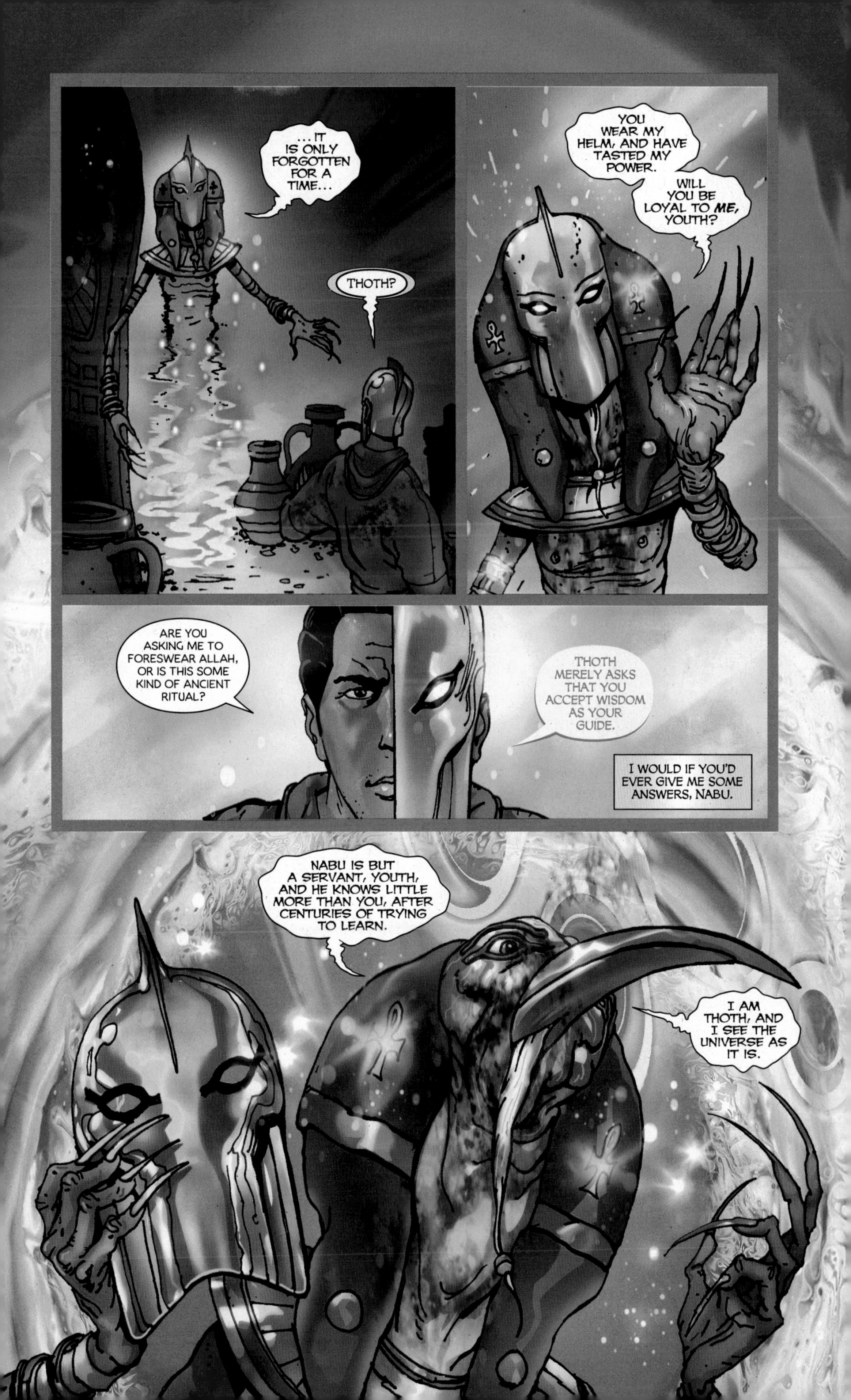
...IT IS ONLY FORGOTTEN FOR A TIME...
THOTH?
YOU WEAR MY HELM, AND HAVE TASTED MY POWER.
WILL YOU BE LOYAL TO *ME*, YOUTH?
ARE YOU ASKING ME TO FORESWEAR ALLAH, OR IS THIS SOME KIND OF ANCIENT RITUAL?
THOTH MERELY ASKS THAT YOU ACCEPT WISDOM AS YOUR GUIDE.
I WOULD IF YOU'D EVER GIVE ME SOME ANSWERS, NABU.
NABU IS BUT A SERVANT, YOUTH, AND HE KNOWS LITTLE MORE THAN YOU, AFTER CENTURIES OF TRYING TO LEARN.
I AM THOTH, AND I SEE THE UNIVERSE AS IT IS.

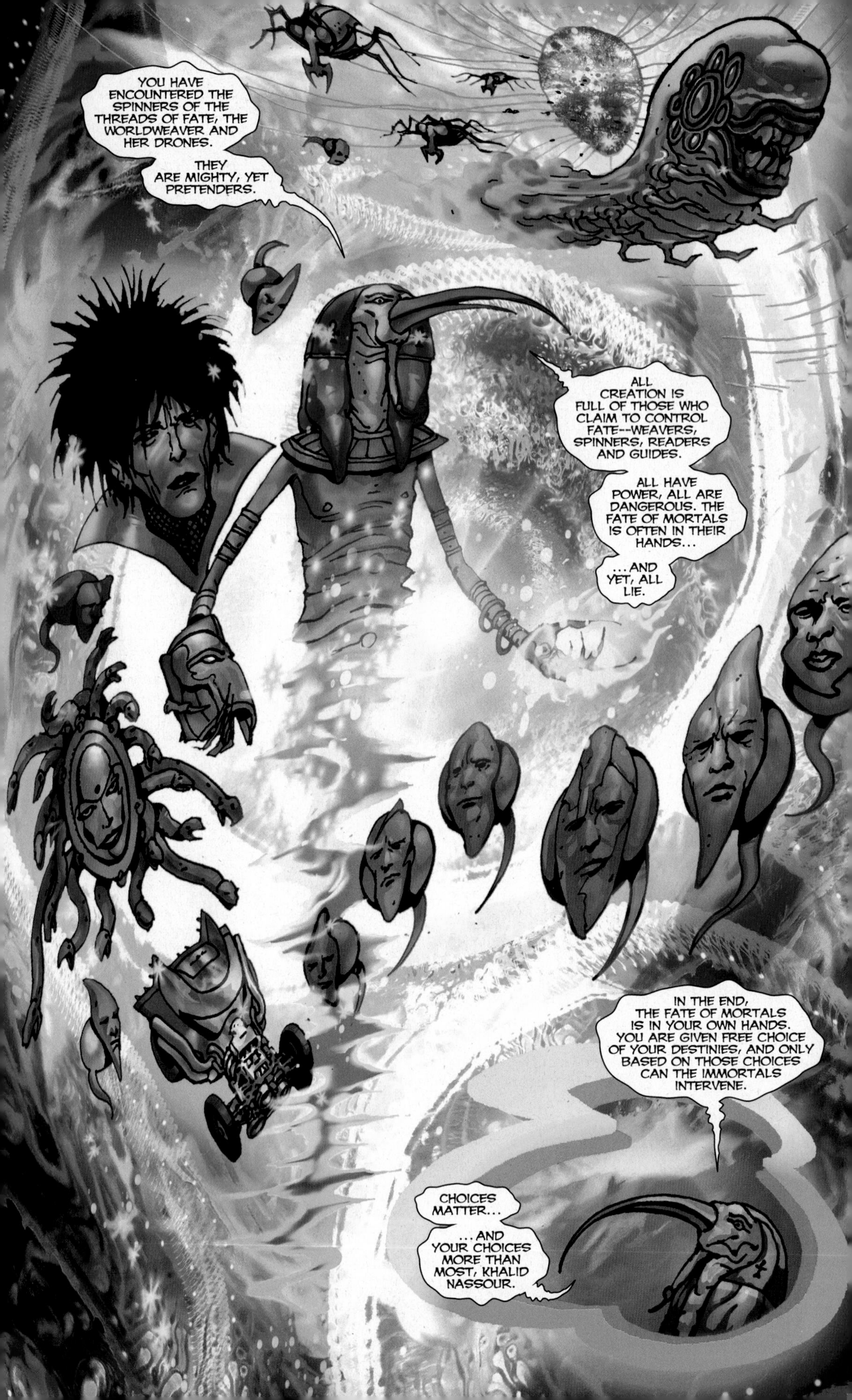
YOU HAVE ENCOUNTERED THE SPINNERS OF THE THREADS OF FATE, THE WORLDWEAVER AND HER DRONES.
THEY ARE MIGHTY, YET PRETENDERS.
ALL CREATION IS FULL OF THOSE WHO CLAIM TO CONTROL FATE--WEAVERS, SPINNERS, READERS AND GUIDES.
ALL HAVE POWER, ALL ARE DANGEROUS. THE FATE OF MORTALS IS OFTEN IN THEIR HANDS...
...AND YET, ALL LIE.
IN THE END, THE FATE OF MORTALS IS IN YOUR OWN HANDS. YOU ARE GIVEN FREE CHOICE OF YOUR DESTINIES, AND ONLY BASED ON THOSE CHOICES CAN THE IMMORTALS INTERVENE.
CHOICES MATTER...
...AND YOUR CHOICES MORE THAN MOST, KHALID NASSOUR.

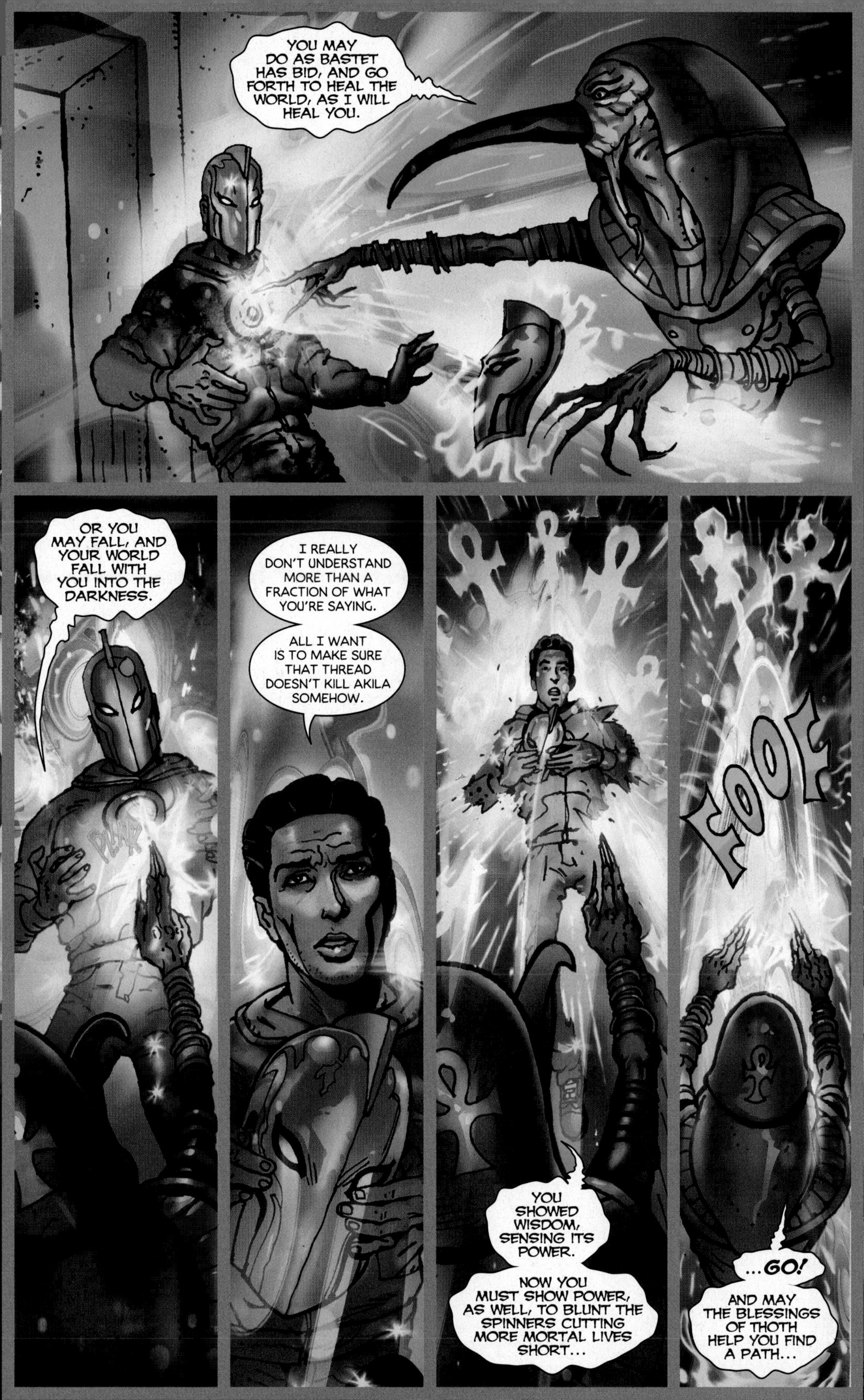
YOU MAY DO AS BASTET HAS BID, AND GO FORTH TO HEAL THE WORLD, AS I WILL HEAL YOU.
OR YOU MAY FALL, AND YOUR WORLD FALL WITH YOU INTO THE DARKNESS.
I REALLY DON'T UNDERSTAND MORE THAN A FRACTION OF WHAT YOU'RE SAYING.
ALL I WANT IS TO MAKE SURE THAT THREAD DOESN'T KILL AKILA SOMEHOW.
YOU SHOWED WISDOM, SENSING ITS POWER.
NOW YOU MUST SHOW POWER, AS WELL, TO BLUNT THE SPINNERS CUTTING MORE MORTAL LIVES SHORT...
FOOF
...GO!
AND MAY THE BLESSINGS OF THOTH HELP YOU FIND A PATH...

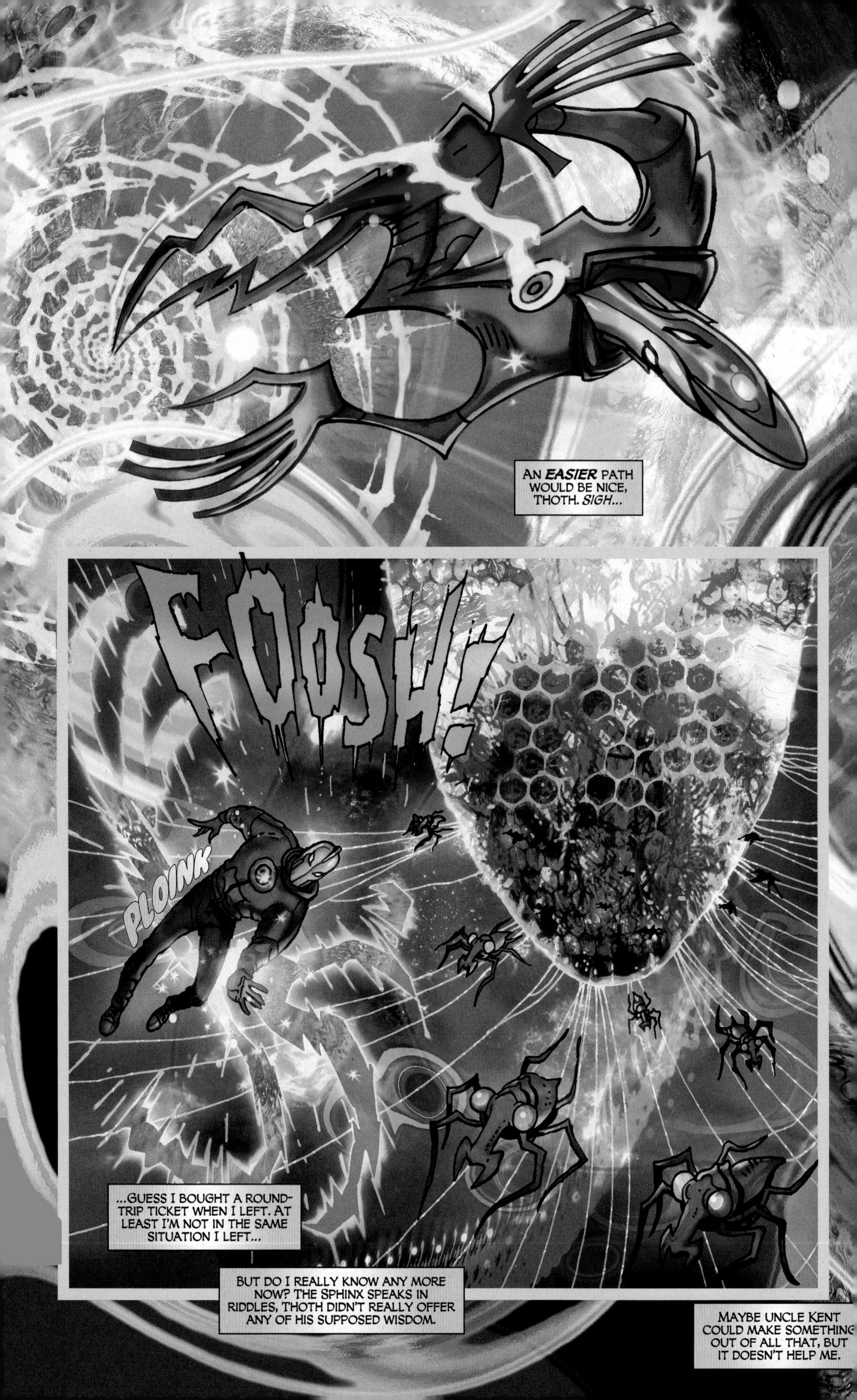
AN *EASIER* PATH WOULD BE NICE, THOTH. *SIGH*...
FOOSH!
PLOINK
...GUESS I BOUGHT A ROUND-TRIP TICKET WHEN I LEFT. AT LEAST I'M NOT IN THE SAME SITUATION I LEFT...
BUT DO I REALLY KNOW ANY MORE NOW? THE SPHINX SPEAKS IN RIDDLES, THOTH DIDN'T REALLY OFFER ANY OF HIS SUPPOSED WISDOM.
MAYBE UNCLE KENT COULD MAKE SOMETHING OUT OF ALL THAT, BUT IT DOESN'T HELP ME.

THOTH CALLED THEM "PRETENDERS"--DOES THAT MEAN THOSE THREADS DON'T REALLY AFFECT PEOPLE? IS THIS ALL A HALLUCINATION? OR NOW THAT I CAN SEE MAGIC, AM I SEEING *REALITY?*

ONE OF THE TRICKS KENT SHOWED ME MIGHT HELP.

LET ME SEE IF I CAN REMEMBER HOW...

THERE.

THE WORLD LOOKS SO DIFFERENT NOW THAT I SEE THESE THINGS.

WISH I COULD GET A *LASIK* CORRECTION AND GO BACK TO NOT SEEING IT THIS WAY.

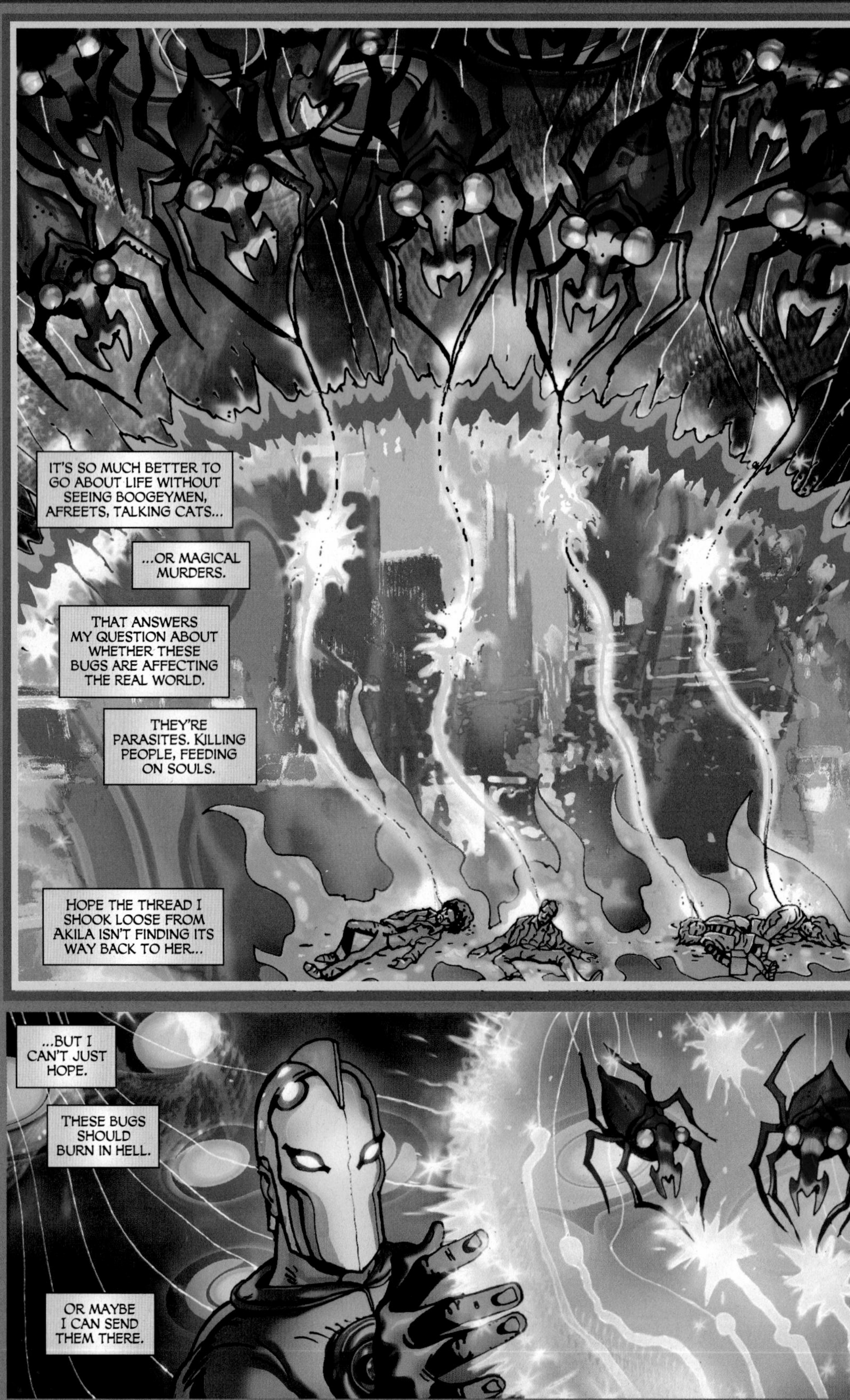
IT'S SO MUCH BETTER TO GO ABOUT LIFE WITHOUT SEEING BOOGEYMEN, AFREETS, TALKING CATS...
...OR MAGICAL MURDERS.
THAT ANSWERS MY QUESTION ABOUT WHETHER THESE BUGS ARE AFFECTING THE REAL WORLD.
THEY'RE PARASITES. KILLING PEOPLE, FEEDING ON SOULS.
HOPE THE THREAD I SHOOK LOOSE FROM AKILA ISN'T FINDING ITS WAY BACK TO HER...
...BUT I CAN'T JUST HOPE.
THESE BUGS SHOULD BURN IN HELL.
OR MAYBE I CAN SEND THEM THERE.

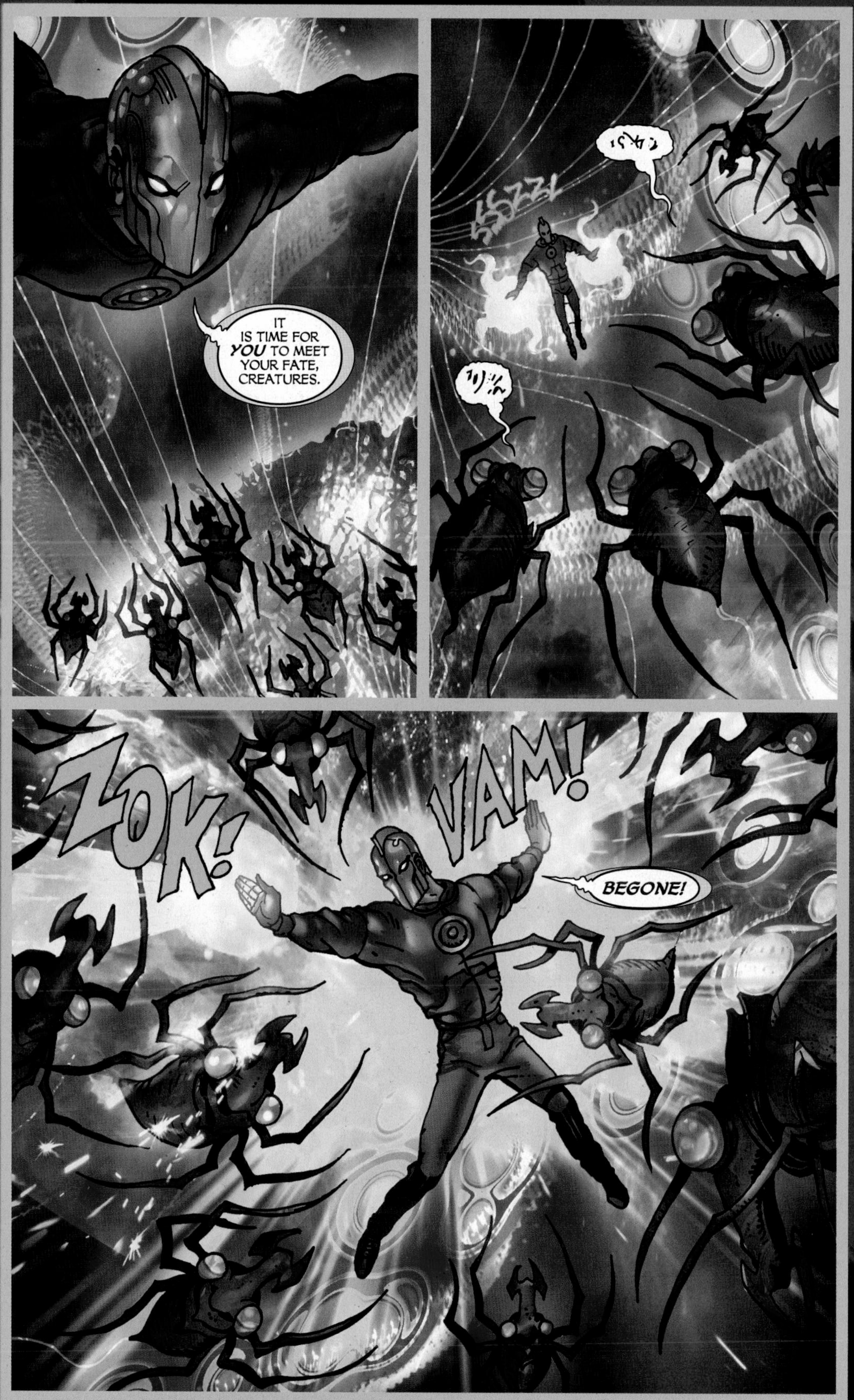
IT IS TIME FOR YOU TO MEET YOUR FATE, CREATURES.
ZOK!
VAM!
BEGONE!

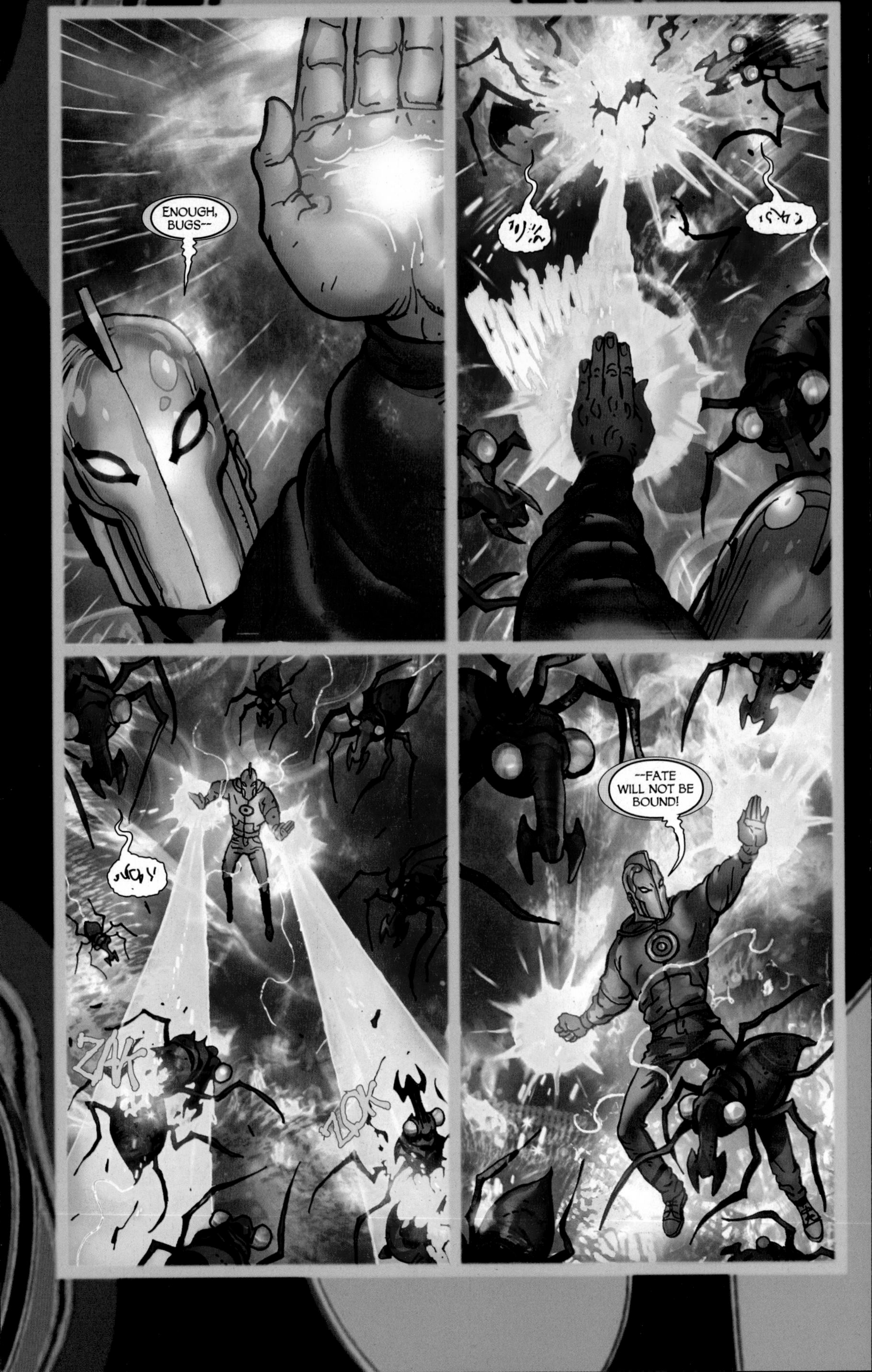
ENOUGH, BUGS--
ZAK
ZOK
--FATE WILL NOT BE BOUND!

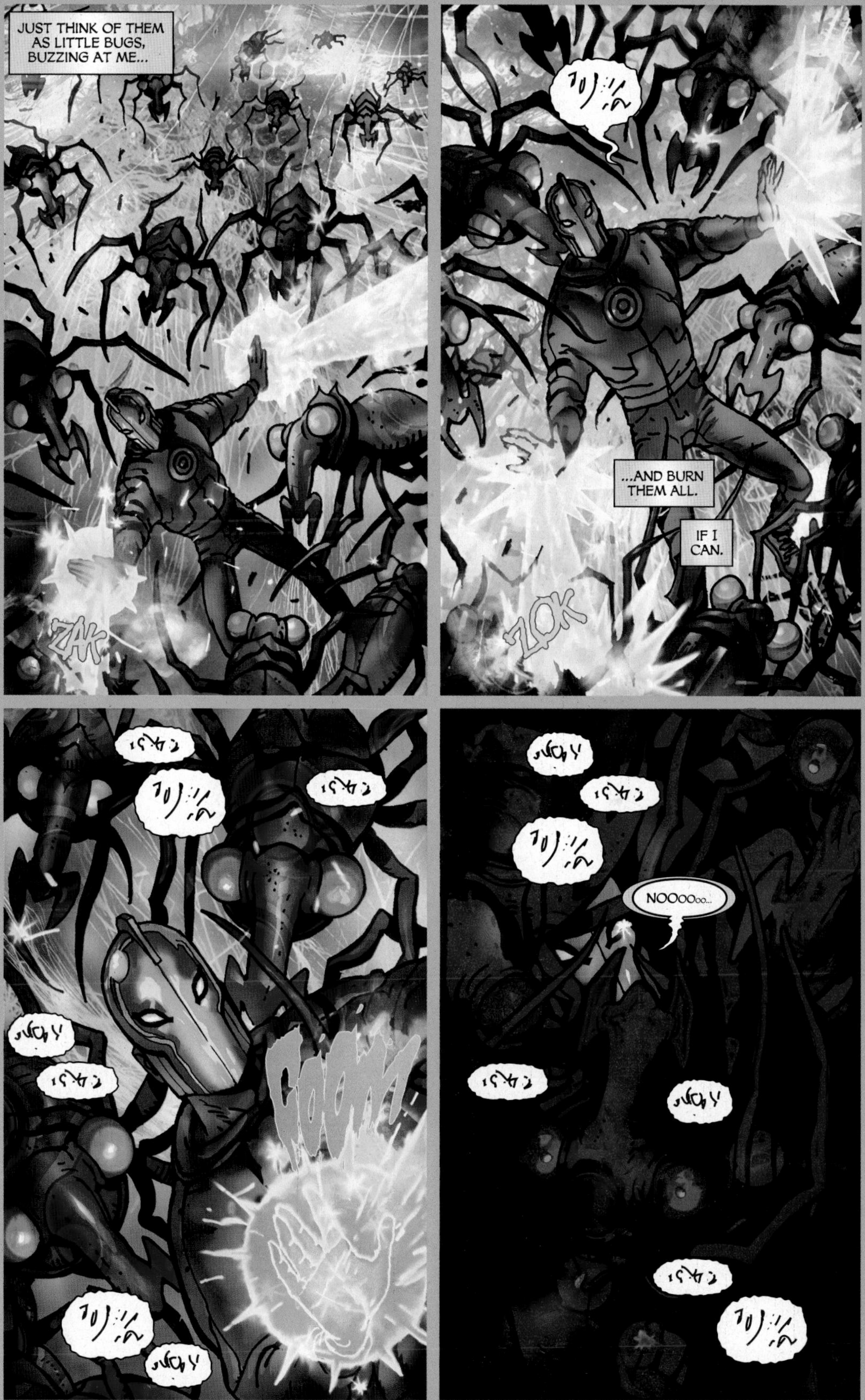

JUST THINK OF THEM AS LITTLE BUGS, BUZZING AT ME...
ZAK
...AND BURN THEM ALL.
IF I CAN.
ZOK
FOOM
NOOOooo...

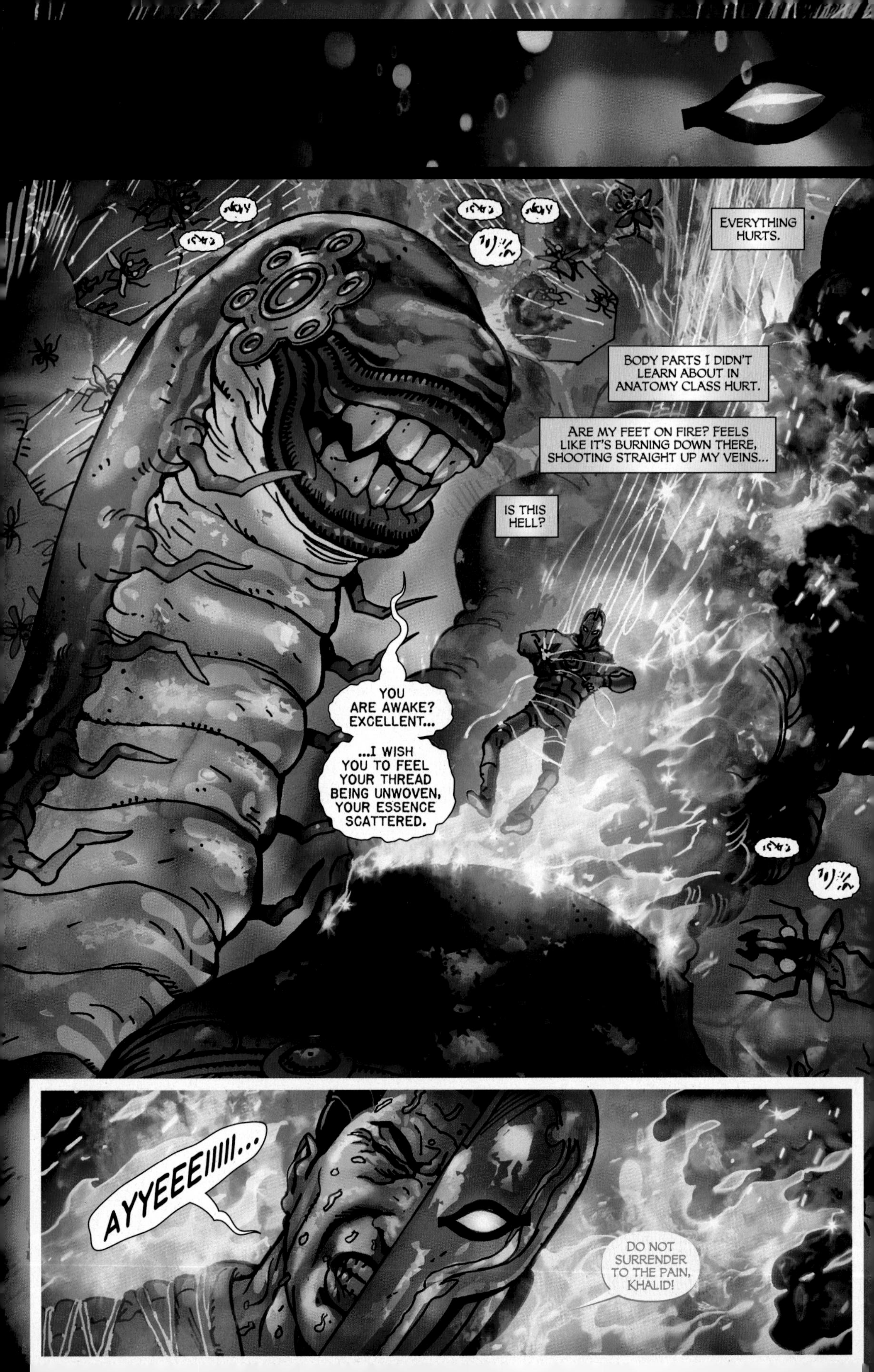
EVERYTHING HURTS.
BODY PARTS I DIDN'T LEARN ABOUT IN ANATOMY CLASS HURT.
ARE MY FEET ON FIRE? FEELS LIKE IT'S BURNING DOWN THERE, SHOOTING STRAIGHT UP MY VEINS...
IS THIS HELL?
YOU ARE AWAKE? EXCELLENT...
...I WISH YOU TO FEEL YOUR THREAD BEING UNWOVEN, YOUR ESSENCE SCATTERED.
AYYEEEIIIIII...
DO NOT SURRENDER TO THE PAIN, KHALID!

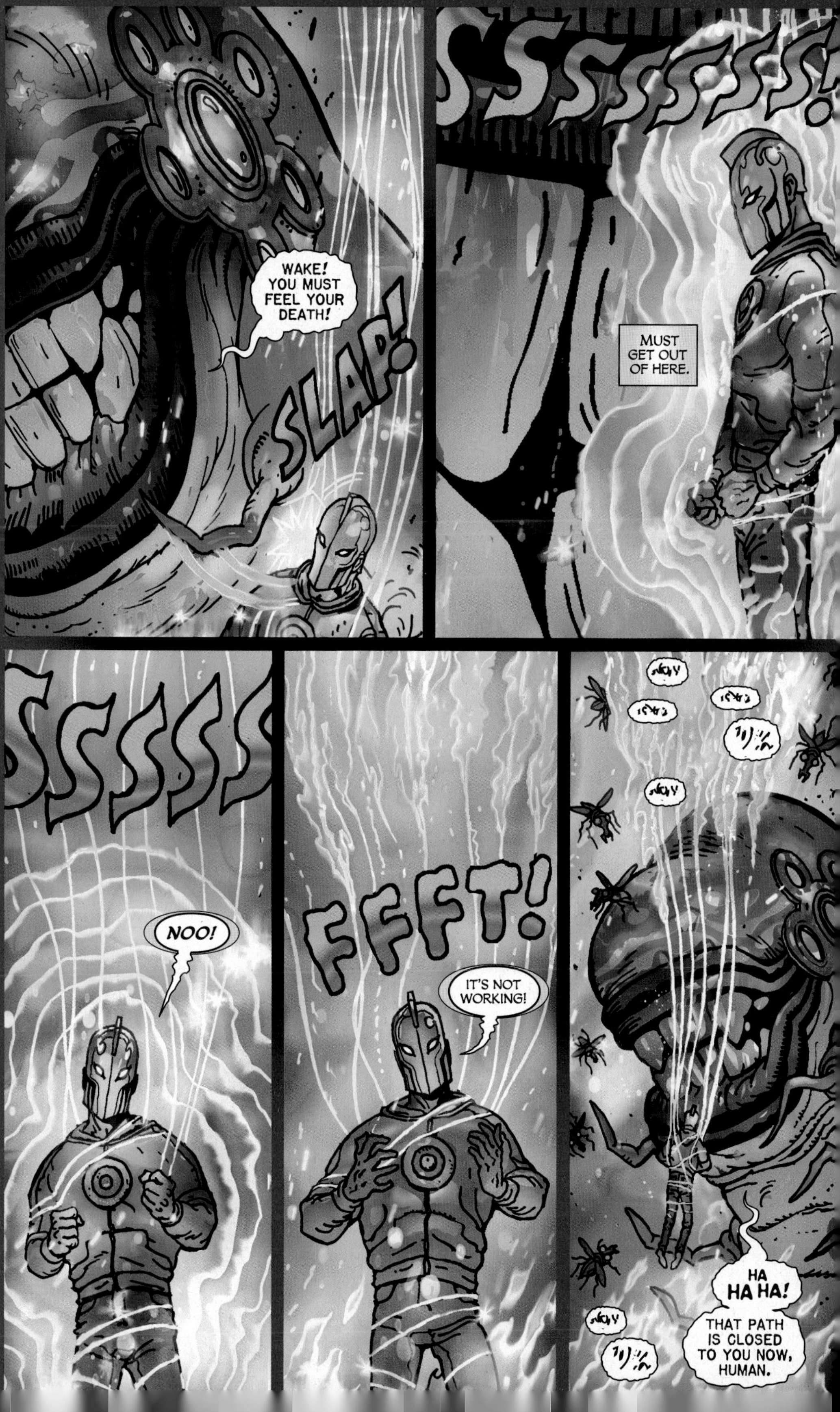
WAKE! YOU MUST FEEL YOUR DEATH!
SLAP!
SSSSSSSS!
MUST GET OUT OF HERE.
SSSSS
NOO!
FFFT!
IT'S NOT WORKING!
HA HA HA!
THAT PATH IS CLOSED TO YOU NOW, HUMAN.

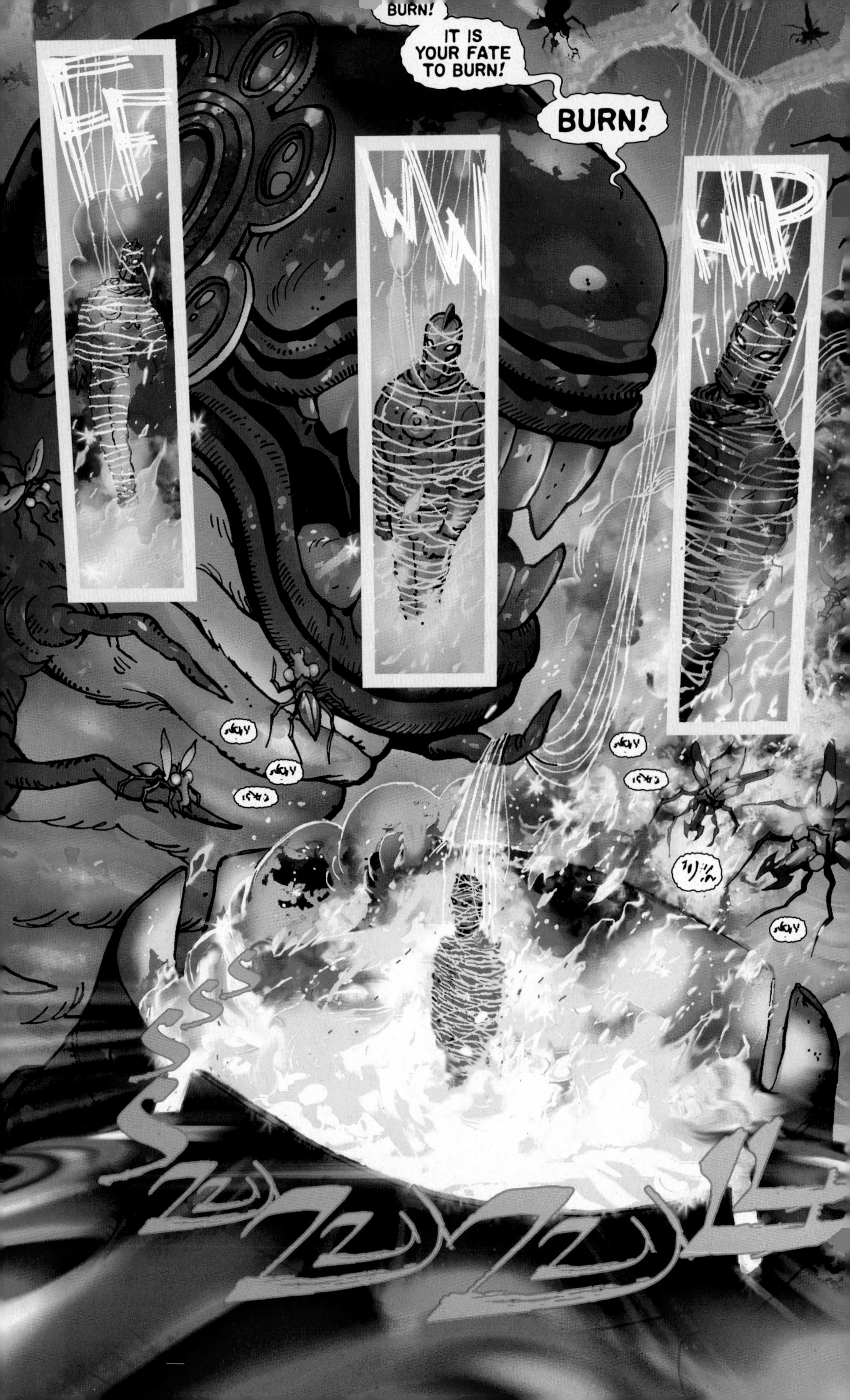
BURN!
IT IS YOUR FATE TO BURN!
BURN!

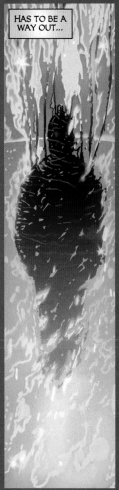

HAS TO BE A WAY OUT...

...INSIDES BURNING UP.

INSIDE?

WORTH A TRY.

MAYBE I CAN GO FROM THE INSIDE OUT?

PREFERABLY BEFORE I'M TOAST.

SSSSSSHSS

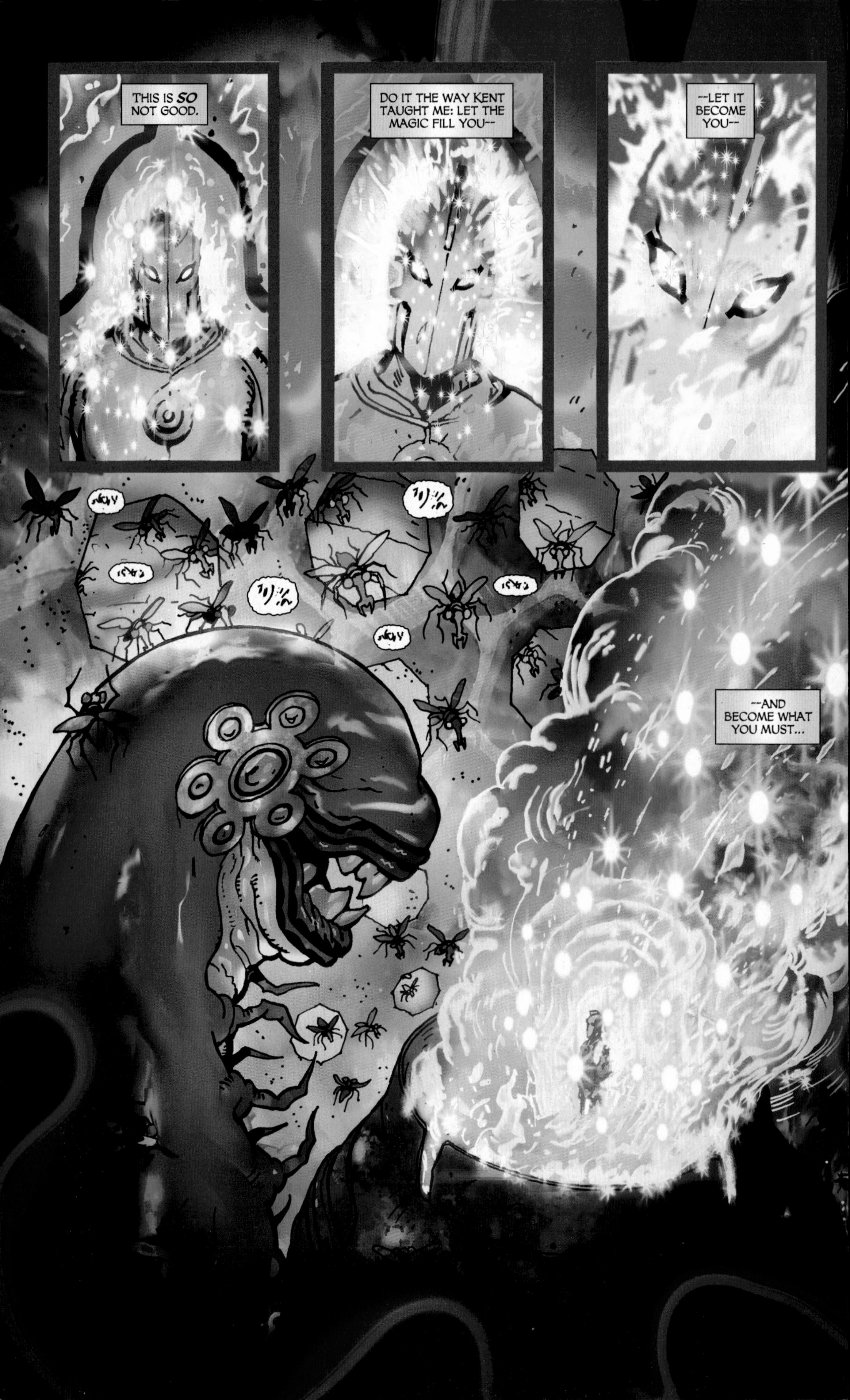
THIS IS SO NOT GOOD.
DO IT THE WAY KENT TAUGHT ME: LET THE MAGIC FILL YOU--
--LET IT BECOME YOU--
--AND BECOME WHAT YOU MUST...

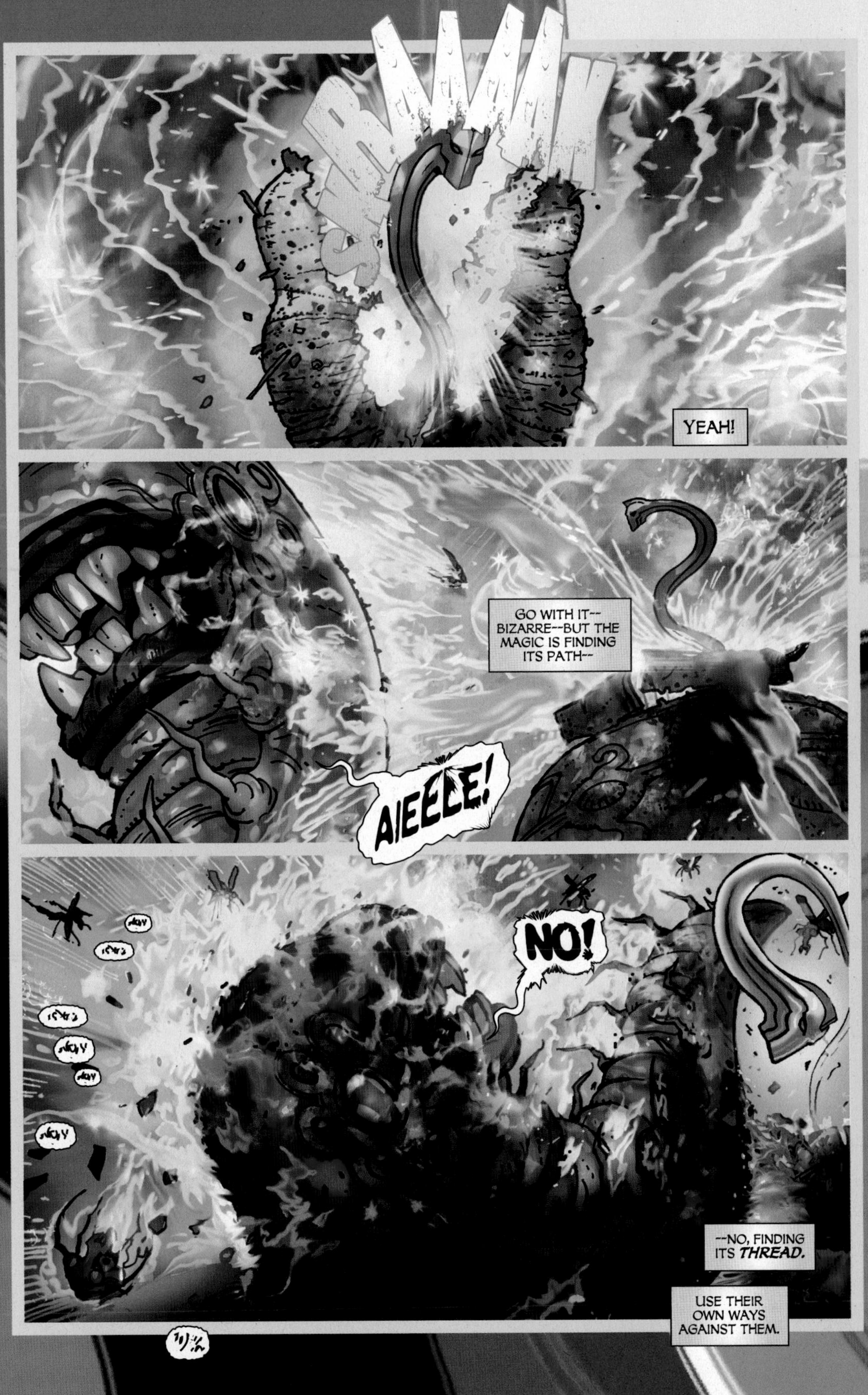
YEAH!
GO WITH IT--
BIZARRE--BUT THE
MAGIC IS FINDING
ITS PATH--
AIEEEE!
NO!
--NO, FINDING
ITS *THREAD.*
USE THEIR
OWN WAYS
AGAINST THEM.

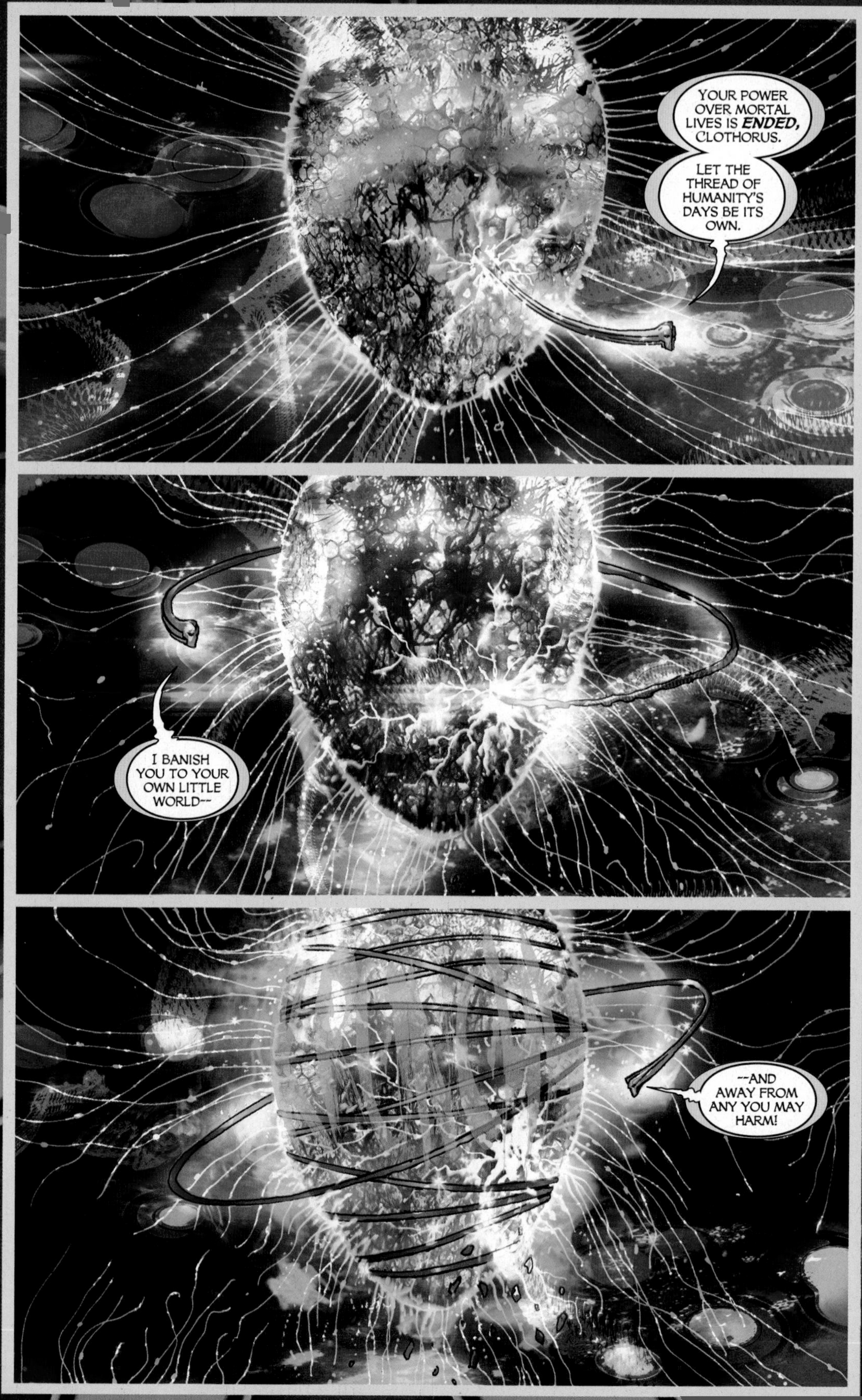
YOUR POWER OVER MORTAL LIVES IS *ENDED,* CLOTHORUS.
LET THE THREAD OF HUMANITY'S DAYS BE ITS OWN.
I BANISH YOU TO YOUR OWN LITTLE WORLD--
--AND AWAY FROM ANY YOU MAY HARM!

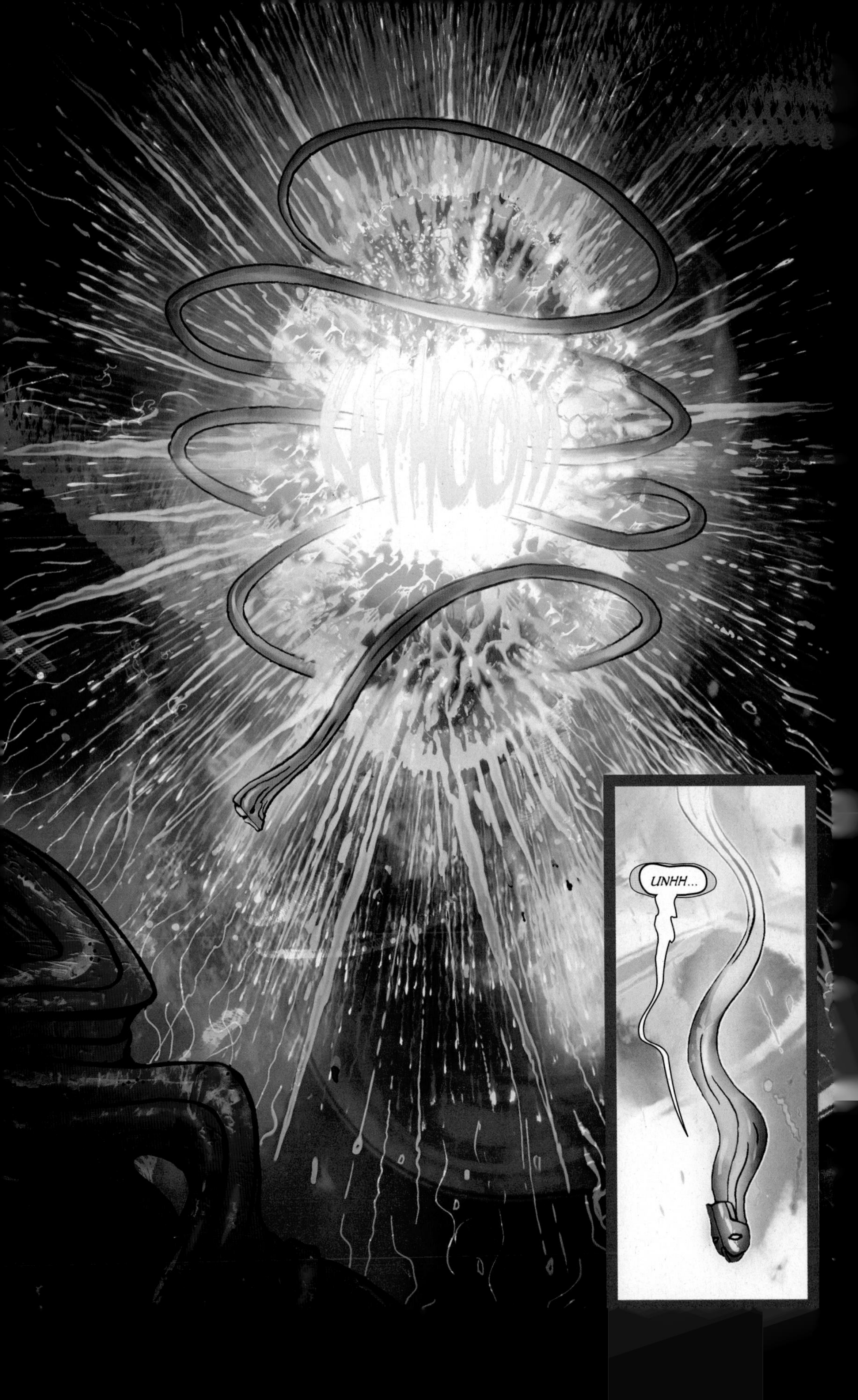
KATHOOM!
UNHH...

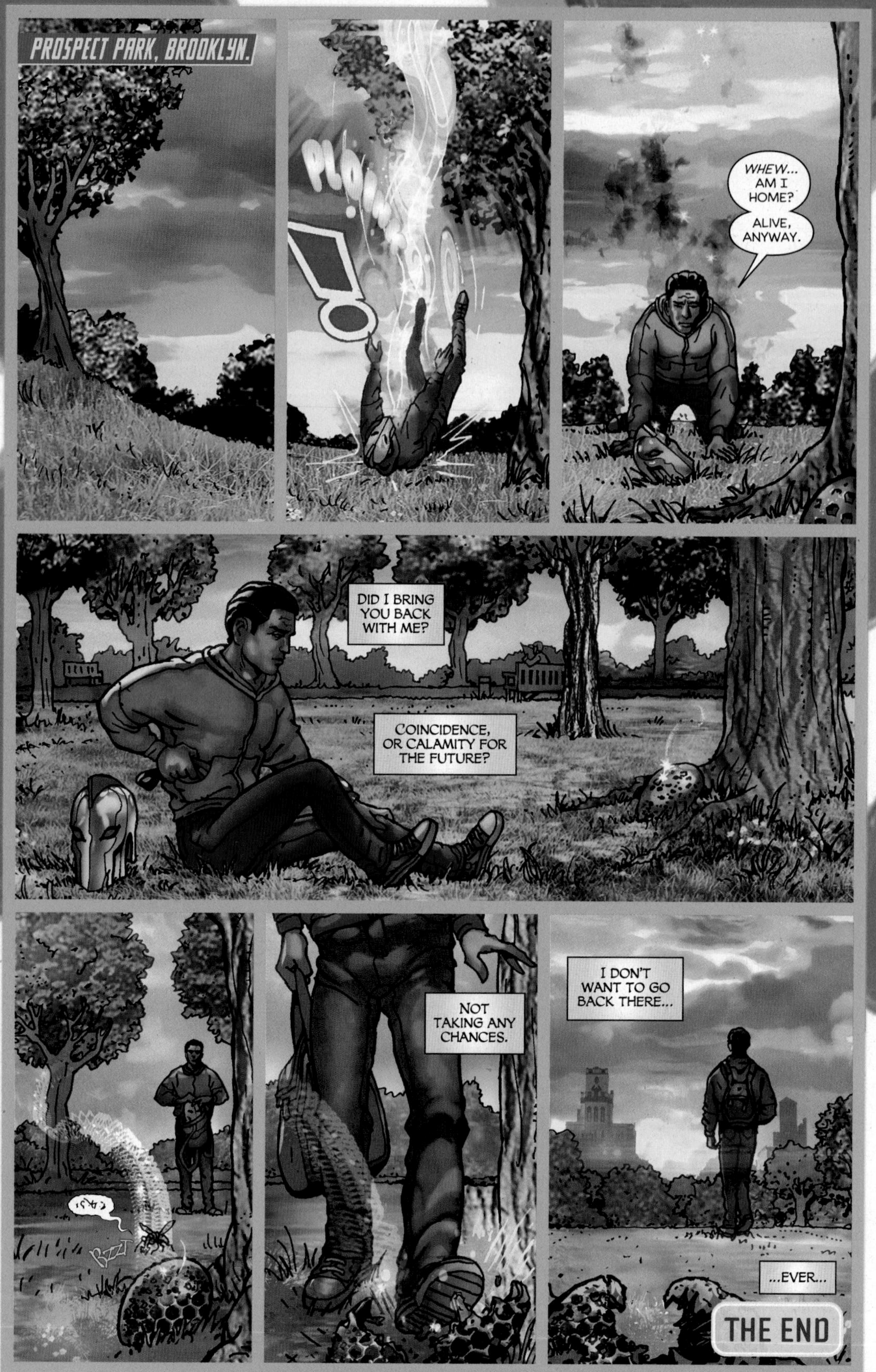
PROSPECT PARK, BROOKLYN.
WHEW... AM I HOME?
ALIVE, ANYWAY.
DID I BRING YOU BACK WITH ME?
COINCIDENCE, OR CALAMITY FOR THE FUTURE?
BZZT
NOT TAKING ANY CHANCES.
I DON'T WANT TO GO BACK THERE...
...EVER...
THE END

_PAUL LEVITZ & BRENDAN McCARTHY
STORYTELLERS

_MARK HARRISON & BRENDAN McCARTHY
COLORS

_SAIDA TEMOFONTE
LETTERER

_DAVID WOHL
EDITOR

_MARIE JAVINS
GROUP EDITOR

_BRENDAN McCARTH
COVER

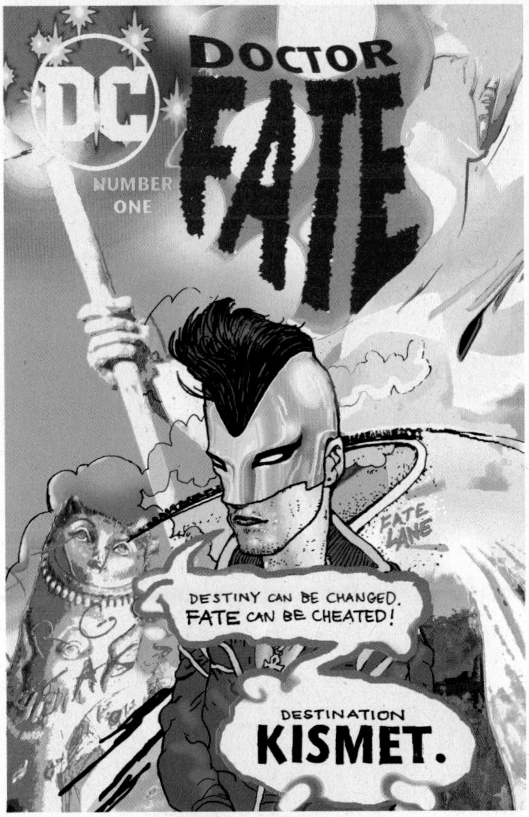
DC
DOCTOR
FATE
NUMBER ONE
FATE LANE
DESTINY CAN BE CHANGED. FATE CAN BE CHEATED!
DESTINATION KISMET.
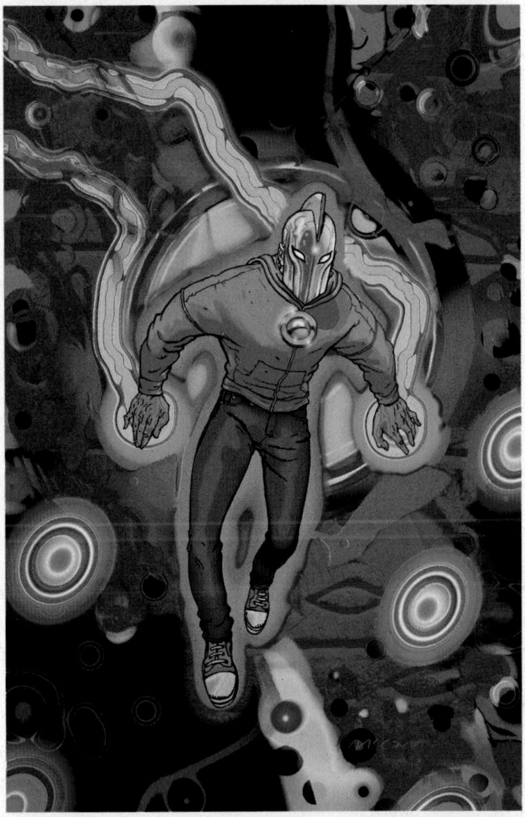
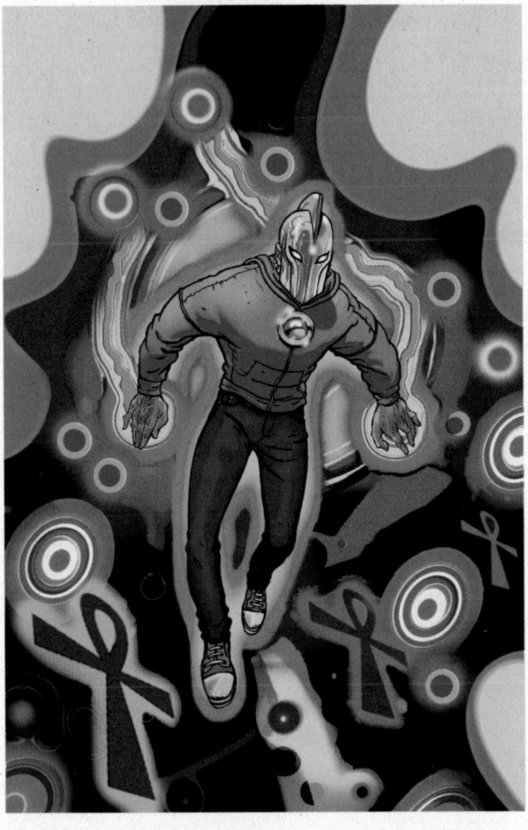
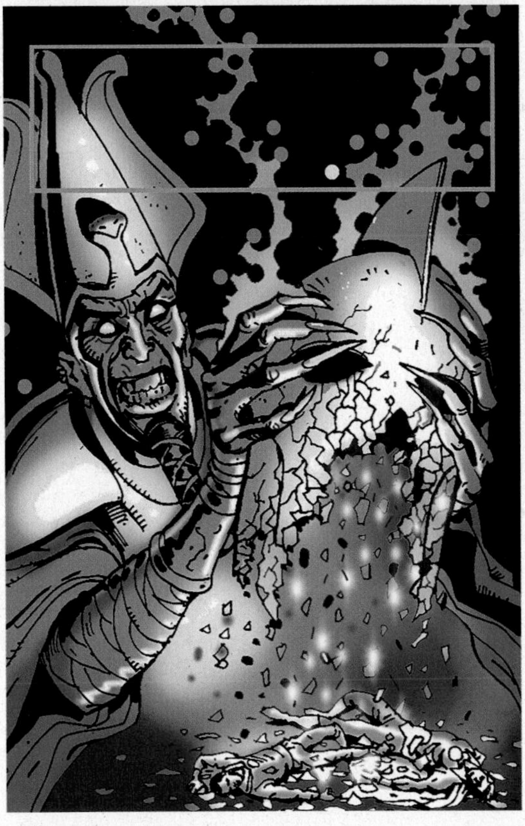

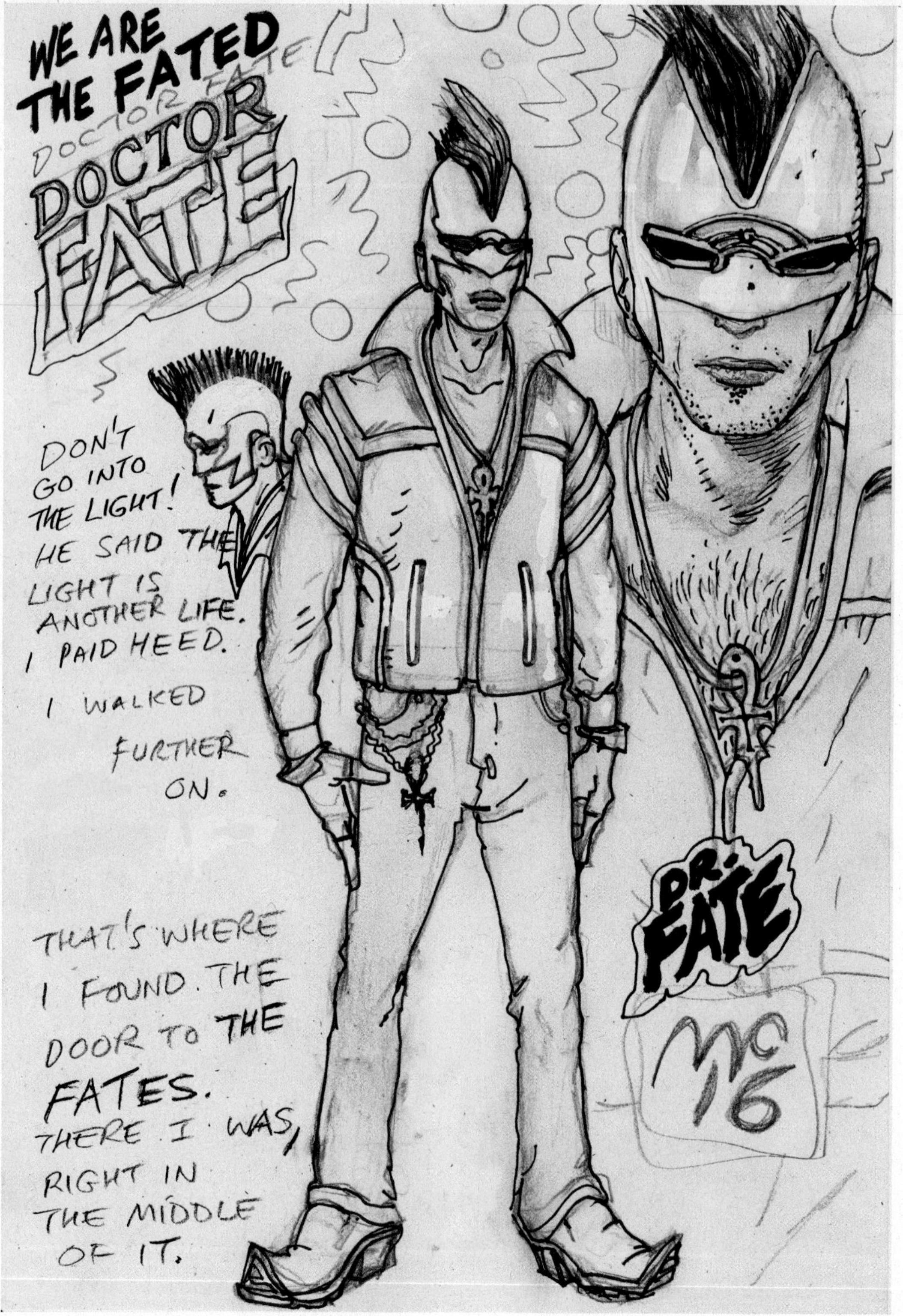
WE ARE THE FATED
DOCTOR FATE
DON'T GO INTO THE LIGHT! HE SAID THE LIGHT IS ANOTHER LIFE. I PAID HEED.
I WALKED FURTHER ON.
THAT'S WHERE I FOUND THE DOOR TO THE FATES.
THERE I WAS, RIGHT IN THE MIDDLE OF IT.
DR. FATE
MC 16

DOCTOR FATE #16 PAGE 2 ART PROGRESSION BY
SONNY LIEW

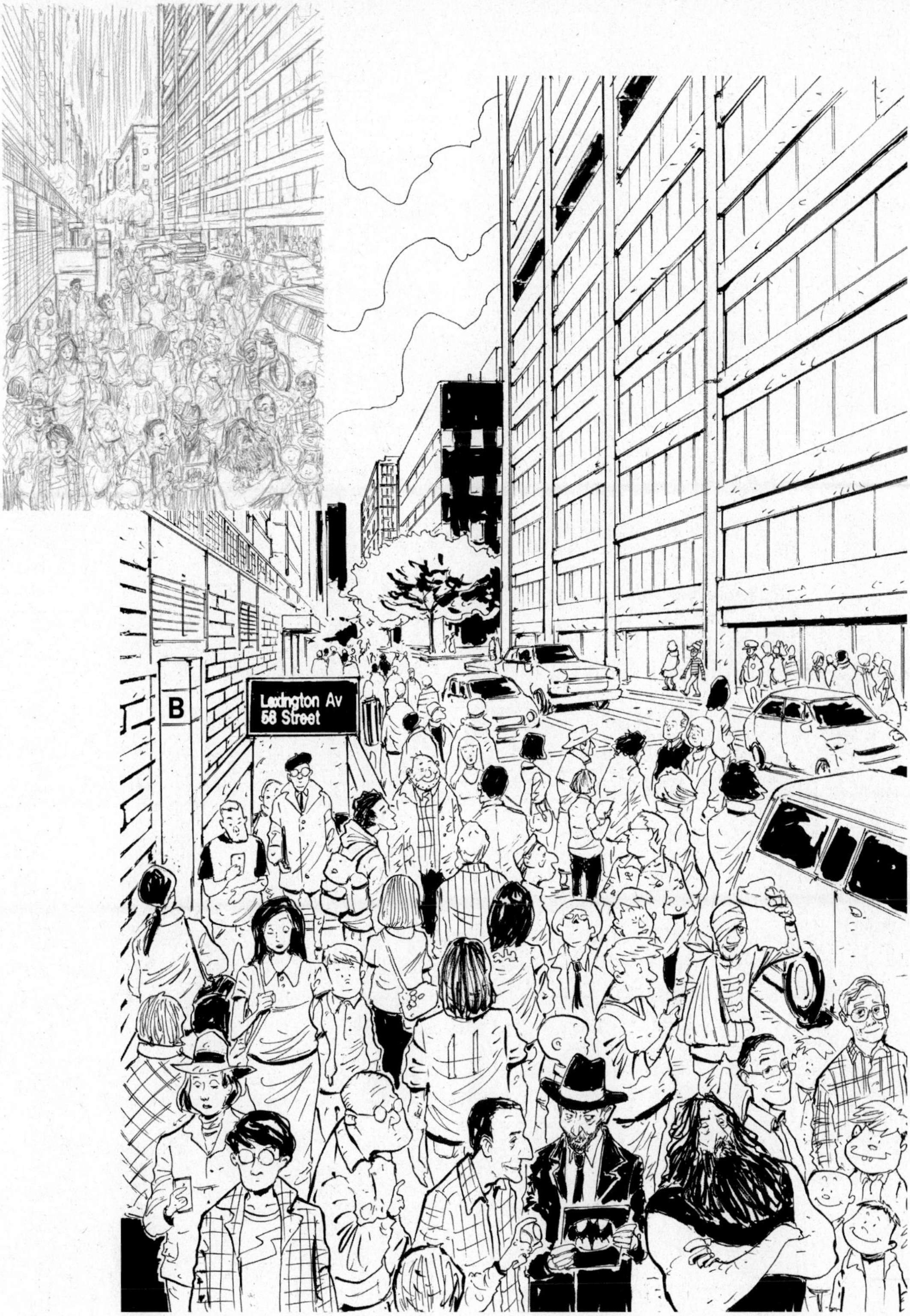
B
Lexington Av
58 Street

DOCTOR FATE #15 COVER SKETCHES BY
INAKI MIRANDA

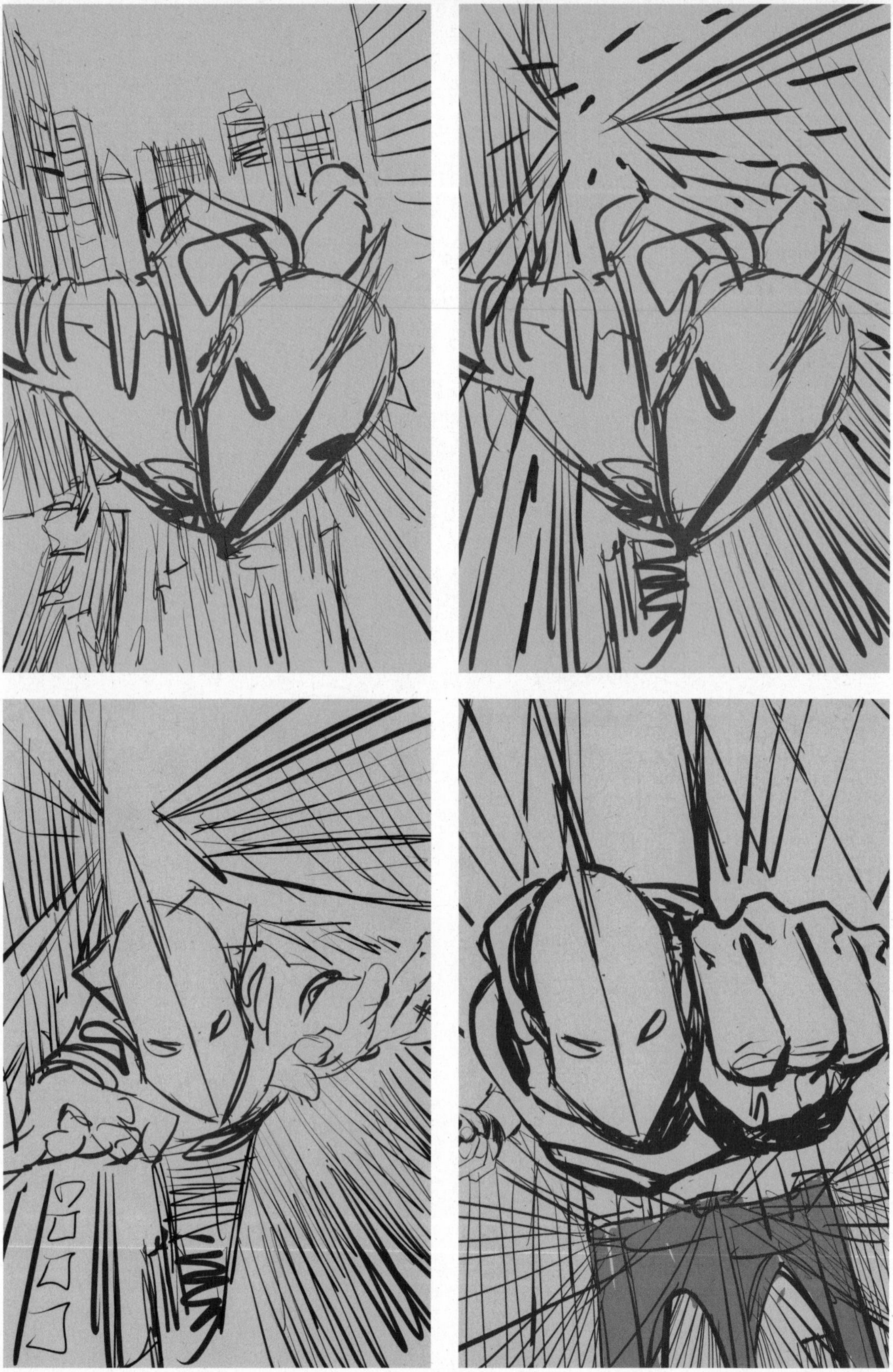

DOCTOR FATE #14 LAYOUTS FOR PAGES 1, 6-8, 10 AND 12 BY
INAKI MIRANDA

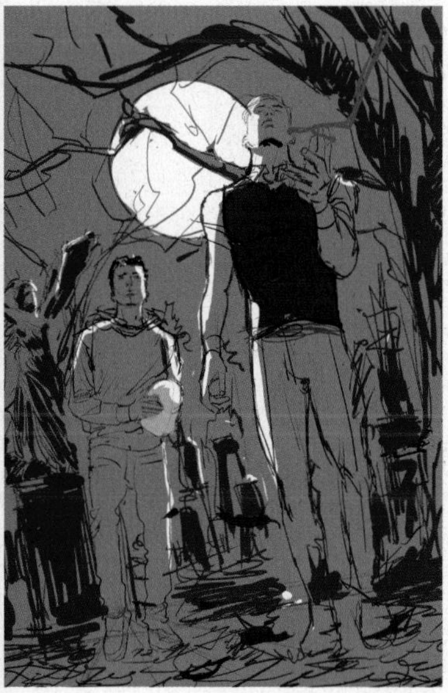

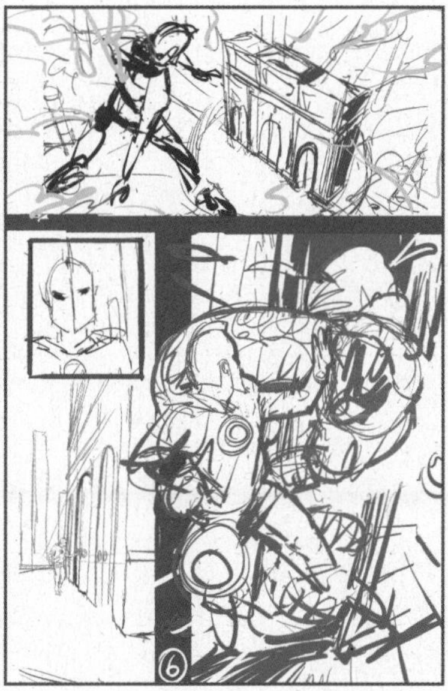
6

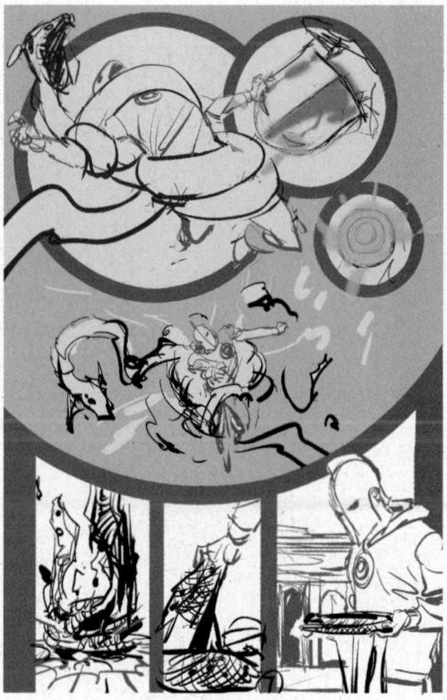

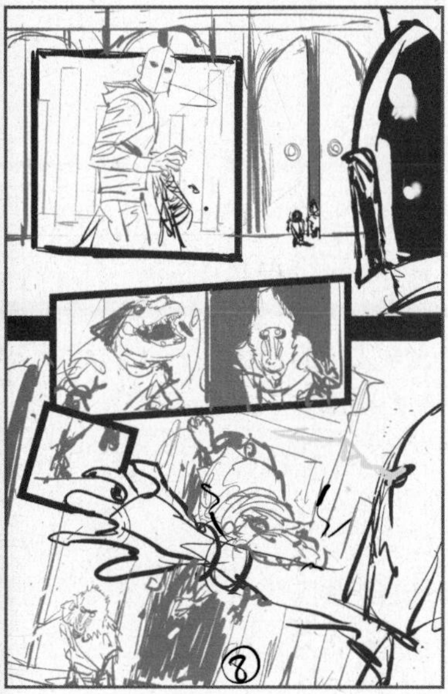
8

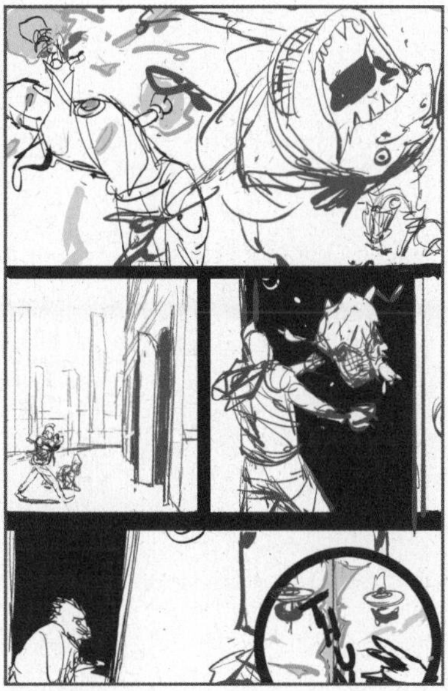

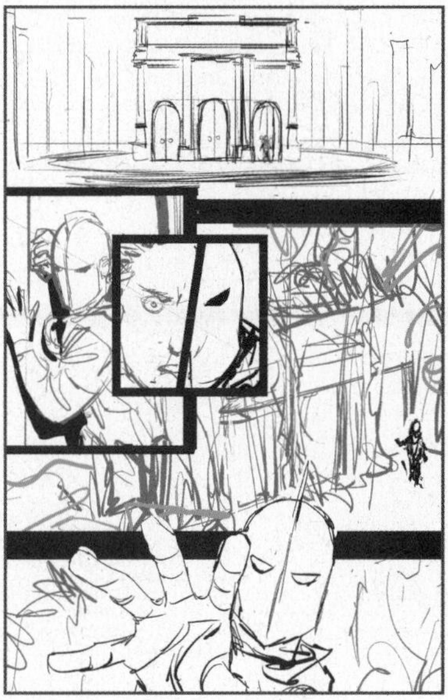

DOCTOR FATE #15 PAGE LAYOUTS BY
IBRAHIM MOUSTAFA

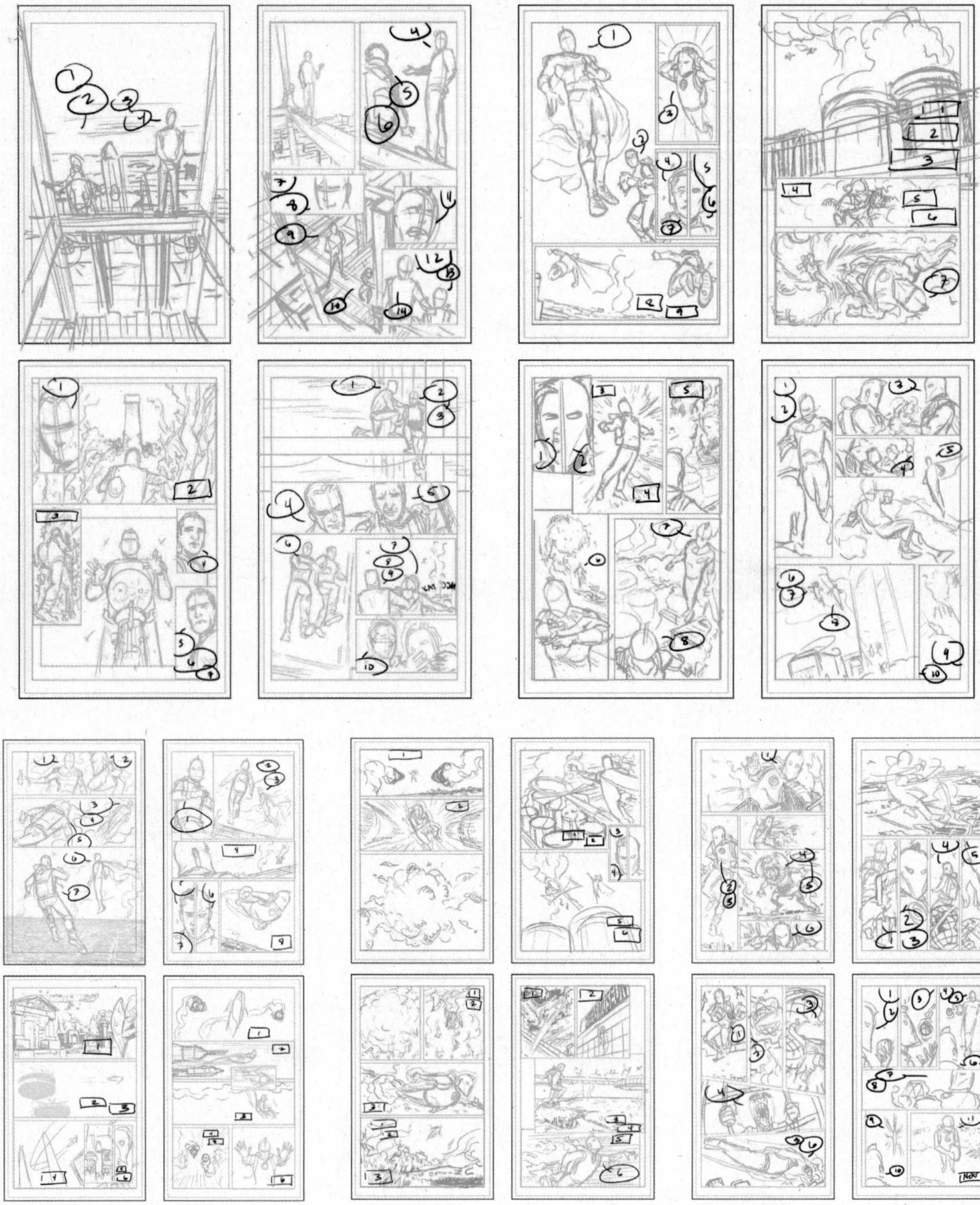

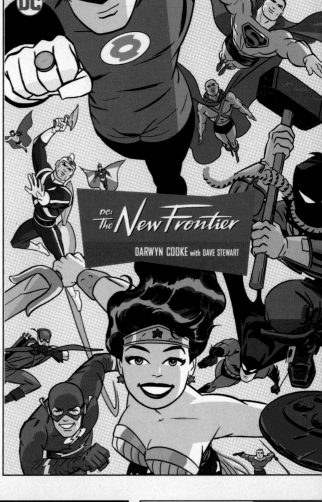